Freedom of Access to Library Materials

By John Robotham and Gerald Shields

Neal-Schuman Publishers, Inc.

Published by Neal-Schuman Publishers, Inc.
23 Cornelia Street
New York, NY 10014

Copyright © 1982 by Neal-Schuman Publishers, Inc.

All rights reserved. Reproduction of this book, in whole or in part, without written permission of the publisher is prohibited.

Printed and bound in the United States of America.

Library of Congress Cataloging in Publication Data

Robotham, John S., 1924–
   Freedom of access to library materials.

   Bibliography: p.
   Includes index.
   1. Libraries—Censorship.   I. Shields, Gerald R.
II. Title.
Z711.4.R6   1982   025.2'13   82-14309
ISBN 0-918212-31-6

For all the librarians on the front lines
—John Robotham

To J. Gordon Burke, Mary Dugan, and Jill Redig,
For making me think it over,
And to Joyce Farley Shields,
For giving me the fortitude to survive
—Gerald R. Shields

Contents

Introduction vii

Chapter One
    What Is Freedom? 1
Chapter Two
    Freedom and the Type of Library 18
Chapter Three
    At What Age Freedom? 36
Chapter Four
    Freedom Denied 58
Chapter Five
    Racism, Sexism and Other "Isms" 88
Chapter Six
    Freedom in the Media 106
Chapter Seven
    Confronting the Complainant 125
Chapter Eight
    Freedom Attacked: A Case Study 146
Chapter Nine
    Freedom Defended 166
Chapter Ten
    Freedom and the Library- and Information-
        Professional 184

Selected Bibliography 203
Appendix 210
Index 216

Introduction

In 1964 the American Library Association published a collection of the McCarthy-era essays of Everett T. Moore, called *Issues of Freedom in American Libraries,* as a sigh of contentment after the trauma wafted through the profession. Eric Moon's 1969 anthology, culled from the pages he edited at *Library Journal,* devoted much of its attention to the censorship practiced by the librarian rather than outside forces (*Book Selection and Censorship in the Sixties*). Charles Rembar celebrated *The End of Obscenity* in 1968, and for one brief moment the forces for the suppression of ideas seemed to be routed.

But the seventies saw the impact of the civil-rights movement, the disintegration of the "guns and butter" philosophy, the cynicism of Watergate and the consequent rise of the fundamentalist, newly and electronically articulate. Censorship turned a corner and accelerated.

As we sail into the eighties, we sense a growing fear of ideas and the pressure to establish social "absolutes." The temperature of debate has risen as positions of racism, sexism, and intolerance are again considered respectable. Librarians and information specialists have become continually pressured to remove, segregate, restrict and, in some cases, destroy materials. New forms of media are appearing, reflecting the diversity of the marketplace; yet they seem to generate additional fears, among both librarians and the general public, as to their ideas and their impact. Consequently they have found unenthusiastic welcome in many print-oriented libraries. And, as if that were not enough, budgets, never high for libraries, are being repeatedly cut, providing additional pressure to reduce access and to avoid the addition of "controversial" materials to library collections.

During all these changes of the past twenty or thirty years, we have been practicing librarianship and have developed an interest in the concept of intellectual freedom transcending the perfunctory introduction received in professional school. We have both served on state-level committees devoted to the issue of intellectual freedom. It was there that we met, and the chance remark of a colleague, carrying the overtones of a challenge, led to our collaboration on this book. The experience has been an educational one, for we have cleared up some confusion in our own minds and have become better able to articulate the place of freedom of access in the professional credo. The purposes of libraries have, after all, never been widely understood. We hope this book will move our colleagues, and other interested readers, to think about issues and philosophies relating to freedom of access to the graphic records stored in libraries.

Although we have concentrated on the censorship of materials, we recognize that many other factors can stand in the way of freedom of access to library materials and other information. Physical facilities can deter many from trying to gain access, as the disabled can so readily testify. In fact, physical facilities are often a deterrent even to many who have no physical disability, for the attitude of those who control access to materials can restrict freedom, as can the library's hours, its location, and the perception of its functions. While we do not dwell upon these factors here, the reader will most likely discover that our philosophy can be helpful in clarifying thinking about all types of access. Our concern here, however, is to provide the reader with an opportunity to think about the purpose of libraries and information services, in order to be better equipped to defend them against the attack of those who would deny freedom of access. It is for this reason that our first chapter discusses the concept of freedom as it has evolved in the Western world. We have taken into account some of the more recent thinking, tempered by some of the problems created by the swiftness and volume of transmitted communications. From there we look at the problems of access faced by libraries defined by type of institutional base, such as academic, public and school. We then look at one of the more recent controversies in the profession: at what age does one have the right to have access to all of the human graphic record? The next chapter explores the various "types" of people who would restrict access, and it should be noted that we do not exclude the librarian from this group. Problems of the "isms" are discussed next, followed by a consideration of some of the problems faced in the acquisition of nonprint graphics. Our next chapter concerns techniques used in confrontation with those who would censor or restrict access to library materials, followed by a case study of a school library media center. We have refrained from commenting on the case, to allow readers to evaluate the circumstance and solutions on their own. We then consider methods that can be used by the professional to prepare for the day when there is a move against the library collection. We conclude with an evaluation of professional responsibility in terms of freedom of access, and its expression as an aspect of intellectual freedom.

Casey Stengel once divided baseball players into ribbon clerks and professionals. Librarianship is, or at least can be, a noble calling. To be a librarian requires courage, learning and judgment, along with a firm belief in service to all people, and in the value of exposure to ideas. Some among us are ribbon clerks—these exist in every profession. This book is not for them. Their minds are all in order, and they will not take the risks or make the effort required for professional dedication. Nor will they reap its rewards. If our effort makes *you* think and move toward a better understanding of your professional responsibilities, then we will be content to suffer the occasional slings and arrows one must expect.

John Robotham
Gerald R. Shields

Chapter One
What Is Freedom?

Freedom is a word whose meaning has been worn smooth by use, its unpleasant edges and sharp points polished by oceans of newsprint and waves of oratory. It slips easily off the tongue, leaving us with a meaningless motto on a license plate or a cheap plaque at a roadside souvenir stand. Freedom has been the subject of long dissertations, classical essays, impassioned dialogues and fervent political documents, but rarely, if ever, has any of us looked at its dictionary definitions. We know what freedom means.

Yet, when we look at freedom closely, like a stone on a beach, it has a variety of colors, some rough spots and indentations and several faces. In conceptual terms and as an emotional experience, it is as variable as the number of human beings currently inhabiting this planet. Likewise, people seem to value freedom differently. For many, freedom is a goal and a dream, a need as fundamental as food, warmth and shelter; in some cases, it is more important than life itself. Other people, apparently, can live happily on a diet of bread and circuses, finding freedom worth neither seeking nor understanding.

This discrepancy may be due, in part, to differences in meaning. For many, the freedom existing in totalitarian countries is as real and meaningful as it is for those living within libertarian social structures.

In the library world, one hears about the free library, freedom of choice, freedom to read (or see or hear), freedom of information, and freedom of access. Do librarians know what they mean when they use these terms? Do others know? If we do know, why do we run into trouble with people who challenge the library's freedom?

2   FREEDOM OF ACCESS TO LIBRARY MATERIALS

In a larger context, is freedom an absence of restraint? Is it immunity from the arbitrary exercise of authority? Is it an exemption from unpleasant or onerous conditions? And does it depend on having a choice? At the very least, we need to understand that all people have their own ideas of what freedom is. And we must know what we mean when we talk about freedom, and realize the person we are talking to may mean something else. Being conscious of the ramifications of the idea of freedom, and having thought out what we mean, we will be on a firmer footing and able to talk more successfully with our challengers.

As a starting point for a brief investigation of the concept of freedom, and the relation between that concept and libraries, we might turn to Mortimer Adler's celebrated exercise in the classification of types of freedom. Adler devoted two thick volumes to the subject, and he drew his ideas from the major thinkers of the Western world. From this extensive exploration, he classifies three major ways in which the human being possesses freedom. He admits these are not "pure" in the sense that each will readily fall into one or both of the other classifications. Nevertheless, he maintains that in all the writings he studied, three classifications of freedom clearly emerge: *circumstantial, acquired* and *natural.*

Circumstantial freedom is either wholly or partly dependent "upon whatever external conditions affect human behavior, in so far as that consists of bodily movements."[1] The external conditions enumerated by Adler may affect human behavior directly, either by preventing or facilitating bodily movement or by contracting or expanding the opportunities for selecting alternative courses of action. Or these conditions may affect behavior indirectly, by occasioning or inducing emotional or other·mental reactions that encourage or inhibit impulses to act in certain ways, including the provision of every sort of social and political impediment.

This is the freedom with which most rhetoric and revolutions are concerned. Possessing it, one would be free from pressures by the government, of the marketplace and of society—free to travel, seek employment, associate with others, and to speak one's mind. It would include both the actual ability to do these things and freedom from the fear of doing them. It is the kind of freedom with which most of us in the library world are concerned and think about. It would include, of course, freedom from the censor. In a number of important ways, however, it overlaps Adler's next classification.

Acquired freedom depends "upon a change or development in human beings whereby they have a state of mind, or character, or personality which differentiates them from other(s)."[2] This, then, is an internal freedom, as opposed to circumstantial, or external, freedom. Acquired freedom may depend on favorable circumstances, but it need not. It is *in spite* of circumstances that some individuals acquire a condition of freedom seemingly denied to others. Adler gives as examples autonomy, exultation, freedom of personality, freedom from conflict; or in the religious sense, a state of grace. If we are freed from the slavery of our impulses, if we can free ourselves from fears and superstitions and, in an autocracy, if we can retain our own values and opinions even though unable to express them, then we have acquired freedom.

Walter Kaufmann, in his book on autonomy, suggests that such people as Goethe, Eleanor Roosevelt and Solzhenitsyn were, or are, autonomous.[3] That is, they acquired freedom in spite of circumstances. He also suggests that if we don't have this kind of freedom, revolutions and radical movements will not bring about external freedom but will only substitute one kind of slavery for another. This may be the great lesson of the twentieth century. Libraries can, and do, clearly participate in the process of acquiring this kind of freedom, in a variety of ways.

Natural freedom is Adler's third category. Its major point is that freedom is "1) inherent in all people; 2) *regardless* of the circumstance under which they live and 3) *without regard* to any state of mind or character which they may or may not acquire in the course of their lives."[4] Therefore, anyone is in a position to determine what he or she wishes to do or become—or, at least, has the ability to do so. Circumstance may prevent complete self-realization, and the requisite virtue or wisdom may not be acquired, but the freedom is inherent. As Thomas Emerson has said, "Man is distinguished from the other animals principally by the qualities of his mind. He has powers to reason. . . . He has the capacity to think in abstract terms, to use language, to communicate his thoughts and emotions, to build a culture. He has powers of imagination, insight and feeling." And since "the process of conscious thought by its very nature can have no limits [and] it is an individual process [and one can neither] tell where it [thought] may lead nor anticipate its end," one might well say we have a natural freedom that no one can take away from us.[5]

And although Adler is careful to distinguish between natural freedom and a natural right to this freedom, one does follow from the other. This is important for libraries, because it is the premise on which our system of government is based, and by extension it is the premise on which the public-library system is based.

When one begins to examine the concept of freedom in this way—and this is only scratching the surface—it is easy to see how conflicts can arise. No doubt, most people—in the United States, at least—would consider themselves free, and would think all should be free. It is the kind, or degree, of freedom that is at issue, and what, if anything, needs to be done about any limitations on freedom that are perceived.

Those concerned with circumstantial freedoms, for example, would be interested in political, social and economic reforms, because they would regard them as necessary for freedom. Others might think the acquisition of wisdom, or virtue, by the individual would suffice. And still others, believing we are naturally free, would think nothing needed to be done.

Within Adler's categories there are all kinds of gradations. Circumstantial freedom—or its lack—is, in some respects, straightforward enough. Throughout history, many people who have spoken their minds have been whipped, mutilated, disemboweled, burned at the stake and subjected to a variety of lesser torments. That is circumstance with a vengeance—and the word vengeance is used advisedly.

But in some respects, circumstantial freedom is not so obvious. We assume, in the U. S. today, that we have a wide variety of circumstantial freedoms. We do, but sometimes we have come to speak our minds, or to assemble peaceably, and discovered that freedom was not so simple. Richard Harris, in a disturbing book, has shown, in detail, how little real freedom we have, at least when it comes to important matters, and how government can take away our supposed freedoms almost when it pleases.[6] (When one considers that at this moment a federal study group is considering a proposal that would require all workers to carry identity cards with their pictures on them, 1984 seems close indeed.) Harris does believe, however, that we can reassert our rights, if we have the will to do so. It will not be easy, of course, but freedom never has been easy to get.

One difficulty is that, since most of us think we have the freedoms we are told are ours, there seems to be no need to protest. Perhaps it isn't until we are directly involved that we realize the limitations of our freedom. Libraries can play an important part here by providing books, films and other materials documenting our crippled rights.

There are other more subtle aspects to the problem of circumstantial freedom, some of which we can indicate. We blithely say we have freedom of the press. It is true that newspapers have freedom of the press—sometimes. But do you have a printing press? In 1980 one could buy a small daily newspaper for a minimum of $20 million. Surely this is out of the range of most people. Thus, even though we have a technical freedom of the press, gaining access to that freedom is no simple matter for the bulk of the citizenry.

There are, of course, other means of access to newspapers. Some have a page open to those with varying points of view, although only a few individuals will ever get to express their ideas there. There are editorial advertisements, but they are very expensive, and tend to be of use mainly to large corporations. One can write a letter to the editor, but more often than not, the newspaper will not publish it.

As to other media of communication, citizens have some access to cable television; and as with newspapers, there is a very limited access to some stations for those holding ideas that differ from the station's. Leaflets can usually be printed and distributed fairly inexpensively. And one can—usually—hire a hall.

On the other hand, even these limited means of access pose problems. Printers, for example, not infrequently refuse to print material of which they disapprove. And it is hard to reach a large audience through the foregoing methods. Obviously, when it comes to enjoying one's First Amendment rights, money, if not absolutely essential, is of the first importance. Freedom is not free.

Another aspect of circumstantial freedom is choice—or the lack thereof. The choice between two candidates whose views are indistinguishable, or the choice among several brands of spongy bread, is no choice at all. And when it comes to news, in many communities, there is only one newspaper and one television station—which, moreover, are often owned by the same company. As Locke notes, a prisoner is free to walk from one end of his cell to the other. This is the kind of freedom many think we have now.

The road to the acquisition of internal freedom is also filled with potholes. "We are born free as we are born rational,"[7] John Locke said, and he believed that freedom was grounded on our having reason. Thus we can acquire wisdom—and freedom—through a rational process. Reason is also one of the traditional bases on which rests our framework of circumstantial freedoms. From this, and similar, notions grew the concept of the "marketplace of ideas," the belief that through a free discussion by rational beings, the truth would be reached. And the truth—as everyone knows—will make you free. This is one of the basic concepts underlying our system of government and, not incidentally, the idea of the public library.

But in the late-twentieth-century, absurdity has reached such a peak that many have come to feel such a course is not possible; indeed, that we are irrational creatures in an irrational world. There seems to be plenty of fuel for this idea. After the assassinations of several prominent figures, after "the best and the brightest" led us into Vietnam, after the Nazis, the destruction of Cambodia and a hundred other horrors, it is not difficult to understand the fascination of tarot cards, the I Ching and other manifestations of unreason. Certainly many novelists, painters and other artists concur in this view of the world.

Modern psychology bears out our observations, suggesting that a person's beliefs are formulated less by reality and discourse than by pressure arising from inner conflict. We apparently experience these conflicts from infancy, and as we mature, we are forced to become more and more preoccupied with the pressures involved in repressing and rechanneling desires. We tend to exclude objectivity or reflection as we confront these conflicts. Instead we develop a series of external reactions and signals that will, we hope, reduce the pressures on the inner self and allow us to participate in social exchange with a low level of abrasiveness. The storms of adolescence are testaments to the growing awareness of the conflicts that exist within us.

As our sense of selfhood develops, we begin to oppose the authorities who previously directed our lives. This is a painful process, and we often make mistakes as we separate from the security of family authority and face the necessity of establishing our own internal authority. There are days of joy and days of fear and loneliness. For some it is a losing battle—the fear and pain are too much, and the struggle for personal maturity is abandoned. Many do not want a freedom that involves carrying so many burdens and offers so much loneliness, and they adopt a number of strategies to avoid it. Walter Kaufmann lists ten major ones, among them drifting, joining a movement, joining a political party, joining a religion and marriage.[8] While he points out that not everybody who acts this way is avoiding autonomy, he clearly believes many are.

Those who do move on, in terms of internal development, discover that they can, for the most part, face new decisions and confront uncertainties. They fight the same battles over and over as the developing self confronts society, conformity battling originality, dependence seeking to overcome independence. And even if we achieve a measure of autonomy, we realize that many of our choices and decisions contain at least an element of irrationality, and are based upon internal pressures and conflicts.

One definition of individualism is "free and independent individual action or thought." This is inseparable from reason as the foundation of our heritage of freedom—the heritage, that is, of which Locke and Mill are the chief apostles. But concurrent with the disbelief in reason is the belief that individualism is no longer possible—even, perhaps, not desirable, that society so molds us that we merely run with the herd. Concurrent with, and probably part of, this belief is the idea that individuals do not matter, that the forces of society are so large and powerful that individuals can't change anything in any case. It is also easy to share this view of our society—and of the world. The suburban street with the blue spruce planted squarely in the middle of every front yard, and with every television set turned on and tuned to the same situation comedy, is only the most obvious sign that mass communications and mass consumerism are turning us into a country of think-alikes.

We watch role models being prepackaged and sent into the national consciousness. Our political debates are staged entertainments, which assiduously avoid issues while concentrating on the game-show race for delegates and the amassing of votes. Technological advance is colored by our need for status symbols, with planned obsolescence its hallmark, and reasoned planning is negated as detrimental to "free" enterprise.

Herbert Marcuse can best exemplify the thinking that reasoned individualism is no longer possible. His work proposes that the individual has always been the victim of circumstance, and as a result of current practice has become the victim of subjugation. Marcuse contends that in preindustrial society the desires and needs of the individual were allowed to flourish in a sort of natural freedom. But as society began to organize, those once freely developed needs and desires got in the way of corporate societal needs. It was then that harsh and repressive methods were used, as the only way to assure obedience.

Marcuse and other like-minded critics claim that our society molds our earliest and most subtle impulses. It now has and uses the means to reach into our very dreams to shape our desires. Thus, overt repression is no longer necessary. Why force individuals to conform, when they can be manipulated? Besides, force is inefficient, and certainly messy. Currently few develop desires and needs that cannot be accommodated without unduly threatening corporate society. (External controls are still applied, however, when—in spite of manipulation—individuals will not conform. Some of these controls we call censorship.)

Let Marcuse speak for himself:

> Under the rule of the repressive whole, liberty can be made into a powerful instrument of domination. The range of choice open to the individual is not the decisive factor in determining the degree of human freedom, but what *can* be chosen and what *is* chosen by the individual. The criterion for free choice can never be an absolute one, but neither is it relative. Free election of masters does not abolish the masters of slaves. Free choice among a wide variety of goods and services does not signify freedom if those goods and services sustain social control over a life of toil and fear—that is, if they sustain alienation. And the spontaneous reproduction of superimposed needs by the individual does not establish autonomy; it only testifies to the efficiency of the controls.[9]

This is a compelling statement. We cannot watch the election process and speak of free choice without wry cynicism. We no longer feel secure about asserting our choice in the marketplace. It is commonly assumed that we will receive shoddy goods. And we feel powerless in the face of the forces that govern our lives—the anonymous multinational corporations, pervasive government, and seemingly autonomous social and economic phenomena. Unable to combat these forces, we seek scapegoats in anything different, or in anybody who does challenge the system. Again we can see the origin of much censorship.

At the same time, we believe we are a free people. We have been told this is so since childhood, and it is one of our most cherished convictions. Society, then, has molded us into something resembling automatons, obeying its dictates and saluting mythical freedoms. But is it only present-day society that molds individuals? Have the inhabitants of any society been internally free? (We know most of them did not have external freedoms.) Clearly, primitive peoples, seemingly the freest of all, are in reality the least free, bound as they are by custom and ritual.

Humans are gregarious animals, and it appears that all societies develop out of some human need to be part of a larger whole. We want and seek to establish traditions. We need to feel we share customs and values, and enjoy sharing similarities. We want, in short, to be like others around us, to be part of the herd. We do not want to be torn away from contact with and acceptance by others.

Is reasoned individualism then possible? Or, to put it another way, is it possible to acquire freedom, to be free internally? Throughout history there have been individuals who appear to have done so (some of them were mentioned earlier in this chapter). And if some individuals can be free, is such freedom not inherent in all of us? It is obvious that there are many who want it; otherwise we would not be witness to the thousands who sacrifice their worldly possessions, and often their lives, to try to achieve it. That they merely exchange one set of controls for another does not alter the knowledge that the longing for some vague idea of freedom is widespread, if not universal.

Meanwhile, we live in a society and we must make the best of it. We *are* reasoning individuals, because we are human. And reason is what we have to solve our problems. It never leads us to the whole truth, of course. At best, all we ever attain is a partial truth. The world is complex and in a constant state of flux, so the truth is ever-changing, even though many want it fixed forever. But through reason, and in spite of irrational elements within us, we reach a kind of truth, and that allows us to function until we can learn more truth. So reason, no matter what the difficulties, is the human way to solve human problems.

Furthermore, individuals can, and do, matter. (Rachel Carson and Ralph Nader are two, among others, who have made significant differences in recent years.) Some will argue that nothing has really changed. But, one suspects, those people want the world changed overnight; if it isn't, they will say nothing works. The truth is that we have to keep battling. To do so is the human condition.

If we, as reasoning individuals, are going to acquire an internal freedom and attain a real circumstantial, or external, freedom, we must also acquire tolerance, and not only for ideas a little different from ours, but for those we really dislike. Tolerance for "the thought we hate," as Oliver Wendell Holmes put it, has usually been honored more in the breach than in the observance, but it is the essence of any real freedom. Although its use is sometimes out of fashion, tolerance is a good word for this purpose: we merely have to bear or endure the ideas opposed to our own, we don't have to like them. Tolerance and freedom of expression are in fact inseparable: if we are free to speak, others must be also.

But must we tolerate everything? In actual practice, we don't, of course. Such things as libel, "fighting words," and a few others have not generally been permitted by the courts—although the latitude we are allowed in these matters varies according to the time and place. This is as it must be, however, because such concepts are not, and cannot, be fixed. So we have to continually adjust them.

Naturally then, there is considerable difference of opinion as to what society should permit. Marcuse, for example, wants an intellectual elite to decide what should be allowed. This is an old and enticing idea, but it doesn't work. The same points have to be made in dealing with all censors, over and over again, apparently ad infinitum. Who is to choose what is to be read? said? heard? seen? And so on. One only has to follow the history of the Supreme Court to see some of the problems involved in making such decisions.

People always ask whether expression that is damaging to others should be allowed. Our answer is that we must allow expression that might be damaging—although we don't, in fact, know if it ever is. Much expression is probably damaging, in some respects, to somebody. Indeed, some may be necessary—in an imperfect world—as part of the toughening process of life. In any case, libraries, if they supply potentially damaging material, also supply a variety of supporting materials to counter it. (See the chapter entitled "At What Age Freedom?" for further discussion of this subject.)

We also must tolerate potentially damaging expression because if everyone is not free, nobody is free. But freedom, once allowed, can lead to all kinds of dangers. When the American Nazi Party wanted to march through Skokie, Illinois, where a large group of concentration-camp survivors lived, many felt the situation was intolerable, potentially damaging to some and that it might lead to violence. Again we must ask: Where do you draw the line? If you don't permit the Nazis to march, should you allow the Civil Rights marchers, or the antiwar marchers? And if only unprovocative expression is allowed, what is the point of freedom? One of the purposes of freedom of expression is to assist in making necessary changes. And this only happens when people are disturbed.

We must even be tolerant of the expression of ideas that might lead to the destruction of the State. The State may be allowed to prevent acts that will destroy it, but as Montesquieu said, "Words do not constitute an overt act; they remain only an idea."[10] In any case, it is doubtful that any government has been overthrown merely through the expression of dissenting ideas. Some, of course, feel that the government should not be criticized. Often this opinion is voiced by those in government, who suggest that any criticism is a danger to the State. Usually it is only a danger to those individuals, however.

Along with individualism and a supreme faith in reason, historical optimism was one of the tenets of our eighteenth- and nineteenth-century forbears. The principle of historical optimism exults in a joyous and spontaneous movement of the human soul toward an ever-more reasonable and orderly life through the practice of individualism and rationality. This was a faith in ultimate perfection, derived—as Tocqueville pointed out—as much from the American experience itself as from Locke, Mill and other thinkers. Tocqueville suggests that equality expands belief in the idea of human perfectibility, and thus faith in progress. While Americans do not presume to have arrived at the supreme good and absolute truth, he said they think they are almost there. He cited as an example a sailor who, when asked why American ships were not built to last, said that every day brings such rapid progress in the art of navigation, ships become obsolete in a few years.[11]

Freedom to reason, and to express oneself, thus had a purpose: it was the road to perfection. This belief was widely held until recently. But one doesn't hear much talk of progress now, and such faith is probably not possible. Nor is it necessary. This makes the fight for freedom even more important; knowing we can't ever achieve it completely or permanently, we must always keep at it.

The principles we have been discussing (faith in reason, tolerance of all ideas, individualism and historical optimism) have had their influence on the framers of the U. S. Constitution, on our traditions, and on the idea of the public library. They are embodied in the Library Bill of Rights, a policy statement developed in 1939 and promulgated by the American Library Association, and most recently revised in January of 1980.

LIBRARY BILL OF RIGHTS

The American Library Association affirms that all libraries are forums for information and ideas, and that the following basic policies should guide their services.

1. Books and other library resources should be provided for the interest, information and enlightenment of all people of the community the library serves. Materials should not be excluded because of origin, background, or views of those contributing to their creation.

2. Libraries should provide materials and information presenting all points of view on current and historical issues. Materials should not be proscribed or removed because of partisan or doctrinal disapproval.

3. Libraries should challenge censorship in the fulfillment of their responsibility to provide information and enlightenment.

4. Libraries should cooperate with all persons and groups concerned with resisting abridgement of free expression and free access to ideas.

5. A person's right to the use of a library should not be denied or abridged because of origin, age, background, or views.

6. Libraries which make exhibit spaces and meeting rooms available to the public they serve should make facilities available on an equitable basis regardless of the beliefs or affiliations of individuals or groups requesting their use.[12]

The idea that libraries are "forums for...ideas," that they should provide for the "enlightenment of all people" and should supply "all points of view" suggests that the origin of this document is in the principles of individualism, rationalism and historical optimism. These principles are, with numerous qualifications, still the backbone of the public-library idea, as well as of all kinds of school libraries. Certainly the notion of libraries represents the apotheosis of individualism, and, in large parts of libraries' collections, of reason.

The question of whether these principles can survive, remains, and thus of whether meaningful libraries can too. We can use the New Left and the New Right to demonstrate why librarians standing up for these principles, based on the essays of Locke and Mill, often find themselves at odds with the society they serve. Both groups would have us withdraw our tolerance of expression of which they disapprove, and subscribe to their collective wisdoms, following the "correct" course of action, or adhering to easily recognized and immutable duties and standards. Meanwhile, the old liberal is still at work, engaged in feasibility studies, and continues to place his faith in more and better social and political agencies. One is reminded of Yeats:

> The best lack all conviction, while the worst
> Are full of passionate intensity.

While the foregoing are admittedly broad generalizations on the state of modern society, they should serve to point out the convergence of various viewpoints, all of which seem to be calling for a sort of communalism, a grouping of effort that swings away from the pronounced individualism and faith in one's ability to make the proper choices of the past. All express a distrust of human rationality isolated from human interaction, and reason and individualism seem to be disappearing. From all quarters there is emerging a historical pessimism stressing that human beings are not about to bring order out of chaos with an optimistic emphasis on individualism and reason.

There may be some hope in those (still relatively few) who are drawing on traditional individualism to find new ways of living outside the corporate blanket. They may even be the new hope for freedom. In the meantime, does the library face a future as an agency of advocacy for collectivism? Too many librarians are already acquiescing in the homogenizing of American life, and are turning their libraries into supermarkets geared only to mass tastes, where circulation takes the place of profits. Should the library remain a steadfast bastion against the forces of social upheaval and continue to stand for the right of the individual to retreat into a world of ideas in order to consider rational and irrational arguments, in search of a truth meaningful in the midst of chaos? What most groups who oppose this notion seem not to understand is that in a free society, ideas are not part of a popularity contest, with the majority deciding which are to be permitted.

Freedom, then, as we started out by saying, comes in various forms and operates on many levels. Furthermore, one person's freedom is another's lack of it. The freedom of some to destroy a wooded area takes away the freedom of others to enjoy it. Affirmative Action programs may limit the freedom of some while promoting that of others. And we all give up some freedoms—such as being allowed to drive on either side of the road—so we may have others. We should all realize, in fact, that we need laws so we can have freedom. This apparent paradox can be resolved if one thinks of a lawless society, where the many will be tyrannized by the few. And librarians are beginning to learn that laws can protect them from censors, just as laws in the past were censorious.

What, then, do we need as a society? Going back to Adler's three categories of freedom, we find that we need them all. We need circumstantial freedom to allow us to fulfill ourselves, and to create a society that is fruitful for all. It includes, not only the negative aspect of laws, which prevent others from infringing on our rights, but the positive aspect, of governments' (and thus libraries') actively promoting freedom of expression. Some aspects of this freedom clash, as when the rights of one infringe on the rights of another. As such it is a protean freedom, which is constantly being adjusted and refined.

Acquired freedom is probably necessary to circumstantial

freedom. We must accept the fact that life is chaotic, and that oppression and suppression must be dealt with on a daily basis. We must truly educate ourselves, learning to understand ourselves and our society. We must learn our history and the sources of our traditions, so that we can free ourselves from the myths and glittering generalities of that history, and at the same time value its basic principles.

Natural freedom is something we have because we are human—because of the qualities of the human mind that cannot be limited. Understanding that we have freedom naturally, we can—and must—try to acquire a greater internal freedom through understanding, and work toward circumstantial freedom because we know it is necessary. Knowing we have freedom naturally, we must also be aware that in some senses it is not negotiable: we can't give it away, nor can it be taken from us. This leads to conflicts, of course—as in a clash of rights—but life is full of conflicting interests, and it is important to know that some freedoms are inalienable.

Where does this leave the library—and the librarian? we all know, or should know, that libraries are not often used for the high-minded purposes we like to imagine. It is rare when library users set out to rationalize their merry way toward changed opinion and to reevaluate truth. Indeed, so innocent are the average users, that they become angry and disappointed in the library when they discover that their values and opinions are being questioned by a piece of material they have found in the collection. Yet, allowing users to exercise their freedom is espoused as a goal of the library.

Still, there are many who realize the function of the library, and some who come to accept the existence of other opinions, although they had not intended to do so. There are even a few who come to the library in search of wisdom.

So it is up to the librarian to provide all users with the means of self-fulfillment, whether they merely want to reinforce their opinions or are genuine seekers, or even if they fall into neither category.

It is also up to the librarian to promote freedom—both internal and external. Equality and freedom were not considerations in the promulgation of library service in earlier years in the United States. And when it came to services to youth, there was simply no place for them in early libraries. As American society evolved, it became apparent that youth should be given some form of library service, but only in tightly controlled situations. (In some library buildings, there still exist entrance doors marked "Children" or even "Boys" and "Girls.") The Library Bill of Rights, in its original (1939) form, reflected this philosophy. Even in 1961, when a paragraph on the rights of the individual to use the library was added for the first time, youth was not considered. Youth services were added to the document in 1967, but the statement that age should not impinge on one's right to use the library caused so much consternation that in 1972 a special interpretive piece, "Free Access to Libraries for Minors," had to be composed and adopted.[13]

Freedom has been limited by librarians in many ways, and for a variety of reasons. During World War I, the American Library Association, in charge of Library War Service, rejected as "improper" certain books being sent to soldiers and sailors.[14] Those who have been librarians for a number of years can remember numerous battles involving this type of problem. But libraries evolve, like other institutions, more or less as the society does, and we are now fighting other battles—both within and among ourselves, as well as with forces outside the library.

We said earlier that librarians should promote freedom. Librarians are also told to be neutral. Are these conflicting statements? Perhaps we should distinguish between kinds of neutrality. Librarians should not recommend one idea or value over another. They might well, however, bring materials with various ideas and values to the attention of users. In fact, they do this all the time, with lists and exhibits and in other ways. Librarians should advocate and promote access to materials for all ages, for every educational level, for those speaking any kind of language found in the community and for those with any kind of handicap. And they should advocate and promote freedom for us all to have access to every idea, and to make those ideas available in whatever format best suits their expression. In those respects, librarians are not neutral. Librarians should advocate these freedoms, not only because freedom is a good in itself, but also because living is chaotic, tumultuous and fraught with obstacles and problems that must be dealt with daily, yearly and across generations. The library is an institution designed by a society that has hopes for the future built upon mistakes of the past, and as such it is a tool for the acquisition of freedom by the individual who seeks self-fulfillment and full participation in a complex society.

NOTES

1. Mortimer J. Adler, *The Idea of Freedom*, vol. 1 (New York: Doubleday, 1958), p. 112.
2. Ibid., p. 135.
3. Walter Kaufmann, *Without Guilt and Justice* (New York: Peter H. Wyden, 1973), pp. 32-34.
4. Adler, *Freedom*, p. 149.
5. Thomas Emerson, *Toward a General Theory of the First Amendment* (New York: Random House, 1963), pp. 4-5.
6. Richard Harris, *Freedom Spent* (Boston: Little, Brown, 1976).
7. John Locke, *Treatise of Civil Government and a Letter Concerning Toleration* (New York: Appleton-Century-Crofts, 1937), p. 39.
8. Kaufmann, *Without Guilt*, pp. 7-30.
9. Herbert Marcuse, *One-Dimensional Man* (Boston: Beacon Press, 1964), pp. 7-8.
10. Baron de Montesquieu, *The Spirit of the Laws* (New York: Hafner, 1949), p. 193.
11. Alexis de Tocqueville, *Democracy in America*, vol. II (New York: Schocken Books, 1961), p. 39.
12. Committee on Intellectual Freedom, American Library Association, "The Library Bill of Rights." Single-page document adopted by the ALA council, January 1980. Copies are available from the Office for Intellectual Freedom, ALA, 50 E. Huron St., Chicago, IL 60611.
13. Office for Intellectual Freedom, American Library Association, *Intellectual Freedom Manual*, Part One (Chicago: ALA, 1974), pp. 14-17. Background on the School Library Bill of Rights can be found in this manual in Part Two, pp. 20-24.
14. Theodore Wesley Koch, *Books in the War; the Romance of Library War Service* (Boston: Houghton Mifflin, 1919), p. 15.

Chapter Two
Freedom and the Type of Library

Libraries have different sources of funding—as well as different purposes—which can and do influence the ways in which they view not only the kinds of materials they should collect, but the amount and kind of access they will provide to those materials. It is commonly assumed that privately funded libraries, regardless of their mission, have the right to collect and to offer access to materials only to those who pay for the library's program. Indeed, it can be safely said that no private institution that has not accepted public monies has been forced to make its library materials available to anyone it did not wish to, or to select or reject any item on a partisan basis.

Some institutions in the education and research field have decided (even where public funding is not a factor) that a more open access and acquisitions policy is in order. But we would do well to remember that such libraries could devote their entire collections to Gothic novels or the promotion of cannibalism, and no one could deny them that right. The authors do know, in fact, of a library that does not collect materials suggesting that the earth might be a spheroid.

Publicly-funded libraries, on the other hand, such as school, college, public, prison or hospital libraries, do have obligations to the public that provides the basis of their fiscal support. These libraries are bound by state and local laws and regulations. Usually such statutes charge them to provide access to any potential user. Beyond that, libraries themselves have evolved a number of unwritten obligations to their communities and to their users, although it should be understood that these obligations are not supported by a wide variety of case law.

Obviously, libraries in educational institutions collect materials at different levels, but they do have some principles in common. They all have a duty to acquire—and make accessible—materials that will enhance and nourish the minds of their users. Such libraries have no pronounced need for materials that serve a purely recreational purpose, although many of the items they acquire will function that way as well. And they are not required to supply material that is outside the educational needs of their users. Educational goals, of course, imply the need for a broad range of materials. If nourishing minds is the goal, those minds must be fed a varied diet—coarse, smooth, sweet, sour, aged, fresh and so on. The difficulty arises because the word education is widely misunderstood; many persons confuse the storing of facts with education, or they confuse education with the indoctrination of orthodox ideas, and they don't condone a variety of ideas. And that's where the censor puts in an appearance. The censor thinks schools should indoctrinate or they should not mention certain things or they should denounce certain ideas.

But the censor aside, the libraries of educational institutions are generally free from public pressure to acquire or reject a particular item. There is, of course, a kind of general pressure on them to adapt to a changing society, but this doesn't apply to any one book or film.

The situation of public libraries is somewhat different. They do accede to public demand in some ways. If members of the public request, or reserve, particular books, public libraries often respond by purchasing those items. If a book is not read for some time, the public library will, in all likelihood, discard it. Within some limits, those are things it should do, because the purpose of the public library is to serve the public. "Ay, there's the rub," said Hamlet, who might have been selecting books for the Elsinore Public Library. What public are we talking about? In any community, there are many publics. (This is a fact censors fail, willfully or not, to understand.) But it is not only censors who seem to fail to see it. When one of the authors was in library school, more than thirty years ago, a controversy was raging in the profession. It still is. That is the controversy between "elitism" and "demand" collection development. Should public libraries buy only the "good books"—the classics, the "wholesome" books, the well-written books, the "important" books? Or should they buy according to public demand, including comic books, formula fiction, punk-rock records, and ninety copies of every best seller? Not many months go by that there isn't an article in one of the professional journals on this subject, and it can raise an argument among librarians at any time. These arguments are usually put in either-or terms, the implicit assumption being that one can't do both. The popularity people will tell you that nobody reads Milton anymore, and that if an item doesn't circulate, it should be thrown out and replaced with something (presumably anything) that will circulate. The bottom line is frequently invoked by this group, as if the library were indistinguishable from the supermarket, and books were so many cans of peas.

Those at the other extreme regard new forms, new media, and new ideas with suspicion, if not disdain. If it isn't a hardcover book written in English and published before 1940, well, who wants it? At the moment, the demand theorists seem to be winning. But, to paraphrase everybody's favorite elitist author, a plague on both their houses. Public libraries can, and should, buy for both kinds of users, and for many other kinds as well. We don't have the money, someone is certain to answer. No, we don't, and that's too bad. But when selecting materials for public libraries, we must serve, not "the public," but all the publics. And we must serve them as well as we can. We are not in business, and we have no right to throw over any portion of the public because there is more profit in another. That means spreading the money around, and it means other expedients such as interlibrary loan and reserve collections. It also means keeping a little bit of a lot of things in the local library—particularly those that are little read or little known—so that people may become aware of them. If we don't, we are not serving the purposes of the public library. (People still do read *Paradise Lost*, by the way.)

But why should public libraries act this way? There are several reasons, all of which assume a belief in freedom. Not everyone believes in freedom, of course. A state prosecutor has recently been quoted as saying, "Americans have genuflected too long at the altar of free speech." Clearly, those who censor anything at all don't believe in freedom for some items or for some people.

Perhaps we should start by trying to explain why freedom is

important, although there shouldn't be any doubt about the reasons, given the number of people through the centuries who have died defending it. But it may be that a full appreciation of freedom is only apparent to those who have felt its lack. A woman who had spent forty years in China, recently appeared on television. She expressed joy at having strangers speak openly to her, and at being able to respond freely.

Thomas I. Emerson, in *The System of Freedom of Expression*, discusses why freedom of expression is important.[1] First, he says, it is essential to self-fulfillment, which he considers the proper end of man. Next, it is essential for advancing knowledge and discovering truth. Third, it is necessary so that all members of a society can participate in its decisions. Emerson goes on to say that once one accepts the premise of the Declaration of Independence that governments "derive their just powers from the consent of the governed," it follows that the governed must have freedom of expression in order to form judgments. Significantly, he says this principle is important, not only in making political decisions, but in all areas of life, including religion, literature, art and science.

Finally, Emerson believes freedom of expression to be important in maintaining a stable society. He says it "provides a framework in which the conflict necessary to the progress of society can take place without destroying society."[2]

The importance of participating in society's decisions, as well as the importance of self-fulfillment, is reinforced by Bettelheim, who says that "a sense of autonomy depends everywhere on the conviction that one can make important decisions, and *can do it where it counts most*" (italics ours). Further, Bettelheim notes, "if one finds it impossible, first to influence one's social and physical environment, and later to make decisions on how and when to modify it, this is harmful, if not devastating, to the human personality."[3]

John Stuart Mill gives us the classic argument about why Emerson's second reason is important, or, conversely, he cites the arguments for not suppressing ideas.[4] In the first place, Mill says, the suppressed idea may be true. On the other hand, the suppressed idea may be false, but it is necessary to hear it to have a clearer apprehension of the truth. In most cases, however, the opinion we hear is a partial truth, and it will be necessary to know of other ideas, to add to that truth. Mill unwittingly demonstrated the importance of that last proposition when he said, "If even the Newtonian philosophy were not permitted to be questioned, mankind could not feel as complete assurance of its truth as they now do. The beliefs which we have most warrant for have no safeguard to rest on but a standing invitation to the whole world to prove them unfounded..."[5] Any censors would do well to ponder that statement, for as all the world now knows, "early in the twentieth century... the foundations on which Newton's work rests were seen to be in need of drastic revision."[6] And as any librarian who maintains a collection knows, the foundations of sacred cows continue to be brought into question in all fields, as they always will be, for our knowledge is never final.

We might adduce many quotations in support of freedom of expression, but we will give only two more. Madison said, "A popular government, without popular information, or the means of acquiring it, is but a prologue to a farce or a tragedy; or, perhaps both. Knowledge will forever govern ignorance: And a people who mean to be their own governors, must arm themselves with the power which Knowledge gives."[7]

Finally, let us quote William O. Douglas, who discussed this subject many times, most pertinently when he stated that

> it is only through free debate and free exchange of ideas that government remains responsive to the will of the people and peaceful change is effected. The right to speak freely and to promote diversity of ideas and programs is therefore one of the chief distinctions that sets us apart from totalitarian regimes. Accordingly a function of free speech under our system of government is to invite a dispute. It may indeed best serve its high purpose when it induces a condition of unrest, creates dissatisfaction with conditions as they are, or even stirs people to anger. (*Terminiello* v. *Chicago* 357 U. S. 1 [1949])[8]

All of these statements are of particular significance for libraries, and especially public libraries, because they are a necessary part of the system of freedom of expression. If there exists a right to express an opinion, then there also exists a right to know about that opinion. Where else but in the library, and especially in the public library, can *all* citizens avail themselves of that right? Robert O'Neil, Professor of Law at the University of Cincinnati, said, in an article of great importance to librarians, that the public library system typically receives substantial governmental appropriations and thus incurs, almost axiomatically, an obligation to serve the entire community from which support is drawn. Moreover the public library really has a monopoly position in the community.... As a practical matter, therefore, countless volumes will be unavailable if they are not carried on the public library shelves. In this respect the responsibility of the libraries may be even greater than that of other components of the public forum.

Further,

Private bookstores and libraries do exist, but are only accessible to those who can afford to pay. For those who cannot pay, the public library is the sole channel of access not only to relatively expensive hardcover books but to less costly items like magazines and even daily newspapers. Thus the public library is as integral a part of the public forum as the municipal park or auditorium, and access to its resources should be unfettered for comparable reasons.[9]

Meanwhile, back at the librarian's office, the decision must be made as to what to buy. And is there any category of materials, or any particular item, a public library should not acquire? Sometimes, restricting parts of a collection, or not acquiring some controversial item, is defended on political grounds. The library's budget, not to mention the librarian's job, is often threatened by the would-be censor, and sometimes that censor is in a position to do a lot of damage. Is that not a justification? Professor O'Neil says,

This is a constitutionally illegitimate consideration. The curtailment of first amendment or other civil rights has never been permitted on fiscal or expediency grounds, Unpopularity or feared loss of legislative support cannot justify denial or abridgement of individual rights.... From these cases emerges a double principle ... constitutional rights ... cannot be abridged or denied because the exercise of those rights may be costly or inconvenient to the community. The possible reduction of support for the public library cannot justify the withholding or suppression of controversial works. Rather, the remedy is to do a better job of explaining to the appropriating body the true character and mission of a public library, and the need to maintain the broadest range of materials.[10]

But sometimes materials are offensive to library users, and, we may personally feel, justifiably so. They may even be offensive to the selector. The quotation from William O. Douglas is appropriate here. We may best fulfill our (the library's) first-amendment function if some materials stir people to anger. The Palisades (N. Y.) Free Library, in its "Book Selection Policy Statement," says that an objection to any acquisition is an indication that it "may well be of more than routine interest and may be likely to be requested by members of the community who wish to judge its merits and demerits for themselves." In other words, rather than withdrawing the item to which there has been an objection, it is the librarian's duty to acquire it. Thomas I. Emerson points out: "Search for the truth is handicapped because much of the argument is never heard or heard only weakly. Political decisions are distorted because the views of some citizens never reach other citizens, and feedback to the government is feeble." He continues,

> the government must affirmatively make available the opportunity for expression ... positive measures must be taken to ensure the ability to speak despite economic barriers. It also means that greater attention must be given to the right of the citizen to hear varying points of view and the right to have access to information upon which such points of view can be intelligently based.[11]

It should be remembered that, in giving his reasons for the importance of freedom of expression, Emerson spoke not only of politics, but also of religion, literature, art and science.

It begins to look as if we were making an impossible job more difficult. But perhaps not. Someone has pointed out that if you prevent one group from using a hall, you give tacit approval to those to whom you grant permission to use the hall. Doesn't the same principle apply to library materials? If we overcome our timidity and acquire as many kinds of materials as we can, not neglecting any significant public demand and recognizing implicit as well as explicit demand, the public may come to realize what we are about, especially if it realizes its interests are not being neglected. It is time librarians discarded selection-policy statements explaining that they don't acquire materials that "foster hate," are "inflammatory," are "sensational" and so on. If materials answering these descriptions are wanted by members of the public, libraries should acquire them. Thus libraries might buy the writings of those historians who deny the murder of six million Jews during the Nazi regime, or the writings of a variety of people who claim that blacks are inferior to whites.

You are, of course, ready with objections. The foregoing are simply offensive, or at worst, distressing. But medical books are another problem; some present new or old remedies for cancer, heart disease, arthritis and other vital problems that are not accepted by the medical profession, and, indeed, are often considered to be positively harmful. And there are popular diets that have resulted in deaths and serious illnesses. We don't want to be responsible for anyone's taking a quack cure when traditional medicine could save a life. On the other hand, a lot of lives are lost through standard medical practices, and they just might have been saved by something else. Given the state of medicine, we don't know. The scientific community is given to dogmatic assertions that particular theories are ridiculous, later only to be proven wrong. It would seem that we have a duty to provide the public with access to these theories, if it wants them. Readers can then make up their own minds, which they have every right to do. Nobody, including librarians, has a key to the truth—unless the truth is on a closed shelf and the key is in the reference desk drawer.

There are other scientific ideas with which librarians should be concerned. Some individuals work outside or on the fringes of the scientific establishment, and their ideas are usually regarded as outlandish. They have difficulty in communicating those ideas, not because they don't express themselves well, but because—in various ways— they are censored. Theodore Gordon, in *Ideas in Conflict*, describes some of those methods.[12] Usually, he says, such individuals are denied access to technical media, they are denied funding, innuendo may be used against them, and sometimes suppression is organized. The only way they can be heard, then, is by going directly to the public. Given the many times the scientific community has proven *not* to have the "truth," it seems apparent that public libraries should acquire the work of any of these individuals in which there is a public interest—or, just possibly, even if there isn't known interest.

Gordon, himself an engineer, says, "I found no formula for distinguishing the potential contributor from the pretentious crackpot."[13] Nobody, in other words, can tell if a scientific theory is valid and will prove useful or if it isn't and it won't. But the public has a right to make up its own mind, or rather, each person has a right to make up his or her own mind, and that is one of the reasons public libraries exist.

But what about the publications of the Flat Earth Society? Everybody knows the earth is round, isn't it so? Obviously some people don't think so. Or, to take a slightly less obvious example, what about those who believe in the Biblical version of the creation of the earth and deny the theory of evolution? Both these groups have their rights, too. If there is a demand for materials that promote those views, public libraries should make them available, whether the demand comes from the true believer or from the merely curious.

Just as there are medical books that suggest alternate cures to those prescribed by doctors, so are there books that suggest bypassing lawyers. These books are often labeled irresponsible or inaccurate by the legal profession. But again, if the public wants them, we have a duty to acquire them. In fact, we should acquire them even if there is no demand. People may not be aware that they can obtain a divorce or process a will without legal assistance, and libraries already have plenty of books that tell the reader to see a lawyer.

But let us contemplate even thornier problems. Many titles in most of the foregoing categories are already in libraries, but there are several kinds of materials that one is very unlikely to find in any library. First, consider what is usually called hard-core pornography, the kind found in "adult" bookstores. Has anybody seriously suggested that libraries collect it?* There are, of course, a few collections in specialized libraries, but we are talking about material for the general public. There is certainly public demand for it, and sometimes even libraries have patron requests. And if there isn't more demand for pornography in libraries, maybe that's because nobody expects to find it there, just as readers in many libraries do not expect to find contemporary poetry, because the librarian doesn't buy it. Librarians often make a point of saying that they don't acquire materials that "offend good taste."

---

*see Rebecca Dixon's "Bibliographic Control of Erotica," *An Intellectual Freedom Primer* ed. by Charles H. Busha (Littleton, Colo.: Libraries Unlimited, 1977), pp. 130–147.

Yet a lot of fiction without sex offends good taste by its mechanical writing, by its stereotyped characters (shrinking-violet women and cleft-chinned men, for example) and by its dull dialogue. Librarians buy it without a second thought, however, because their readers want it.

Why shouldn't librarians buy "adult-bookstore" items? Actually, they do buy some materials that are almost indistinguishable in content from such titles. Consider the writings of the Marquis de Sade, for example. There are some arguments for collecting his writings; his name is part of our everyday language, he is much written and talked about and his work is important. But there are other titles that have been published in recent years, usually anonymously, that parade under the guise of science, or self-help, or something respectable, and they are little, if any, different from *Teacher's Sex Class*. Nevertheless, libraries buy them and circulate them, maybe because they are in hard covers and therefore presentable. And libraries probably should have them if they are in demand. These titles, however, have been heavily promoted by large publishers. The titles on the special rack in the corner of the drugstore have not been advertised, and libraries don't buy them—nor would they dream of doing so. But there are those who hold that pornography is socially useful, that it provides an outlet for frustrations, even that it may help those who have psychological problems with sex. Whether it contains positive values or not, people want it, and libraries buy many other books for no better reason. No doubt it would be tempting fate to buy such books, and some segments of the community would be outraged, but if we are to be consistent, at least in our thinking, we, as librarians, should consider purchasing the kinds of materials found in "adult" bookstores.

We are not suggesting that any public librarians actually buy this material, of course, unless they feel they have community support. We all compromise our principles sometimes, and maybe there are better places to hold one's ground, but we should think about all kinds of materials and know why we are selecting or rejecting them. Unless we have thought through all the ramifications of acquiring, or not acquiring, every kind of material, we cannot well defend ourselves against those who would attack our selections or our rejections. And indeed we won't have a very good collection.

But there is an area of pornography that may be even more troubling than the common garden variety, which simply has explicit descriptions of sex on every page. That kind has been condemned as degrading to women—although it seems just as degrading to men—but there is now some evidence that when pornography is linked to violence against women, the consumers may themselves become more violent. At any rate, as *The New York Times* has reported, some researchers are coming to that conclusion.[14]

Whether or not such experiences can lead to crime or other antisocial behavior is another question. In any case, it appears that all kinds of experiences, some of them apparently innocuous, have triggered criminal behavior in unstable individuals. Furthermore, the evidence cited in the *Times* article is far from conclusive. What is bothersome for libraries, in this case, is that some of the films studied by those researchers have been widely shown commercially, and include movies libraries might possibly show themselves. We have heard, for instance, of an alleged gang rape by a group of drunken teenagers after they saw *A Clockwork Orange*. Since many people have seen *A Clockwork Orange*, and similar films, without, apparently, engaging in such activity, and since the charge that books and films lead to criminal behavior is an old one that has been leveled against a great variety of materials, we must conclude that libraries should acquire whatever they think they need, and, having made those acquisitions, should firmly defend their decisions.

The *Covert Action Information Bulletin*, for example, has been charged with causing the deaths of CIA agents, by printing their names. But it alleges activities on the part of the United States Government that citizens surely should know about. Libraries, therefore, have a good reason to buy it, as long as it is legal to do so.

Let us take an extreme case. There are books available that describe methods of assassination, that give instruction in knife fighting, or that tell the reader how to make a variety of lethal weapons. Library patrons may have a variety of informational needs that can be best filled through these materials. If that is so, libraries should make them available.

Much of the argument for public libraries' acquiring the material—or a good deal of it—that has been described in the previous pages is based on public demand. Libraries, usually, don't have much problem with those items for which the demand is widespread, such as best-selling diet books, for example, even if the diet is dangerous. But when the demand is small and the material is less generally acceptable, such as where extreme political opinions are expressed, the argument is that we should select the best. This is closely tied to the argument that we have neither the space nor the money to buy everything. If we merely buy what the public wants, so the argument goes, where do book-selection skills come in?

There is plenty of room for selection, and we do need, insofar as possible, to satisfy not only the widespread demand, but also the minority demands; the demands of the many small, or special, interest groups. The preceding arguments have some validity; it is true that we don't have the money or the space we need. We have a duty to try to satisfy all needs, however. And as far as selection is concerned, we must also acquire, or attempt to, for unexpressed demand, and that will include finding the best in every field. As W. S. Gilbert might have said, a librarian's lot is sometimes not a happy one.

One of the many areas in which librarians can put their selection skills to work, and one that librarians often ignore, is small-press publishing. There are some fairly good reasons for this. Small presses tend to be short-lived. Finding out about and acquiring small-press materials is more difficult than acquiring from larger publishers. Furthermore, much small-press material doesn't fit the expressed standards (which are useful) of many libraries. Among these standards of selection are the reputation of the publisher, the authority of the author, the format, the quality of the bookmaking and expert opinion. These standards are helpful because time is limited and because the librarian often lacks the knowledge to judge the book entirely on its merits. (How could it be otherwise, when 30,000 books a year are published, on thousands of different subjects?)

Nevertheless, this situation works to the detriment of the library's public, since much good material is bypassed. Publishers are taking fewer and fewer chances with unknown authors, with innovative fiction, with subjects not likely to sell well and with different political, social and economic ideas. Small presses publish exactly those, and while much of it is poor or mediocre (as is the output of larger publishers), much is also exceptional. Thus librarians are denying their users access to some of the best and most imaginative creative writing, as well as to opinions that have no other outlet. Some of the most artful bookmaking is also being done by small presses. Some of this material will, no doubt, be offensive to some users, but so will some of the regular commercial-press items.

Many of the types of materials discussed in the previous pages are of interest primarily to public libraries, but some of them could also be of interest to libraries of educational institutions, depending on their level and their goals. Certainly some small-press materials would be useful in any kind of library. So might publications espousing fringe ideas in science, politics and economics. The essential differences between the private and public library are three. The latter serves *all* the public; in the public library, *demand* is *one* of the factors in selection; and the entire purpose of educational institutions is to educate, while it is only *one* of the purposes of the public library. Otherwise, for school, college and public libraries, materials should be selected to serve the goals of the particular library, from any source, on any subject and in any medium of communication.

There also exist publicly funded libraries in hospitals, old-age and nursing homes and prisons. Although there are those who want to protect everybody from harmful library materials, when it comes to special groups, such as the elderly, the blind, prisoners and so forth, there seem to be more people who want to protect them from more materials. Witness the United States senator who wants to prevent the Library of Congress from distributing a braille edition of *Playboy*. (Perhaps he thought all those raised dots would be too erotic.) The elderly, the sick, the blind and prisoners are not, essentially, any different from the rest of us, and they are just as varied. As W. S. Gilbert pointed out in the *Pirates of Penzance:*

> When a felon's not engaged in his employment,
> Or maturing his felonious little plans,
> His capacity for innocent enjoyment
> Is just as great as any honest man's.

Not only is there no reason for libraries to deprive them of enjoying all types of materials, but the need of these groups is even greater than the general public's, due to their limited mobility. Furthermore, the rights of these groups—with one exception—are the same as the rights of the general public, although it is easier to deprive them of those rights since they are relatively helpless. Hospital personnel, administrators and librarians should be aware of their varied needs and should pay particular attention to seeing that their rights are guarded.

The one exception to full rights is among prisoners. They have, after all, already been deprived of freedom of movement, and it seems sensible to assume that there is a small class of materials that prison officials are justified in keeping out of their hands. Unfortunately, prisoners have frequently been denied access to needed library materials, both officially and unofficially. Most of this censorship is unofficial; one prison librarian reported being told not to bring "any of that political garbage" and "any Commie stuff" into the institution.[15]

Prisoners have fought for, and sometimes won, the right to library services, particularly to legal materials. As we know, however, there is often a large gap between having a right and being able to exercise it. Yet prisoners should have access to the wide range of materials available to the general public, with a few minor exceptions.

And so it is our not-unexpected conclusion that libraries of all kinds should acquire those items their population needs, whatever the source or subject. But since items still must be selected—because of lack of space and money and because judgments differ about what the library's patrons need—there is a controversy about who should control that selection. This controversy centers mostly around school libraries, the contention being that parents have a right to control the schools their children attend and therefore have a right to select books for the school library. Sometimes advisory groups have been suggested for public libraries, too. Personnel in other institutions doubtless have the same ideas sometimes.

The questions we are considering, then, are not only who controls the selection, but also whether there is any difference among the kinds of libraries in this respect. School libraries are obviously different from others. Their patrons are all young and still, ostensibly, under the control of their parents. Furthermore, parents should have some rights, since they have the duty to raise their children, in saying what constitutes the education of their children. Those who want parents to control book selection never explain, however, to which parents they refer, the assumption apparently being that all parents agree. Obviously, in any community, they do not. Some courts have recognized that diversity of opinion. In an article in the *Connecticut Law Review*, Julia Turnquist Bradley finds, after reviewing a number of pertinent cases, that "A local school board must be ... proscribed from limiting a minority's access to books which a majority of parents might find objectionable." She goes on to say that it is irrelevant whether the complainants are in the majority, for parents do not have the right to control what other people's children read. "Indeed, no case has been found which permitted parents to impose their views of suitable subject matter or books on all the children in the community. Therefore, a [school] library must provide for a wide variety of tastes and beliefs, with the realization that nearly every book has the potential to arouse some parental objection."[16]

We are, of course, talking about two kinds of parents here: the majority simply have a child in school; the other are members of the school board who probably have a child in the school or had one there in the past. It should be obvious that the first kind of parent has no say about what other children should read, although sometimes they do. There is a bit more logic in the position of school boards, who believe that they should decide what books are to be in a school library. They are, after all, charged with running the school. But that logic doesn't carry us very far. In the first place, school boards change every year or so. Are the books that are permitted in the library going to change too? Such a situation could quickly become farcical. More importantly, can the majority limit the freedoms of the minority? It can when deciding on speed limits is concerned, although many Americans resist even that limitation. But when it comes to education and the access to ideas, the notion of censorship is most reprehensible and un-American. No Americans should allow their rights—or those of their children—to be voted away.

In addition, students, as we have noted elsewhere, also have rights, and these rights are violated when books are removed from the school library. "The United States Supreme Court has stated emphatically that 'neither the Fourteenth Amendment nor the Bill of Rights is for adults alone.' Nor do students 'shed their constitutional rights . . . at the schoolhouse gate.' The State . . . may not abridge their rights of freedom of speech or religion, even at school, without compelling justification."[17] Furthermore, "Young people's rights have been recognized independently of parental rights of control," and

> Students' . . . first amendment freedoms can be infringed only to prevent grave and immediate danger to interests which the State may lawfully protect. The State does have a legitimate interest in protecting the welfare of young people. However, the State cannot satisfy its burden in a school library context. Even assuming that students are influenced by what they read, the mere presence of a controversial book in a school library falls short of a "grave and immediate danger."[18]

Moreover, not only are the rights of students violated, but they are damaged in other ways. Students "may conclude that the first Amendment is not to be taken seriously." And that breeds contempt for the country's laws, and the principles on which the country was founded. "They may [also] be convinced that school officials consider students too immature or unintelligent to make rational decisions."[19] Thus the students' intellectual growth is stunted. That growth may also be stunted because students didn't read a particular book, and thus could not become aware of some new idea or point of view. As for older students, "The maintenance of a school library as a marketplace of ideas is especially crucial since high school students are expected to emerge shortly as full-fledged members of an informed and intelligent citizenry.[20]

If neither parents nor the school board should select books for the school library, then selections should be made by the librarian. And if that is true of the school library, where the users are young and impressionable and in which the parents have such a stake, it must also be true of other kinds of libraries, where the users are adult.

It has been said, by some of those who wanted to remove books from libraries, that librarians are no smarter than other people, and are therefore no better at selecting library materials. That librarians are no smarter than anyone else goes without saying. But they do have some training in selection for libraries, and they do have the experience of working in the library daily; others do not. Furthermore, they can see the collection as an entity, and they can see the library community as a unit. They are also familiar with the wide range of materials published. For all these reasons, they are in a better position than others to judge the needs of the library and its users. The question does not simply involve leaving the decisions up to the professionals because professionals know best. After all, there are bad professionals in every field, and those employing them or using their services have every right to look elsewhere.

But professionals have rights too. They have a right to practice their profession, without the public's telling them how it should be practiced. And librarians have duties and responsibilities; they have the duty to serve all of their public, not just a part of it—even a very large part—who might want a book removed. In this respect, all publicly funded libraries are alike.

NOTES

1. Thomas I. Emerson, *The System of Freedom of Expression* (New York: Vintage Books, 1970), pp. 6–7.
2. Emerson, *Freedom*, p. 7.
3. Bruno Bettelheim, *The Informed Heart* (New York: The Free Press, 1960), p. 69.
4. John Stuart Mill, "On Liberty," *Prefaces to Liberty* (Boston: Beacon Press, 1959).
5. Ibid., p. 262.
6. Collier's *Encyclopedia*, vol. 17, p. 470.
7. Letter to W. T. Barry, August 14, 1822, quoted in Robert M. O'Neil's "Libraries, Liberty and the First Amendment," *University of Cincinnati Law Review* 42, 2 (1973): 220.
8. Quoted in Haig Bosmajian's *Justice Douglas and Freedom of Speech* (Metuchen, N. J.: Scarecrow, 1980), pp. 34–5.
9. O'Neil, "Libraries," p. 240.
10. Ibid., p. 251.
11. Emerson, *Freedoms*, pp. 628–29.
12. Theodore Gordon, *Ideas in Conflict* (New York: St. Martin's Press, 1966).
13. Ibid., p. 251.
14. *The New York Times*, September 30, 1980, page C1.
15. William Zukowsky, "The New York Public Library and Institutional Library Services," *The Bookmark* (Winter 1979): 56.

16. Julia Turnquist Bradley, "Censoring the School Library: Do Students Have the Right to Read?" *Connecticut Law Review* 10, no. 3 (Spring 1978): 763.
17. Ibid., p. 762.
18. Ibid., pp. 763-64.
19. Ibid., p. 755.
20. Ibid., p. 771.

Chapter Three
At What Age Freedom?

The age at which children and teenagers should have access to certain subject materials and/or the adult collection in libraries concerns many people. Parents, schoolteachers and administrators, organized and unorganized clergy, politicians and the judiciary are among those willing to expound on their firm conviction that certain materials and subjects are harmful to the young. There are also those who, although uncertain about the effect of certain materials and subjects, are willing to restrict access for the young, and to demand that librarians be responsible for policing such action. Librarians generally share these ambivalent feelings about library materials and access for children and those termed young adults. Librarians are aware of the possible adverse reaction of adults if alleged controversial materials are placed either in the children's or the young-adult collection, and as a result often choose not to select such materials. A recent letter to *American Libraries* suggested that librarians place controversial children's or young-adult material only in adult collections, thus avoiding confrontations with those adults concerned about "harmful" matter reaching minors.[1] The letter-writer stated that everyone would win, because the material would be available, while objections based on access to the material by the young would be thwarted. The writer did not seem to anticipate problems in determining at what age the young person would be allowed access to the adult collection containing this material, nor was a method proposed for defining either controversial or non-controversial material. Such a "way out" is actually used by some public libraries in the U.S., even though a cursory look at librarians' solutions to objections to library materials for the young reveals placement into the adult collection of titles and subjects that would be classified as noncontroversial by many.

Librarians have a right to be nervous about this touchy subject. Value systems differ as much as do the individuals holding those values. Those concerned about youth access have many differing positions. Some have a fear of the young being exposed to the so-called four-letter words, although it has been determined that most children hear these words every day, see them written on walls and sidewalks and generally by the fourth grade are able to discuss their use and definition. There are others who fear that children will be harmed by exposure to descriptions of sexual activities, pictures of humans nude, advice and explanations about human sexuality, violence, social problems and other facets of society, including defiance of authority, both governmental and parental, disrespect for religion, patriotism, capitalism, and the like.

The objectives of those making complaints will often differ. Some will ask that the material be restricted in some manner, while others will ask that the offending material be labeled, indicating the type of material, or age level at which access is to begin. Others will request unequivocal removal of offending materials from the collection. The complainant often cites the lack of maturity of the young or simply notes that the subject, or a passage within the material, is unsuitable for a specific age group.

A parent recently complained about *Daddy Was A Number Runner*, a young-adult novel with a realistic urban setting, by Louise Merriwether, stating that even high-school students were probably not mature enough to read the book, let alone intermediate-level students. Another parent, complaining about *Run, Shelly, Run,* by Gertrude Samuels, said that its treatment of a foster child sent off to a detention home was too mature for a twelve-year-old. Another found Isaac Asimov's *Fantastic Voyage,* a science-fiction picture book, unsuitable for an elementary-school library.

Nudes are a constant concern of parents, and in recent years they have been turning up in what were once considered unlikely places, causing a flurry of distress and complaints. Several issues of magazines including *Time, Life, Newsweek, Glamour, Popular Photography* and (yes!) *Car and Driver* have been removed from school and public libraries, because they contained photos of partially unclothed women. Sometimes speakers invited into libraries or institutions containing libraries have been banned, particularly if they are to discuss anything connected with human sexuality or drugs. An ironic experience of one of the authors of this work involved being asked to discuss censorship in schools, at a special in-school workshop for teachers, and being told that the word "censorship" was not to be used in the title of the program.

Films are a frequent target of censorship, and as with books, the same titles reappear in news accounts of suppression. *About Sex* (Texture Films), a presentation of human sexuality designed for teens, is often attacked by antiabortion and antiprofanity interests as being unsuitable. *Death of a Legend* (National Film Board of Canada), a film about wolves, was banned by school officials because a parent complained that students were "sickened" by the mating and birthing of the wolves. *The Lottery*, a film based upon the much-honored short story by Shirley Jackson, is often attacked on religious grounds, or because it contains violence. Yet both the film and short story have been praised for their affecting plea for tolerance and their warning about the result of blind adherence to majority pressure.

We could continue to cite specific library materials thought to be unsuitable for various age groups, but the pattern and subject matter would become quickly repetitive. The question that emerges is whether Anglo-Saxon words plus newly minted words for bodily functions and parts, pictures of genitalia, depictions of the more distressing realities of life or *anything* will harm the child or the teenager. Unfortunately for the librarian, no one knows for certain. Therefore, whichever side one takes is difficult to challenge authoritatively.

What is clear is that words and pictures have effects upon people that are as different as are the individuals who see them. One librarian has said that the death in *Little Women* haunted her for years. At the same time another librarian tells of being given a piece of pornography at the age of thirteen and being bothered by it for a number of years after. W. H. Auden, on whom one would expect words to have an effect, has testified that he could be aroused sexually more by words than by people. One of the authors remembers spending several sleepless nights at the age of nine after seeing the film version of H. G. Wells's novel *The Invisible Man*. (He has since enjoyed the film, as an adult, several times.) Many children's librarians have stated that *The Wizard of Oz* stories often produce considerable distress in young readers. And there is the individual who told us that upon seeing the Walt Disney film *Fantasia*, at the age of six, he cried and screamed for several nights thereafter; the music still upsets him, and he doesn't like to hear it. Another librarian has said that as a preteen she had read *Peyton Place*, a once-notorious novel of small-town life and sexuality. It made her nauseous. It was not the sexual scenes that upset her, however, but the description of the body of a pregnant woman.

Just as testimony can be collected on the ill effect of a reading or viewing experience, so can statements on how individuals have been inspired to positive thoughts and resolutions, if not to action, by the things they have read or seen. It should be noted, however, that in a great many instances there is no discernible effect whatsoever.

It is even *possible* that an ill effect could be beneficial. The dilemma involves determining if the effect is permanent and crippling. In the *Fantasia* example, the damage seems to be permanent, since hearing certain passages of music continues to produce an unpleasant effect. Such a reaction may be unfortunate, but it is doubtful that the playing of themes from Moussorgsky's *Night on a Bald Mountain* has caused that librarian to embark on any antisocial action. Yet the question is, and seems likely to be for some time to come: will materials housed in libraries trigger antisocial behavior and thus "harm" the individual? At the same time we must consider whether, should it become clearly established that certain kinds of materials collected by libraries may sometimes inspire crime and violence, such material should be provided anyway. It must be decided which is the greater risk to the individual and society: not having access to a variety of information and ideas, or having restrictions placed upon access only to materials and ideas that might inspire antisocial reactions. Many people, including some librarians, believe it is not worth risking possible harm to the individual or provoking antisocial behavior by providing everyone with access to all materials.

It is held by many to be commonsensical that reading, watching movies and television, listening to radio and recordings, can and does lead directly to crime and other antisocial behavior. J. Edgar Hoover, who never seemed to have any overt doubts about anything during his tenure as Federal Bureau of Investigation chief, was credited with saying that "indecent literature is making criminals faster than we can build jails to house them."

The U.S. Commission on Obscenity and Pornography reported on a survey taken of police chiefs and other professionals who worked with juveniles in trouble with society. Those polled were asked the following question: "Do you think that reading obscene books plays a significant role in causing juvenile delinquency?" Over half (57.6 percent) of the police chiefs were affirmative, while 77.1 percent of other professionals (psychiatrists, social workers, etc.) said no.[2] Another survey of opinion found that 48 percent of the population of the U.S. believed that reading or seeing sexually oriented materials leads to rape.[3]

A case in California appears to be in support of those arguing that a link exists between exposure to ideas and criminal action. In a suit brought against the National Broadcasting Company, a parent contended that four days after the showing of a television movie, *Born Innocent*, in which a sexual assault in a girls' detention home was depicted, a group of young girls staged a similar sexual assault on the nine-year-old daughter of the plaintiff. The lawyer for the plaintiff asserts that he will prove that one of the girls staging the attack got the idea from the film, thus making the network showing the film liable for damages. Apparently, it is not only material with some sexual content that can be considered a cause in crimes of a sexual nature; in Germany a mass killer of women was prompted to commit his crimes after he saw the movie *The Ten Commandments*. In England, a so-called vampire committed his sexually oriented crimes, including murder, after watching an Anglican church service.

In a case known to the authors, teenagers burned a cross on a neighbor's lawn, claiming inspiration from a *Life* magazine article. A county sheriff received considerable attention from the press when he contended that the showing of the film *Mandingo* (a violent depiction of slavery conditions in antebellum U.S.) was causing black youths to attack whites. It is interesting to note that the showing of *Roots*, a television film of the history of a slave family in the U.S., produced considerable speculation that its content would inspire civil rioting and unrest in black communities. No discernible reaction of this nature was recorded, after the film had been witnessed by the largest audience in television history.

It is almost impossible to give examples of incidents in which materials have promoted distinct prosocial action. People do not make headlines if they announce that the showing of *Holocaust* on television caused them to abandon their anti-Semitic prejudices. Any of us would be considered a bit affected if we announced that we had undertaken a series of helpful acts as a result of reading "Mary Worth" in the comics section of the newspaper. Yet it should be borne in mind that a majority of adults reach their maturity exposed to allegedly harmful material without embarking on a career of crime and debauchery. For many of us the experience of one of our librarian acquaintances is very familiar. When she was ten or eleven, she was reading Erskine Caldwell's *God's Little Acre,* a depiction of poverty-stricken, illiterate Southern whites once infamous for its earthy sexuality. Her father took it away from her, explaining that he didn't want her to read it because it would harm her. She was determined to discover what harm a book could do, and she managed to get hold of another copy. She found it disappointing and boring, a phenomenon often shared by those who finally get the chance to read or view "forbidden" materials.

The U.S. Commission on Obscenity and Pornography made a thorough survey and several scientific studies of cause and effect. After examining the evidence, it came to the conclusion that

> if a case is to be made against pornography in 1970, it will have to be made on the grounds other than demonstrated effects of a damaging personal or social nature. Empirical research designed to clarify the question has found no reliable evidence to date that exposure to explicit sexual materials plays a significant role in the causation of delinquent or criminal behavior among youth and adults ... the Effects Panel has examined popular and scientific literature and has initiated new empirical research. In drawing conclusions we have been sensitive to both the quantity and the quality of the research. The conclusion to be drawn from the totality of these research findings is that no dangerous effects have been demonstrated on any of the populations which were studied.[4]

The research mentioned was admittedly limited when it came to children: "access to populations of younger age groups was restricted. Although the research involved several surveys of adolescent and experimental studies with young adults, children generally were deemed inaccessible for direct inquiry."[5]

"In U.S. society—and perhaps in most Western societies—to learn about sex is to learn about guilt. To develop a commitment to sex is to learn about techniques for the management of guilt."[6] When research was, for the most part, privately funded, in the 1930s and 1940s, research concerning children, particularly their sexual development, was fairly steady and consistent. However, it seems that now, with the majority of money for research coming from public sources, activity in this area is sparse. But we do know that children are confronted by strange adult behavior when the question of sexuality appears. Adults generally respond to a child's interest in sexuality as either unequivocally wrong and refuse to provide an explanation as to why it is wrong, or ignore the sexuality of the child by trying to distract his or her attention or by substituting "cute" words to describe the sexual act.

Richard Cox and Dee Ann Davidson, marriage and family counseling professionals, have stated the case very well.

> In other areas of education (reading, science, social studies, math) . . . we start from the child's level of comprehension and work from there as he is ready to understand the material. In the area of sexuality, however, we behave quite differently. Because of well established societal taboos against discussing sexual matters, we tend to gloss over important questions our children ask and to label such inquiry as "naughty" or "dirty" or to ignore the child's interest altogether.[7]

Children get most of their information and learn their attitudes, whatever their worth, from the society in which they live. By the time they are eleven years old, they have a primitive understanding of the reproductive process, based for the most part on procreation through marriage. By the time they reach fifteen and sixteen years of age, they regard sexuality as an integral part of a relationship between two people, not necessarily dependent upon marriage. And, most significantly, teenagers feel very strongly that they have a right to their sexuality.[8]

Teachers, librarians and others who work with the young have often expressed the opinion that it is not exposure to explicit sexuality in itself that harms children. Clifton Fadiman, a one-time teacher, has said that as a child he read some of the forbidden books of the period, considered by that society to be pornographic, and that as far as he knows the experience had no effect upon him. He went on to say that as a teacher of literature, he could not find any reason to censor the reading of his students, because he believes that what a child is not emotionally ready to absorb is automatically rejected.[9] Indeed, some research indicates that concern over the effect of media materials and video programs should focus on violence rather than pornography.[10] A young-adult librarian has stated that she believes nothing people read, see in a film, or hear on a record will harm them. She goes on to say that "the imagination is quite capable of conjuring up perceptions of the unknown far more excessive than in reality."[11]

Support for this contention comes from a survey cited by the U.S. Commission on Obscenity and Pornography that found "imaginary stimuli" to be about twice as arousing, sexually, as either literary or photographic stimuli.[12] As a children's librarian has observed, "A child is not going to be traumatized by a book or set in a rigid pattern for life by what we offer in libraries. There are too many influences in an individual's development."[13] It is this very multiplicity of influences that frustrates many a parent or group concerned about children's welfare. Because a library is visible within a community, it is used as a focal point by those concerned about negative influences on their children. It is usually subject to local tax support, and thus susceptible to attack by those who feel threatened or shaken by constantly shifting social values. It is more difficult for a parent or group to mount an attack on the television networks, street-corner peer groups or the child's best friend than it is to attack school curricula or library collections.

So far, we have been discussing materials related mostly to sexual matters. There are, however, other subjects to which children and teens have access that are problematic for the librarian. Not long ago one of us was in the library browsing through a copy of *Publisher's Weekly.* An interruption came in the form of a telephone call from an outraged mother. Her eleven-year-old son had borrowed *The Underground Dictionary* from a bookmobile, and the woman was distressed by what she had found in it. Under the subject entry "High" (ways to get), cleaning fluids were listed, among a number of other dubious substances. The entry provided no explanation about the effects of sniffing cleaning fluids. Another entry, "Carbona," did not provide such a description either. However, under the entry "cleaning fluids," an explanation of the effect is provided. The results of sniffing such items could result in liver, kidney, bone-marrow, brain or chromosomal damage.[14] The mother of the boy explained that her neighbor had urged that she burn the book immediately, but she was asking that we remove such a dangerous item from the collection.

Reference librarians were consulted, and they felt that the book was needed because they could not find handy access to much of the information collected in that work. It was decided that the book should remain in the collection. Should children and teens have access to such information? Should the book be on the shelf in the bookmobile, or should it only be available in a large reference collection? Should it be restricted and placed on a closed shelf? These are legitimate questions, and librarians are constantly being asked, and are asking themselves how, to resolve such problems.

It is not very difficult to imagine a child or teenager experimenting by sniffing cleaning fluids, as suggested in this book, and not seeing the entry describing the effects of such an act. This could be a dramatic example of the ill effects of reading, and would undoubtedly arouse the community against the library. At the same time, neither is it difficult to imagine that a child or teenager planning to give cleaning fluid a try as a method of getting high would decide against such an act because he or she discovered its harmful effects. If the book is controlled or limited in terms of access and circulation, the librarian will never know how many young people needing the information were reluctant to ask or "blow their cool" by approaching the "authorities." Such young people would have to rely on peer-group sources for their information, which could be just as damaging as the misuse of library materials.

The Bible is an example of a book that is in all but the most special of library collections. It is doubtful that there have been many complaints about allowing children access to this work. Nevertheless, in *Mark:* 16, one finds the statement, "And if they [believers] drink any deadly thing it shall not hurt them." The same passage makes other potentially dangerous statements. Adults have taken such passages literally and suffered the consequences, on Biblical authority, by handling snakes or denying themselves and their children medical attention. Do we allow access to the Bible in all our collections? Do we restrict it only to large reference collections? Do we offer only expurgated editions? Do we deny use based upon the age of the potential user?

The Anarchist Cookbook poses another kind of problem; it contains information potentially dangerous not only to the user but to others as well. This work is devoted, as one might guess from the title, to methods of sabotage. Some are simple and often seen in action films; e.g., stringing a cable across a highway. Others are more arcane and vicious, such as making a very effective weapon out of a tin can. Once again, it is not difficult to imagine someone deciding to test out some of the propositions in this work.

William O. Douglas, one of the strongest defenders and more purist interpreters of the First Amendment of the U.S. Constitution, said in 1951:

> If this were a case where those who claimed protection under the first amendment were teaching the techniques of sabotage, the assassination of the President ... the planting of bombs, the art of street warfare and the like, I would have no doubts. The freedom to speak is not absolute; the teaching of methods of terror and other seditious conduct should be beyond the pale along with obscenity and immorality.[15]

By 1957, Supreme Court Justice Douglas had apparently changed his mind about at least part of that stand. In a case involving alleged obscenity, he cited studies that show that juvenile delinquents are far less inclined to read than those who do not present society with problems; that there are many other influences besides reading that can be harmful; and that reading as a cause of delinquency is so insignificant that it is not worth investigating.[16]

In terms of this discussion, it is the First Amendment that forms the basis for making decisions on risktaking. In the case brought against the television network showing *Born Innocent,* cited earlier, the judge threw the case out of court when the plaintiff could not address the charge on a First Amendment basis; i.e., it could not be proven that it was the intention of the network, in producing and showing the film, to invite sexual attacks on young children. The plaintiff wanted only to prove that the result of the showing of the film led to a violent attack on the child, thus making the producers and distributors of the film liable for damages. Justice Douglas's statement on advocating methods of terror in order to violently overthrow the government would seem to apply to *The Anarchist Cookbook*. Should libraries acquire it (even if there is a demand)? Should it be available to children and teenagers? Who makes the decision as to the purpose of the work and whether it is protected under the First Amendment? The answer is provided, not by the librarian, but by the courts. The decision to acquire a work and make it available to the young involves policy, and is made by the librarian. That decision involves a profound responsibility to the community being served by the library. Too often the librarian will rule something out of the collection, not from sound selection principles and policies but because the subject is considered likely to be troublesome to the librarian.[17]

Depictions of violence also disturb those who would protect the young; violence begets violence, they believe, and examples such as the television movie cited before are offered as proof of their contention. Again, no one knows the answer. The studies cited by Justice Douglas and those contained in the reports of the U.S. Commission on Obscenity and Pornography provide some indication that there is a basis for speculation. Bruno Bettelheim, among others, thinks that violence in fairy tales serves a useful purpose. In speaking about the classic tale "The Goose Girl," he says that the cruel punishment of an evil person fits the crime. Instead of upsetting most children, it reassures them that justice will eventually prevail. He points out that children feel unjustly treated by adults, and that it seems to children as if nothing is done to rectify that. Thus, children want those who cheat and degrade them to be severely punished. If, through stories, they can vicariously experience the punishment of evil, children feel more secure and less resentful.[18]

The interpretation of the positive and negative effects on children of viewing and being exposed to violence seems to vary, depending upon the circumstances. After viewing the television film *Holocaust*, a fictionalization of the Nazi concentration camps and the pogroms, a mother reported, in a letter to *The New York Times*, that her nine-year-old son "broke into hysterical tears within a half-hour [of the beginning of the broadcast] and threw up at the rape of Anna Weiss."[19] He would watch no more of the program, but the parent testified that she was satisfied that her son would never forget that infamous period of human degradation and persecution of the Jews. She obviously believed the experience to be a positive one for her child. One librarian remembers having read some pornography at thirteen. She has forgotten the book's content but has never been able to forget her horror at reading that the Nazis used their victims' skin for lampshades.

It is just this dichotomy of differing values that faces the librarian in developing collections and providing meaningful services to the young. There most certainly were parents who did not allow, or shortly withdrew permission for, their children to view *Holocaust*. For some parents it would be anathematic to subject their children to depictions of such inhumanity, and they would not have viewed their child's hysteria and throwing up as a positive reaction.

A growing number of those who deal with youth recognize that children and teenagers need more than peer-group relationships against which to test their growing sense of self and their interpersonal relationships. Too often the parent is unprepared for this responsibility. Such shortcomings in parental preparation are among the reasons for the growing number of adult and continuing-education programs about "parenting." Librarians are not anxious to become surrogate parents, either from a practical or an ideological stance. Librarians feel the young (and in particular teens) need to have a resource that their peers consider reliable and confidential, where information can be sought without fear of peer and/or parental reaction.

Joseph Sorrentino is a judge in juvenile court. His background is unusual. He was once a member of an urban street gang, he has been an inmate in reform school and he has been in jail. He is disturbed by the violence surrounding the young, pointing out that the average person will see some fifteen thousand killings on television before leaving high school. He considers such exposure to casual violence one of the five causes of teenage crime.[20] A recent study in England supports the judge's contention that exposure to casual violence has an effect on the young. A researcher studied 1,565 males aged twelve to seventeen over a six-year period and concluded that "constant exposure to violent acts leads to a breakdown in inhibitions against violence." It was found that the group that watched a greater number of violent programs on television committed a greater number of violent acts. It was also discovered that some types of violence on television produce more violent acts than other types; among these were realistic violence, gratuitous violence, physical violence between two people with a close relationship and violence committed by *good* guys for *bad* reasons. The investigator concluded that constant exposure to violence did not change the youths' conscious attitude toward violence and did not make them callous; instead, television violence seemed to work on a subconscious level.[21] It should be noted that in England, unlike most of the major metropolitan areas in the United States and Canada, there are relatively few hours of television broadcasting and there are only three stations.

Does the foregoing mean that libraries, with their growing use of films and television, might be contributing to the problem? Probably not. In the first place, those who watch television many hours a day are less likely to have the time or inclination to use libraries. Then, too, many of the materials in the library in which violence is a factor do not contain the kind of violence found to be significant in the British study. Cartoons, science fiction, sports, comedies and contemporary fiction for the young do not tend to incite violence even when they involve violence. Finally, it must be noted that it was the *steady* diet of violence that was affecting the youths studied. Materials in a collection for children and youth that may contain even gratuitous violence is intershelved and classified with other materials (and, it is hoped, not labeled), so that a young person would have to go to great lengths to seek out a steady dose of violence.

At the same time, it should be observed that television and libraries work at different levels. Commercial television relies on audience size for income, and therefore reduces its programming to a formula dependent on fast action and clichéd characterizations in order to hold the audience until the next commercial. Materials collected by libraries do not need to cater to a mass audience. Indeed, the collection must reach across a broad spectrum of interests and needs. A plurality of values has a chance for representation in a library collection, whereas such a variety of interests are served on television in small and often isolated amounts.

It is not our intent to imply that mass tastes are not represented in library collections. Many public library collections are built for

At What Age Freedom?

the most part around popular demand, but within those collections will also appear such materials as do not foster traditional stereotypes but rather provide creative, thought-provoking role models who encourage the acceptance of responsibility and choice in human relationships. One of the quiet and constant pleasures of library service to youth is to witness the mental growth and development of children who, through independent exploration of library materials, plug into the wealth of information about themselves and the world they live in.

As can be observed, there is considerable uncertainty about the total effect of books, films, television and recordings on children and teenagers. The evidence to date does make it doubtful that the users of a library collection would be permanently harmed by anything they happened to find in the collection unless they were predisposed to harm themselves or others. There may be occasional damage done and certain risks involved in constant exposure to violence of certain types, whatever the source, but research to date is so limited that no one can be positive about how much this is true. But it would seem that libraries, with their less-than-mass audiences, would tend to offer counteractive alternatives to the diet of television violence, rather than reinforcing the subliminal effects of such violence.

Nevertheless, many persons wish to prevent children and teenagers from any exposure to certain subjects. Many librarians, in turn, respond with a variety of restrictions placed on access for certain age groups, in the hope of forestalling any public criticism of the collection and service. However, collections that avoid contemporary life and concentrate on trying to reinforce a traditional morality are ignored by the young, who only patronize them when forced to by a parent or teacher. Some libraries, as a matter of policy, label certain subjects and titles of materials and require written permission of the parent before allowing access. This practice may allow for the inclusion of a few more materials needed by young people, but it still sets up a barrier that precludes many from having access to the materials.

Libraries vary in the degree to which they have restrictions. Some openly restrict certain types of material. One library would not place Erich Fromm's *The Art of Loving*, a small but effective discussion of the personal commitment we must make to ourselves before we can offer love to another (containing nary a "naughty" word), on the open shelf, for fear a teenager would check it out. Some libraries restrict the use of adult materials until a predetermined age or school grade level is reached. These restrictions seem to range from the sixth through ninth grades and/or in age from eleven to fourteen years. A variation on this system is to have the person at the check-out point look at the material, and if it is decided that it is too "hot," considering the reader's age, to cross-examine to determine if the use is "serious" or legitimate. This has the effect of discouraging the youthful library user, because the person at the check-out desk may well know or communicate with the parent of the questioned user. However, most librarians allow access to the adult collection from age fourteen. Many children are adult physically, if not mentally, by that age, according to recent studies.

Dr. Dorothy Broderick, renowned youth services specialist for libraries, stated the case rather startlingly.

> While most adolescents make the transition to legal adulthood (age 18) uneventfully, girls 15 and under are the only group in America experiencing a rise in the birthrate; young adolescents are the only group for whom the rate of first admissions to mental institutions has increased recently; the number of teenage runaways has doubled in the last five years; youth unemployment is pervasive; suicide ranks second only to accidents as the cause of death for this age group; delinquency appears to peak at 16 or 17 and then drops off; the decision to drop out of school is usually made before 16...[22]

Members of this group do not find the collections in many libraries, and the special services provided for teenagers, to be significant to their lives. Many libraries do not purchase much of the material aimed at this age group, in the belief that teenagers are nothing more than older children. In a *growing* number of libraries, services for this age group are either nonexistent or have been phased out in the name of economy.

As we indicated earlier, libraries and the librarians imposing such restrictions have developed a rationale for their actions. They operate in a climate of often real, but more often imagined, intimidation. There have been too many examples of librarians being fired or "let go"; librarians listening to or receiving vicious threats of violence against themselves and their families; librarians facing long and costly court battles; librarians discovering that to be involved in a censorship battle often means being abandoned by their colleagues, who do not wish to compromise their professional position. H. L. Mencken once said, in the process of defending Theodore Dreiser, "this is still a great moral republic, and there is plainly such a thing as tempting its pious sentiment too far."[23] Librarians encounter pious sentiment not only in the adults using their libraries but in many of their colleagues as well.

What is a librarian to do? While we do not urge librarians to push their book trucks into battlements and stand waving a symbolic red flag, it seems obvious that they could and should be tempting the republic and their colleagues' pious sentiments a good deal more than they do. That is the librarian's basic claim to professional responsibility. Certainly, the agreement to provide library services to children and teenagers carries with it a moral commitment that should rank with that in the fields of social work, medicine, education and law. More and more professionals in those fields are considering the possibility that children and teenagers have rights, rather than having to serve out a sentence of oppression until they reach their majority. Imposing blanket restrictions on all because they are minors fails to recognize the differing needs of the young, and can cause denial of information to the teenager who needs to cope with a newly discovered confusion about sexuality, or to better understand mental depressions that can lead to thoughts of suicide, to alienation and/or senseless acts of violence.

It is important that children be allowed access to adult collections when they so desire. But it is even more important to provide children's and young-adult collections with a wide variety of materials and programming in different formats, in order to insure that youthful patrons will have access to information as it is needed. Such collections must be developed and staffed by people who, through temperament, training and commitment, understand the maturation process, with all its attendant joys, fears and frustrations. In a world shrinking to a village, and with all the pressures implied in a multi-cultural society, the young cannot be expected to survive as mindless innocents turned out to fend for themselves at age eighteen.

Elaine Simpson, teacher and young-adult librarian, has explained that for a book to meet the needs of today's young people, its characters should speak in their language, its problems should be those currently most pressing to them; details of action and reaction to events and attitudes toward life should agree with psychologically valid patterns of behavior among them. If we feed children and young adults a steady diet of pap—of the false, the trivial, the phoney—we will produce adults who will continue to believe lies and cheap sentimentalities because they do not know the truth.[24]

And what is the truth? The truth is what has been so for ages. There are drugs that harm, there are rapists, there is abortion, there are mothers without wedding licenses, parents can be cruel, true love may end, and starvation, poverty, injustice and inhumanity surround us. Understanding and withstanding these realities requires a mature and balanced mind.

A parent opposing the removal of 150 titles from a district high school library said simply, "If you raise your children right at home, he is going to know how to accept the books he reads away from home. Sooner or later he is going to face life and would be better suited to face the world knowing what's in it."[25]

A children's librarian from an area in which a well-publicized book-burning incident took place has said that "it is better to learn about the harm of prejudice and persecution; the horror of war, the dangers of drug abuse; from the safety of the printed page... there is greater protection in awareness. Children acquire knowledge that may very well protect them from a very dangerous encounter."[26] A trustee of a public library was moved to make this comment:

> One more word should be spoken to reassure those who fear for the young adult or for the children. Freedom may be the greatest safety for our young people, for it may be better for them to learn about sex in books with literary value than in back-street, under-the-counter pornography. We apparently cannot stop the supply of such contraband material. It will always be available for the curious and the emotionally disturbed. It is not pornography, we have noted, which causes emotional imbalance, but emotional imbalance which impels the child or an adult to seek pornography.[27]

Finally, we must remember that great authority on education, Sam Weller's father, who said he took great pains with the "eddication" of his children; he turned them out into the street. That method may work for those who survive. Yet the turning of the child into the streets to learn of a reality larded with mythology and superstition seems to be preferred by many adults as a method of education. The two major rules adopted by the young forced to survive this way is never to discuss what you learned on the streets with adults and never get caught trying out some of the theories advanced by the street pedagogs. Therein is the basis of lifelong alienation.

We believe that the communication media have an effect upon all people, from those watching Captain Kangaroo to those reading large-print materials. The media are the life blood of our culture. The effect of their activities can and does sometimes lead to antisocial behavior, but the effect upon all of us and the risks taken in terms of the growth and development of our children is greater and more devastating if we suppress and distort the truth. We believe that librarians must, by the very nature of their commitment to themselves and the institutions wherein they practice, take risks. They must take the risk that they will be attacked by the fearful and the immature, in order to hope that tomorrow's world will be populated by less of that unfortunate breed. The risks that librarians take in behalf of children and young adults must be informed, and founded in the knowledge and understanding of their needs. The librarian must be a source of strength and guidance for those adults in the community who wish to see their children profit from the use of media materials. And the librarian can consequently be able to win the support of those who would resist efforts to purge library shelves of "harmful" matter.

Oliver Wendell Holmes said that "every idea is an incitement," and libraries, if they are to be worth anything, must incite. To do so, they will have to house ideas and information that may be dangerous. Parents must be helped to understand that all of us need to understand danger in order to resist it. The traditional library approach is to say that a parent has the right to determine what a child sees, reads or hears. However noble that sentiment, it is blind when it is used as an excuse to deny children the right to exist in a real and meaningful world.

The courts decided long ago that a child had a right to be educated regardless of the parent's wishes. In many cases the courts have decided that a minor has the right to proper medical attention without parental permission. In some states it has been established that "for the public good," minors can obtain abortions without parental knowledge or consent. In a recent case, the right of a sixteen-year-old woman not to have an abortion was upheld although the parents had ordered their minor dependent to have the operation. A growing number of states are providing venereal-disease information without parental consent or awareness. And in the past few years the right of the parents to physically abuse their minor child has come under strong legislative and judicial attack. The young do have needs and rights, and they must have librarians who will help them take advantage of these rights and fulfill their needs.

Parents often go to great lengths to withhold information from their children on such subjects as human sexuality, drug use, birth control, venereal disease, abortion and alternate life-styles. Many schools provide considerable information about these areas but, owing to group and parental pressures, others have abandoned many of the instructional components, if not entire programs. In the United States it is estimated that there are about two million young people a year who are not in school.[28] Often these children have no source of information other than the media. Librarians are beginning to discuss the role of libraries as information sources in meeting the alternative information needs of the young. This debate is still in its early stages.

Richard Farson, president of the Esalen Institute, is but one of a growing number of individuals beginning to speak out in behalf of minor's rights. He has proposed that "a child must have the right to all information ordinarily available to adults—including, and perhaps especially, information that makes adults uncomfortable." He believes that children should be able to design their own educations, including nonschool forms. He advocates that children should be free to enter into binding contracts, to work, to make money, to develop credit ratings. He is particularly critical of society's efforts to deny children and teenagers information about their own sexuality and that of others. He deplores the philosophy espousing innocence and ignorance as the best defense against unwanted sexual advances.[29] If one can believe reports by the press and letters to the editor, one of the books in circulation today most feared by adults is the widely acclaimed work on female sexuality, *Our Bodies, Ourselves*. One librarian stated that the work contains "the kinds of information young people need.... They are in a period of their lives when they have many questions about their bodies.... This book can help them answer some of these questions."[30] Yet the book has been yanked out of many collections, both adult and young adult, upon the complaint of a parent or special pressure group.

Librarians are asking that the young be allowed to grow and develop the ability to make important decisions about themselves and to be able to profit from their mistakes. In order to accomplish this, librarians are beginning to give serious consideration to the rights of children and young adults to have a free and open collection of materials to meet their needs. Mary Kohler, director of the National Commission on Resources for Youth, has her own list of children's rights, which often matches those of many librarians. She points out that the young learn best by involvement, doing, experiencing and engaging. She maintains that children have a right to learn by trial and error, through a variety of experiences. The young, she maintains, have a right to participate in decisions that affect their lives. She points out that the education system often stifles and that uniform curricula may well contribute to learning difficulties. Significant in her list of children's rights is "The Right to Societal Mechanisms to Make the Foregoing Rights Effective."[31]

In summing up the question, at what age freedom? let us quote a children's librarian:

> Our dilemma has been that, whether we want it or not, the tradition of library service to children has placed us in a role of protector, not advocate. Children and children's books are tough and full of spirit. Instead of trying to protect children and launder their reading, why don't we show our respect for them, give children and older people as well the chance to discover in our libraries the true wealth of children's literature, and take on our proper role of child advocate by being the first in the defense of a child's right to full library service.[32]

NOTES

1. *American Libraries* (April 1978): 196.
2. U. S. Commission on Obscenity and Pornography, *The Report of the*

Commission on Obscenity and Pornography. (Washington, D. C.: U.S. Government Printing Office, September 1971), p. 161.
3. Ibid., p. 157.
4. Ibid., p. 139.
5. Ibid., p. 140.
6. J. H. Gagnon and W. Simon, *Sexual Conduct: Theoretical Sources of Human Sexuality* (Chicago: Aldine, 1973), p. 262.
7. Richard H. Cox and Dee Ann Davidson, "What Do Children Know About Sex?" *Journal of Marriage and Family Counseling* (July 1976): 259–68.
8. Kari Schoff-Tams, Jurgen Schlaegel and Leonard Walczak, "Differentiation of Sexual Morality Between 11 and 16 Years," *Archives of Sexual Behavior* (September 1976): 353–70.
9. Clifton Fadiman, "Children's Reading," *Party of One* (New York: World Publishing Company, 1955), p. 370.
10. Schoff-Tams, "Sexual Morality."
11. Rayme Meyer, *Young Adult Alternative Newsletter* (January 15, 1978): 3.
12. U.S. Commission on Obscenity and Pornography, *Report*, p. 172.
13. Patricia Finley, "Advocating Children's Rights," *Newsletter on Intellectual Freedom* (September 1974): 130.
14. Eugene E. Landy, *The Underground Dictionary* (New York: Simon and Schuster, 1971), pp. 46, 103.
15. *Dennis v. United States* 341 U. S. 494 (1951).
16. *Roth v. United States* 354 U. S. 476 (1957).
17. See Lester E. Asheim, "The Librarian's Responsibility: Not Censorship but Selection," *Wilson Library Bulletin* (September 1953): 63–7.
18. Bruno Bettelheim, *The Uses of Enchantment: The Meaning and Importance of Fairy Tales* (New York: Knopf, 1976), p. 141.
   For those of you who do not remember The Goose Girl, the villain was stripped, put into a barrel that was studded inside with pointed nails and dragged up and down the street by two horses until dead. In Cinderella, another story cited by Bettelheim, the two sisters mutilate their feet to get them into the slipper, and later birds pick their eyes out. These versions of both stories are told by the Brothers Grimm. Needless to say, Bettelheim doesn't approve of the various sugared versions.
19. *The New York Times*, April 30, 1978, Section 2, p. 30.
20. "From Juvenile Delinquent to Judge," *Scholastic Action* (March 23, 1978): 14–15.
21. Howard Muson, "Teenage Violence and the Telly," *Psychology Today* (March 1978): 50–54.
22. Dorothy Broderick, editorial in *Voice of Youth Advocates*, (April 1978): 3.
23. H. L. Mencken, *The New Mencken Letters*, ed. Carl Bode (New York: Dial Press, 1977), p. 67.

24. Elaine Simpson, "Reason, Not Emotion," *Newsletter on Intellectual Freedom* (September 1974): 129.
25. Ken Donaldson, "Forty Iceberg Tips: The State of Censorship 1972-1978," *California Librarian* (July 1978): 32-8.
26. Stella Fried, "Freedom From Fear," *School Library Journal* (October 1976): 84.
27. Alex Allain, "Public Library Governing Bodies and Intellectual Freedom," *Library Trends* (July 1970): 62.
28. Beatrice Gross, and Ronald Gross, eds., *The Children's Rights Movement; Overcoming the Oppression of Young People* (New York: Anchor Press/Doubleday, 1977), p. 113.
29. Ibid., p. 326.
30. *American Libraries* (January 1978): 22.
31. Gross and Gross, *Children's Rights*, pp. 228-29.
32. Finley, *Advocating Children's Rights*, pp. 130-31.

Chapter Four
Freedom Denied

Censorship activity has always been a part of our history, and there is no current evidence that would convince us that such activity is either on the wane or unknown in some corner of the world. The writings of Protagorus were burned, Ovid was banished, and Goethe reported witnessing a merry little fire fed by then-despised French romances. More recently, and closer to home, a library trustee burned a book on the steps of the library, and a school board had the janitor feed the furnace with some disapproved titles taken from the school's curriculum collection. One of the authors of the burned collection might have commented, when hearing of the fate of one of his works, "And so it goes."

Histories of censorship abound, so there is no need to recount it here. The reader is already aware that no civilization is free from censorship activity, and the roster of materials attacked could well go toward the start of a good shelf-list for a library. In this chapter we are going to offer some observations that can help those concerned with libraries make decisions about how to approach the problem of censorship in libraries.

There are several categories of individuals who currently appear quite regularly in accounts of attacks on libraries and their collections. Members of one of the more consistent groups classify themselves as parents. Many people, as parents, are concerned about what their children see and hear, as they should be. Unfortunately for the librarian and the teacher, some parents also want to prevent children other than their own from seeing and hearing about certain subjects—at least, the manner in which their demands are made would have that effect. We remember an attempt by a woman in Oak Park, Illinois, to have a photograph removed from an exhibit in the high school. She commented to the press that it was not her children's morals with which she was concerned; it was those *others'* morals. Whatever the motivation, the object of parental complaint is to demand the removal or restriction, in terms of either circulation or availability, of library or curriculum materials. School-media librarians are the ones most likely to be under attack from parents. Watchers of the scene, such as the American Library Association and the National Council of Teachers of English, report that such incidents are accelerating as we move further into the 1980s. However, public libraries are far from immune to such attacks. Occasional forays into community-college libraries by disturbed parents have also been reported.

Sexuality would seem to be the primary preoccupation of parents attacking library materials. The use of certain well-known words pertaining to sexual activity, excrement or descriptions of the human body are usually the basis for objections. Catchwords such as vulgar, filthy, obscene, cuss words, profanity, moral content, trash, offensive and unwholesome are repeated constantly in reports of attacks. The attacks are usually highly emotional, and the statements made about the material are often phrased in such a way that those rising to the defense of the materials are made to appear violators of childhood innocence.

The clergy constitute another category of individuals frequently appearing in reports on censorship activity. They too seem to be interested in the depiction of sexual activity in available materials, and the same catchwords appear in their attacks on specific works. Of course, religious doctrine or interpretation can sometimes be the basis for the complaint, and the source need not be works on that subject. One case involved a vigorous complaint by a clergyman over the inclusion in the library collection of a certain cookbook that contained a quote from the Bible that spoke approvingly of beer, followed by recipes using that ingredient. The clergyman insisted that the Bible was being misquoted and misinterpreted, and demanded that the cookbook be removed from the collection. In this case he was not successful, but this example does demonstrate that the cause for an attack can be the most seemingly inoffensive materials.

Politicians, political candidates, law-enforcement officials, school administrators or board members and public-library trustees comprise yet another group involved in censorship activity. Police chiefs, sheriffs, district attorneys, mayors and even city managers have all appeared from time to time as protagonists in complaints against library collections. These individuals are often acting on their own initiative, ignited by one or more members of their constituencies. Not only are the usual catchwords for sexuality or bodily functions quoted, but it is here that political and sociological materials are made targets for suppression.

Because those in this last group have some authority in their communities and because they have the means of publicizing their concern, their complaints can bring about swifter and stronger pressure upon the librarian than can the activities of the nonaffiliated citizen. Many of these officials have economic or legal power. Their positions may be such that they can directly threaten the job security of the librarian. Although burning at the stake, placing the accused in stocks or sending them for a ride on the "dunking" stool have disappeared in North America, political and law-enforcement officials can create an atmosphere in the community comparable in intensity and anxiety to the witch hunting of yore. Librarians and teachers having gone through such experiences tell of the harrowing feeling of being alone, and abandoned by colleagues and the community, when such attacks are underway. Librarians have reported intense feelings of unease and intimidation induced merely by a visit from a member of the police force or a law-enforcement agency. Occasionally these officials do more than visit or place a phone call to make a demand on a library. One police chief conducted a search of a library for "smut." Trustees and school-board members, acting on their own, have been known to remove or mutilate materials of which they disapproved. When an official takes such action without respect to established "due process" procedures, librarians caught unprepared are uncertain of their rights and duties, or they may be honestly afraid to oppose such authority figures. Those librarians who have themselves prepared in advance, through the establishment, promulgation and strict adherence to procedures for handling complaints, are less likely to be caught unaware by a complaint or an attack. They are able to react coolly, dealing with the situation as if it were nothing out of the ordinary. Those who panic or become visibly disturbed by a complaint or attack often create the impression that they have been caught "being naughty" or have added materials to their collection of whose suitability they are uncertain.

There are many other kinds of people who come to libraries with a variety of concerns, including complaints about the political, social and economic, religious and philosophical materials they feel are an attack on themselves and their personal values, their group or their interpretation of society. As has been noted, tolerance for a variety of viewpoints and for different approaches to life-style comes only to those who feel secure in themselves and in their ability to live with themselves. Such tolerance is often more evident among those who, through educational experiences, have learned to adapt to variety and change. However, educational credentials should not be used as criteria for classifying those likely to engage in censorship activity. Teachers, lawyers, doctors, philosophers, and other highly educated individuals have frequently complained about materials they found offensive and have sought some method of suppressing those materials. A New York lawyer sought to ban the iconoclastic magazine *National Lampoon*, on the grounds that its content was occasionally blasphemous. Scientists tried to prevent Velikovsky's dissertations on natural cataclysmic effects on world history, geology, astronomy and anthropology from being published, and once published, they sought to prevent the works from being distributed. Not only government officials, but some physicists, were involved in the recent attempt to forestall publication of an article on how the hydrogen bomb is constructed.

Age is not a factor either. Too often, because censors happen to be parents, public officials or senior members of the citizenry, it is assumed that there is a connection between such activity and aging. Those who work with youth, such as a young-adult-services librarian we know, report that teenagers, when given the opportunity to participate in a program where they reviewed library materials for their peers, would often declare that they liked a particular work but would not recommend it for use by younger people.

All of these types of individuals sometimes form groups to bring pressure more effectively upon institutions in order to censor or restrict materials they consider undesirable. A school board was recently visited by a representative group from a local evangelistic church, who demanded that books about handwriting analysis be removed because such practice was blasphemous. At other times, censors do not band together in groups devoted to removing offensive materials, but instead work through existing groups that were initially formed for other purposes. Either group may be local, and possibly affiliated with a state or national organization, which may be church-related, political, patriotic, racial or ethnic in origin. Or its members may form a special-interest group concerned with such issues as gun control, environment, energy, abortion or human rights. They may also be affiliated by occupational interests, such as police, business, commerce, education or health services.

Local censorship groups organize under such "buzz" words as "concerned parents," "citizens against pornography" or "guardians of traditional education." It is difficult to find groups organized to oppose censorship or the tactics used by those groups who undertake such public stands. State- and nationally affiliated groups seeking some form of censorship have adopted such names as Parents of New York United (PONY-U); Florida Action Committee for Education and Missouri Citizens for Life. And organizations with concerns other than censorship who have engaged in such activity include the American Legion, the Ku Klux Klan and some chambers of commerce.[1]

Finally, there are official groups. School boards, library boards of trustees, town councils, state legislatures and the courts all have engaged in censorship actions at one time or another. In some cases such groups have the authority to control, either directly or indirectly, materials that go into library collections. To counter their challenge can be a long, costly and often personally damaging legal process. The individual librarian or teacher usually does not have a financial base from which to challenge actions taken by boards and legislatures, which can use the public tax monies to support their own actions. The burden of providing for personal legal representation, including, in some cases, lost income while litigation is underway, and the physical and emotional strain of being under constant pressure has often proved to be the deciding factor in keeping librarians and other individuals from overtly opposing censorship activities by official tax-supported groups.

In the case of school-board activity in removing materials from school media centers, their authority and methodology have come under question, and in a few cases have been challenged in the courts. In some very few, the challenge has been successful in terms of offering redress from the removal of materials and the loss of employment by librarians or teachers. However, to date, no case has gone high enough in the federal court system to have set a precedent that would relieve the attack on the selection and circulation of materials in a library collection. The cost and emotional strain are not the only barriers to active participation by librarians and teachers in these challenges. The ability of official and peer-group activity to exact reprisals in the form of harassment and fiscal penalization of libraries and schools may drive individuals out of their chosen profession; this is not uncommonly the reward for having the courage of one's convictions.

Lower courts are too often willing to restrict materials, leaving the publisher or distributor of the material no other recourse but the costly appeal in a higher court. *Titicut Follies,* an early film by the award-winning director, Fred Wiseman, deals rather graphically with conditions in a mental institution in Massachusetts (although the institution is not identified as such in the film). Its use was restricted, by the Supreme Federal Court of the Commonwealth of Massachusetts, to certain professionals (legislators, judges, doctors, social workers and a few others). Even those who meet the criteria have difficulty obtaining the film. As an example of the ripple effect of such action, the copy of the film owned by the Instructional Communications Center of the State University of New York at Buffalo is shown only to controlled audiences, and its availability for off-campus loan is severely restricted. Elementary and secondary schools are not the only ones affected by censorship.

Sometimes the federal government is involved in censorship activity. In the case of the *Progressive,* the magazine that was going to publish an article on how to construct a hydrogen bomb, a Federal District Court judge issued a temporary restraining order, at the request of the U.S. Justice Department. According to the editors of the magazine, all of the references used in the preparation of the article came from materials already available to the public, primarily in library collections. The objections raised by the federal government included citations of widely circulated physics books and some illustrations taken from published encyclopedias.

Circulation records of libraries have from time to time been of interest to the federal government. In 1970 the Milwaukee Public Library resisted initial attempts by the U.S. Treasury Department to inspect circulation records for names of individuals using materials on explosives. The library was pressured into complying because of a decision by the city district attorney. At the same time Treasury agents were visiting other libraries; Atlanta reported visits to 27 branches. A prompt and dramatic stance by the American Library Association (ALA) against such practice without proper court procedures brought a halt to the activity.[2]

In another incident the Justice Department made life difficult for the Tricontinental Film Center, a distributor of third-world films. Tricontinental was ordered to register as a foreign agent; their films would be required to carry the label "foreign political propaganda" (although not all of the films in the catalog dealt with political subjects), and customers' names would have to be turned over to the federal government for filing, within forty-eight hours of rental or sale.[3] The ALA pointed out to the Justice Department that many libraries and educational institutions already owned films sold by Tricontinental and that labeling such films as "propaganda" would jeopardize the tax-exempt status of these institutions. In addition, the blanket application of "propaganda" to all of the films sold and distributed by Tricontinental was questionable under law, and the ALA asked what procedures would be applied for "review of such determinations by courts of competent jurisdiction."[4] The ALA did not receive a formal answer to its inquiries, and, coupled with the outcry from other individuals and organizations, the order was dropped.

The Customs Service has the authority to seize items it considers to be obscene or that urge or advocate treason, rebellion or forcible resistance to any law. Lengthy delays can occur in the importing of materials, and in some cases the items are simply destroyed or disappear. Nor is action consistent. In February of 1980, Unifilm, a U.S. distributor and the Los Angeles International Film Exposition imported a copy of the Cuban film *Retrato De Teresa (Portrait of Teresa)*. The Customs office in Los Angeles seized the print and threatened to destroy it. No reason was given for the seizure, and several days were required to gain release of the film. What was puzzling about the incident was that the film had passed through a New York customs checkpoint in August of 1979 and was being shown in the San Francisco area.[5]

Librarians have discovered that prison officials do not want materials that, according to the officials' evaluation, will cause trouble. If, as has happened, their evaluation violates prison policy, including the established "rights" of prisoners, they have been known to go to great lengths to circumvent that policy. Librarians working in prisons or providing library services to prisoners are often instructed to exclude "political stuff," any materials on sexuality and any that could incite violence. If such materials *are* purchased, they often disappear before they can be shelved. But things are not always as bleak as they seem. Not too long ago the State Library of Idaho undertook to improve library services to prisoners in the state institution. When they asked about the policy for selecting materials, the librarians were told that the only item to be excluded from the collection would be road maps of the State of Idaho.

The United States Post Office has, from time to time, been involved in censorship activities. The notorious Espionage Act, passed in June 1917 and bolstered by sedition sections in the Espionage Act of 1918, allowed for almost wholesale censorship of the mails. Under a directive from the Postmaster General, materials were confiscated widely, including those stating that the U.S. was involved in World War I for the wrong reasons, that the government was a tool of Wall Street, and any other statement that could be construed as criticism of or resistance to conscription into military service. As the Red Scare took over in the 1920s, materials were not only held up for inspection, but many were often seized, and the intended recipient was never informed. By the 1930s and 1940s, sexuality had become a concern of the post office, and materials were seized if they contained information on divorce, birth control and research studies of human sexuality. Librarians had a difficult time receiving as well as sending materials via the mails.

The Central Intelligence Agency (CIA) has, in recent years, attempted to suppress books, either in whole or in part. These are primarily being written by former employees of the agency, who signed away their right to publish anything without prior submission of materials shall be required to turn over all royalties to the CIA, pending formal determination of violation of other laws. The CIA has generally been able to delete materials critical of its operations. Victor Marchetti's *The CIA and The Cult of Intelligence* and Frank Shepp's *Decent Interval* are two of the titles recently tied up in litigation with the CIA.

Organized Groups in Challenge Actions

Assorted other business and occupational groups have tried to prevent materials of which they disapprove from reaching the public. Among these have been distributors of films and periodicals, book publishers and printers. One distributor of materials to libraries has been inserting pink slips into processed books sent to libraries as a warning that complaints have been received about those titles. The distributor disclaimed any responsibility when charges were made that the action "labeled" materials, stating that he was merely supplying a service to customers, and no judgment by the firm was involved. The pink slip was added only when the distributor received complaints from its library customers about the content of the book.[6]

Obviously, official groups and large organizations are difficult to oppose, if only for economic reasons. At the same time, materials that are suppressed, even if libraries are not directly affected by that suppression, cause problems to librarians. These works, peripheral to libraries' interests though they may seem, often represent ideas that need to be heard. In addition, successful suppression of materials by extralegal means such as those mentioned here can create a climate wherein the library becomes the ancillary target. We remember being engaged in conversation with an executive of a group with a national affiliation promoting the censorship of materials, and being told that the organization was not currently interested in focusing on the public library. The executive coolly stated that the group would concentrate on the school libraries first, and once it had succeeded there, would bring the public libraries into line. It is because of just such strategies that librarians are constantly being encouraged to resist censorship activities wherever they appear.

Certain features are common to many organizations that seek to control materials. One characteristic appears to be the members' inability to read anything but someone else's list of what *not* to read. As a result the same titles seem to constantly appear and reappear in challenge actions across the country. Sometimes the same title will be attacked at various geographic locations at about the same time. Similarities have been noted in the language used by these complainants. One might think that they are being told that such and such is *bad* and are joining in the crusade against it. It is remarkable how often complainants have not read the material being questioned, and will cite that as being one of their virtues: "I would not read [view] ———."

One tactic of would-be censors is to extract certain words or passages as examples of why they are concerned. In Randolph, New York, a complainant about the school media collection set up a card table in the shopping district and displayed underlined passages from books currently in the school's collection. In Riverside, California, when dictionaries were under attack, a mimeographed list of offending definitions were reproduced and widely distributed, to the great delight of many readers.

Another tactic often witnessed is the defense of freedom and a denial of censorship. Thus complainants will loudly proclaim that they are not advocating censorship, nor are they interested in starting a witch hunt. They just want to make certain that this particular work be removed, for it has violated freedom by *going too far* to enjoy reader access.

Turning our attention to the fund-raising activities of these groups, we find that they have been stepped up in recent years, and although exact figures are difficult to obtain from "tax-exempt" agencies, it is easy to see that activity in this area is expensive. Attacks on a public library in Utah in 1979–80 were well funded, and the group involved is reputed to have raised $200,000 to assist in its fight to rid the community of unwanted library materials. When so much money is involved, the library is faced with an even more serious problem. It does not have budgeted monies to promote its role in the community.

The following advertisement, telling one side of a story, and undoubtedly costing a good deal of money, appeared in a local newspaper:

> We have investigated our Centre County Library and have found several communist books which are very vile.... Everyone wants to

68   FREEDOM OF ACCESS TO LIBRARY MATERIALS

give to the library, but many are forgetting just what they are giving and paying for. Namely, Socialism [sic] or Communism.

How long will it take all groups in Bellefonte and surrounding areas to awaken? This is not a child's game, but rather a dangerous one after morals have been destroyed. In the Morrisdale area police have been called pigs—all because a book was made available in the library.[7]

While such advertisements are comparatively rare, letter-writing campaigns are not. Newspaper editors are often receptive to such letters, and not infrequently use their position to support censorship of items of which they disapprove. Letters can and often do appear without prior notice or warning to the librarian involved. In some cases the complainants have approached a member of the library staff and been rebuffed, and thus feel forced to take their grievance to the public. Librarians have been known to receive threatening letters (often anonymous), obscene phone calls and, in one known incident, threats against the members of the librarian's family.

It is difficult to chronicle some of the attacks on librarians and members of boards concerned with libraries because such acts are kept from public view. In one of the more famous cases, in Kanawha County, West Virginia, the campaign to remove materials from the school library and curriculum reached beyond verbal violence into shootings. School-board, and occasionally library-board, meetings are disrupted by groups demanding some sort of restriction of materials. Such highly emotional tirades are difficult to interrupt and threaten to turn violent. An example of this kind of situation exists in a recording of a public meeting in Riverside, California, when an underground newspaper was under attack.[8] Such events are not common in the lives of most librarians, but they almost always occur unexpectedly, and with such vehemence as to leave the librarian shaken and disoriented. The need for a well-organized plan for dealing with complaints is evident. It is important that the complainant and the librarian have some rules set up so that the fight may be fair, if not "clean."

Some organizations have the names of prominent people on their letterhead, which adds to their prestige. The librarian confronted with such an array of power may think twice about how much a confrontation over a single item is worth when the odds seem to be so stacked against the library. The organization, as we have said, may not have been formed for the purpose of censorship, and some of those whose names are on the letterhead might find it personally offensive to be dragged into an attack on a library collection. Those individuals may not even be aware that their names are being used. One tactic librarians can use is to send a letter to some of those whose names are on the letterhead and inform them of what is being done in their name. If the librarian is acquainted with any of them, a phone call may start the wheels moving in another direction. Those involved in public libraries in which the trustees have been well versed in the need for preventive measures regarding attacks on library collections may well know some of the people in the censoring organization, and can use their contacts to cut off the complainant at the pass. Trustees are often the best source for forestalling open warfare against a library and its collection. But trustees must be informed and appreciative of well-developed policies and procedures in this area.

The "big lie" is another tactic enjoyed by groups attacking libraries. Whether or not the teller of the tale knows it to be untrue is unimportant. If librarians do not check out the facts, they too can be caught up in a censorship activity based upon false premises. The librarian is on the defensive and the complainants are often simply repeating what they have been told. Even if the complainant is believed to be genuinely disturbed and annoyed, the librarian must apply a jaundiced eye to the source of the complaint. If he or she does, there is a chance of some headway being made. The complainant has been told or has discovered something which creates a situation of fear and frustration. There is a real fear at work in the complainant: the fear that comes with feeling that suddenly the world as envisioned was not what it seemed. If the librarian understands why the individual is concerned and tries to help that individual collect the facts so that a proper investigation can be undertaken, then the chances are that a potentially explosive situation has been disarmed. Such reasonableness doesn't always work, but it is far superior to rebuffing a complainant or mechanically filling out a bureaucratic form.

Sometimes the "lie" is so vague that it is difficult to deal with successfully. We know of a filmmaker whose product is often purchased by libraries. The complaint was made that the producer was a maker of pornographic films for a well-known distributor and that one of the shots used in a film sold to libraries came from one of the pornographic films. This kind of non-fact is almost impossible to disprove.

A series of textbooks was charged, in a recent campaign, with advocating wife-swapping. This custom of the social group in question was mentioned in the teacher's guide but not in the students' text. This did not concern the complainants, who maintained that the mention of such a group in the text was in effect supporting the practice of wife-swapping, and so the text must be removed. Again, we are dealing with a difficult situation. It is here that setting and following procedures is necessary, and a strong policy-making group will find it must stand its ground. Proving anything to such complainants is most unlikely.

Economic factors figure prominently in pressure on libraries. In particular the public library can be hurt severely by an attack by a group or an individual applying such pressure. A recent incident was reported to us by a staff member of a major public library system on the East Coast. In question was a popular book on human sexuality aimed at the high-school-aged student. The county executive was informed by a group of the presence of the book in the collection. He in turn called the director of the library system and stated that he wanted the book removed from the collection. When the librarian began to explain book-selection procedures, the county executive demanded immediate removal of the book and said that otherwise he would severely cut the library's budget. The library director ordered all copies of the title removed from the collection, to the consternation of some of the librarians who serve the youth of that county. In a staff meeting, the director announced that he had foresaken the policies and procedures of the library in this case because he felt it was more important to protect the staff's jobs and salaries. He received a standing ovation for his devotion to staff welfare, according to the report made to us.

It is easy to view such action as practical, and for the moment, at least, that library seems to be on a steady keel. Yet one cannot help but take into account the fact that a work that had been debated about and selected, following the policies and procedures of the library, for its usefulness to the youth of the community was suddenly withdrawn because of an extralegal threat by someone whose hand rests on the purse strings. The threat worked. And those who put the county executive up to it know that it worked. The library and its staff now have a new policy and procedure for selecting materials that are to go into the library. If the "right" materials are not selected, job and family security of the staff will suffer. Suddenly a new selector sits in on all deliberations of the staff. Is this subject, this opinion, this image, or this sound likely to be disapproved by someone in the community? If so, does it disappear from the collection after a phone call from the county executive? These questions are probably never stated by staff members in their deliberations, but the specter of the county executive looms across every bit of material in the library from that day forward. The censors know it. The staff knows it. But the public probably doesn't know who is screening access to the materials in the library.

Certainly many on the staff can live with an attack on their *circumstantial* freedom, and may even feel that those in the community will exercise their *acquired* freedom and find access to the material elsewhere. Others may feel that they still have their *natural* freedom and can wait for a better time to use it. But the price paid so easily would have been less costly if the librarians knew the board and the community well enough to stand firm in defense of their selection of material. Yet they were not certain that they had made the right selection, and rather than admit it, they gave the county executive an ex-officio membership on the acquisitions team.

We Have Met The Censors

The foregoing discussion leads naturally into the last, but certainly not the least important, group of censors. To paraphase the cartoon opossum Pogo, we have met the censors and they is us. We, the librarians, do a good deal of censoring, and it is all the more insidious because it is not easily detectable. There have been two noteworthy studies made by librarians on the unprofessional activities in the acquisitions of materials that lead to censorship.[9] These studies make it clear that librarians, in fear of losing their jobs, and being somewhat timid and wishing to avoid controversy,[10] betray their professional responsibility to provide materials. Instead they avoid acquiring certain materials, or remove those to which they feel certain members of their community might object. In many cases librarians themselves do not approve of the materials they are excluding from the collection.

A rather mild example of this attitude occurred in a recent meeting of librarians. A school media librarian reported that she had a paperback copy of the novel *Jaws* (which was also one of the most popular motion pictures of all time), which she kept in a desk drawer, because, as she stated, she was serving grades 7 through 9 and felt that there were many in that age group who would not profit from reading it. She said that she didn't exclude the title from the collection because it was so much in demand, and finished her account by stating that so many students came to the desk, asking to read the book, that she got rid of it. She told the students that it was lost and she didn't have the money to replace it.

A librarian employed in a major metropolitan public library told us that in her library, "controversial" titles are purchased and immediately placed in the closed stacks. The staff has been told to evaluate anyone who wants the material enough to seek it out by asking for it at one of the service desks.[11] "Funny-looking" people and youths are often told that the book is in circulation. One professional staff member was heard to turn down a high-school student's request for some material on homosexuality, recommending that the student visit the office of a local homophile organization to try to find material. When questioned by other staff members as to why such evasive action was taken when there was material in the stacks suitable for the student's age group, the librarian replied that she did not want to be responsible for the youth's becoming a homosexual.

We know of another librarian who kept a copy of *Das Kapital*, by Karl Marx, behind the charging desk, rather than letting any interested member of the public have access to it. Circulation desks are often used as control points. They can easily intimidate the young, and staff members are often heard to caution some of the steady clientele with such statements as, "I really don't think you're going to want to read this."

As you can see, control of access by librarians takes various forms. The closed shelf is the most common, and comes in many models, sizes and constructions. The material may be kept behind the reference desk, behind or under the circulation desk or in a desk drawer. If it is the library policy never to circulate reference books, controversial titles are sometimes placed under that classification, for "protection." Other collections can spring up in the office of the head of adult services or children's services. Most remote of all is the shelf set up in the office of the director of the library. In one library, we know of a special room for "problem" materials and an interview with the director is required before admission is granted (or denied). We know of a major Midwestern library where for years a large uncataloged collection of classic and near-classic erotic and pornographic materials was kept in a tiny room near the furnace room, in the bowels of the building. The director was the only one who held the key. How do we know of the collection? Because some of the more enterprising of the professional staff discovered that by removing the screen from an air duct in the furnace room they had direct access to the materials by crawling. That collection maintained a high but selective circulation record for years before it finally joined the rest of the "rare" books upstairs.

Sometimes these "problem" items are listed in the card catalog; other times they are not. Sometimes a listing in the card catalog is misleading to the public, because there is no indication that the material is receiving unusual treatment. In many cases a special symbol or code is used, which is only understood by the staff. For this reason, the more sophisticated library user can spend considerable time trying to find materials on the shelf, while, if the truth be known, they are languishing in some out-of-the-way place. This is a very effective way to control access to materials, but one that can create real wrath when discovered by the user.

Restricting part of the collection to a particular age group, storing materials in obscure places, labeling materials and even mutilation are favorite methods of librarians wishing to control access to the collection. The very existence of children's and young-adult rooms in public libraries can be misinterpreted as an attempt to control or restrict access to materials, especially when they are used to keep those patrons from using the remainder of the collection and services. Storing materials in closed stacks has been a valid method of controlling materials in terms of security, but it should be clear to the user how to gain access to that collection. The undergraduate library, which has been separate from the research library on many American campuses since the

1950s, has been used by some librarians as an excuse to exclude the undergraduate from the research collection. The purpose of the separation of the two collections was originally to provide more meaningful and open access to each level of user.

The mutilation by librarians of books, periodicals and films has taken several forms. One librarian removed a page from *Sylvester and the Magic Pebble,* a picture book for children showing animals in human situations, because of a complaint that one of the pigs was wearing a policeman's uniform. More than one librarian has painstakingly covered the nudity of the charming boy in Maurice Sendak's *In the Night Kitchen,* usually with white tempera or a felt-tip pen. One woman reported to us that, as a clerk in a system's processing department, she had to provide shorts for the boy in each of thirty copies going out to member libraries.

Films and filmstrips are edited for all kinds of reasons. Some librarians distrust the "values" to be found in film and have been known to restrict access because "too much time can be spent looking at film instead of reading." Don Roberts, noted multi-media-minded librarian, has done some basic research that documents the bias of librarians against nonprint communications materials."[11]

Such alterations of materials seem on the surface to be ridiculous and worth little more than a chuckle and perhaps a "tch-tch." Yet librarians who feel so strongly about the material selected that they are willing to spend time and money altering the material into some "acceptable" form should not select the material in the first place. Hypocrisy has a way of showing its face. The user of the materials will know they have been altered. If the librarian feels that the library should not have any materials depicting the human form nude, that policy should be made known to the user of that collection. If other materials are going to be restricted in some form, the public has a right to know how, and on what basis, so that they can judge if they wish to use that library's collection. The high-school librarian of our youth who used to apply Band-Aids to photos of young women and reproductions of artwork was at least consistent. The students appreciated this and would always stop by the library to check up on the latest application of adhesives so that copies of those materials could be sought out and studied in the local drugstore or bookstore.

Labeling takes many forms. One library put a "Q" on the spine of books, to keep track of "questionable" materials in the collection. Another uses a red band of tape on the spine. There are whole collections of symbols used on spines to single out materials in order to prejudice the user. We have seen rockets or atomic symbols to designate science fiction. Deer-stalker hats, guns, magnifying glasses and the like have been used to signify mysteries. Gothic romances, westerns, novels of international intrigue and now books with larger print, all have been marked and segregated. Whatever the method, the effect is the same. By placing a label on the book, the librarian is trying to make up the reader's mind about the work. To wrap such action in the flag of providing a special service for those who only read that type of material is contrary to the goals of the library. If such labeling is permissible, then why cannot the library label those books that are of interest only to the sports-person, the business executive, the doctor, the teacher or religious groups? Moreover, how can the librarian argue that it is permissible to label some books but not all books? Is it possible to reach the desired goal through special browsing collections and bibliographies rather than sending materials out of the library marked with a symbol that to many is prejudicial?

The selection of potentially controversial items points up one of the more difficult problems facing librarians. All librarians reject items for inclusion in the collection, and they do so for a wide variety of reasons. Certainly the following must be considered: the budget; the item's place, both physically and in terms of subject, in the total collection; the need for the item in the community being served; the pressure of popular demand, and so forth. But when the item in question is also potentially problematic or controversial or concerns a subject beyond the knowledge and experience of the librarian, professional evaluations can waiver and a good deal of rationalization and self-delusion can enter the selection process. One librarian, upon being questioned as to why the library sold rather than acquisitioned a collection of "pornographic" books that included scholarly works on human sexuality, marriage, birth control and biology, very frankly replied that there was no demand for that type of material in the library.

All librarians face this problem if they are involved in any way with the development of their library's collection. Lester Asheim dealt with the problem in his now-famous essay, which is cited every time this dilemma between selection and free access is discussed.[12] Asheim maintained that the selector looks for positive values, while the censor is negative and looks for flaws. Further, the censor judges by external criteria; that is, by considering the author or publisher's political affiliation or sexual preference, whether virtue is ascendant and so on. The distinction between censorship and selection seems an obvious one, and if we make a conscious effort to follow Asheim's principles, we can go a long way toward sidestepping excuses when we avoid selecting controversial materials. However, it should be pointed out that professional librarians must know what their personal prejudices and moral values are, in order to avoid making subjective decisions during the selection process.

Once materials are selected, we encounter the problem of protecting them from theft and mutilation by library users. Self-appointed censors constantly appear in the library stacks, carrying their personal fears into action via knife, scissors and felt-tip pens or outright theft. One technological advance that has helped reduce theft, while possibly increasing mutilation, is the electronic device that prevents the removal of materials by setting off an alarm. (It should be pointed out that theft of materials is, surprisingly, performed in large part by the staff. This condition is well known in manufacturing and commercial retail establishments but has not significantly penetrated the minds of those who plan for library security.)

In terms of security (where electronics are not being used), one question is paramount: is the material being protected for the good of the librarian or the user? Pictures of nudes or of sexual acts tend to be removed or mutilated by some users. When such is the case, the librarian is faced with having to decide whether to absorb the cost and replace the material or to drop the title from the collection. In some instances the act of replacement is costly. More than the price of the material is involved; so are staff time, searching, ordering, processing and so forth. When librarians see copy after copy of stamp catalogs, art books, auto-repair manuals, exam-preparation workbooks and the like disappear as fast as they are replaced, the question of cost becomes most serious. And it is for such reasons that closed collections develop. Yet libraries, once using such a protective device, can suddenly find that they have hundreds of items in closed shelves. And when they find titles by Nabokov, O'Hara, Miller, Inge, Vidal and Bellow alongside the Arco test-book series, the tropical-fish catalogs, gun-collection books and chemical-formulae handbooks, it becomes obvious that more than the materials are being protected.

In addition, librarians have developed a newer and more subtle form of restriction of access, which, according to a growing number of reports, has been widely debated and practiced recently. It is not called censorship, nor is it intended to be, but charging fees for certain library services can have the same effect. Librarians have long charged fees for reserving materials and for providing copies of materials (usually in the form of special equipment for the user). More recent is the nonresident borrower's fee, and a few unconfirmed reports have surfaced that libraries are contemplating charging fees for admission to programs in the library. Of course, the most classic fee of all in library service is that for keeping material beyond the return date.

Libraries should be able to charge for a number of fringe benefits for users, such as copy machines, coin-operated dispensers of paper and pens, tote bags and refreshments. We feel that libraries should long ago have pushed to be not only depositories of state and federal documents, but retail outlets for some of them. At the same time, we recognize that the elderly, the poor, and the young in particular are punished by the imposition of any fee that denies them use of the library collection. We realize that setting fees is not about to be universally adopted in American libraries, but we feel strongly that the imposition of fees and fines for use of library materials limits the access to a significant segment of the public. It may already be too late to reverse this state of affairs, as library policy-makers and legislators eye the income to be generated from charging fees for the use of the collection or of the various electronic devices that provide special access to information. Yet imposing such limitations weakens the librarians' credo that collections should be easily and openly accessible to all.

Words Without Music

Censors, regardless of who they may be, have personal reasons for wanting materials removed or restricted. The most often-heard battle cry rallies those who have a desire to protect the young, a laudable virtue easily translated into a misguided ambition. Others want to protect everyone from what they term the offensive. Others just want to make certain that their views and personal values are the only ones being promoted. Attempts at censorship seem to come from a misunderstanding of the nature of education, a misunderstanding of the nature of freedom and democracy and, in some cases, from a deep-seated belief that if one witnesses someone walking down the street in a horsebridle, one has in fact seen a horse. Most censors are, however, sincere in their complaints.

One side effect of censors' activities never seems to occur to them (or if it does, they don't care); that is, any attempt to censor material focuses public attention on it and increases demand. This seems to be true everywhere and always. Goethe, writing about the burning French romances, reported that people immediately rushed out to buy copies of the accursed book. In more modern times, the banning of books in Boston was a sure signal for increased sales in the remainder of the nation. In Rochester, New York, in 1973, *Steal This Book,* by Abbie Hoffman, was attacked, and within twenty-four hours all copies in the city were sold.

What materials do people want to censor? The answer is: almost everything. When one looks at a list of censored materials it becomes apparent that nothing is immune from attack; subjects range through the library classification system, starting with the most innocuous-seeming light novels, continuing to the bestsellers and going on to the classics. Thousands of titles have been reported censored over the years; Anne L. Haight's *Banned Books* provides a thorough list of the types and varieties.[13] But one must bear in mind that many cases of suppression do not make the recorded pages of history.

Words are often the target of attack by censors. We have mentioned that censors often underline words or passages in offending materials or make multiple copies of the words they have found in the various sources they wish to suppress. True, there are taboo words in all cultures. To some, words seem to have a magical quality, so that the word becomes the thing or the act. James Lewton Brain summarizes his behavioral study of the effect of language:

> ... there is no doubt of the universality of language and, arising out of

that, a knowledge of our own mortality. Also seemingly universal are fears and anxiety about sex and incest, the concept of incest, of marriage, and of kinship being rooted also in the capacity for categorization inherent in human language. Because we know about death, we fear it. Present in our cultural memory (if not genetic memory) is the knowledge that corpses rapidly putrefy and produce odors that we, alone among the animals, regard as disgusting. Because of our posture, gait, and partially our diet, humans have to clean themselves after defecation, an action that has to be learned. The nature of the feces is disgusting to humans, though not to other animals, presumably because of association made between the smell of feces and putrefying bodies. Thus many mothers inculcate in their children the notion not only that feces, and indeed other bodily emissions, are dirty, but everything connected with sex is dirty. At one level, then, sex reminds us of death. And at another level, all aspects of sexuality prove to be anxiety-provoking because of the perpetual ability of males and females to engage in sex, unlike other animals that have oestrus cycles and mating seasons. The anxiety arises from a fear that incest might take place and thus disrupt and shatter the social structures we have erected based upon prohibition of sex between close kin, a concept of marriage, and the idea of parents, siblings, grandparents, cousins, uncles and aunts, nephews and nieces. The very idea of incest, marriage, and kinship is, as I have noted, totally dependent on language. If sex reminds us of incest, it also reminds us of death because we consider sex with feces and feces with death.[14]

The foregoing attests to the power of language to be translated into the very act it symbolizes. The process of translating the thing into a symbol is the only explanation for an example cited by S. I. Hayakawa when he reported that, in 1939, the City Council of Cambridge, Massachusetts, passed a resolution making it illegal to "possess, harbor, sequester, introduce or transport, within the city limits, any book, map, magazine, newspaper, pamphlet, handbill or circular containing the words Lenin or Leningrad."[15] And if 1939 seems to be a quaint place in time, let us remember that very late in the 1970s *Drums Along the Mohawk* was removed from a school reading list only because the words "damn" and "hell" were used.

Dictionaries are attacked from time to time. The *Dictionary of American Slang* was attacked in the late 1960s and began to reappear on complaint lists in the late 1970s along with the more recent *American Heritage Dictionary of the English Language*. In the latter work the censors were horrified by such definitions as "bed: 4. A place for lovemaking. 5. A marital relationship, with its rights and intimacies" or "shack-up. *Slang.* 1. To live, room, or stay at one place. 2. To live in sexual intimacy with another person, for a short time." Such words are keys to attacks on all kinds of books, films, television productions and recordings. The words are often described as "filthy language," "profanity" and "dirty." One of the outcomes of the oft-printed lists of offensive words published by the censors is that they move readily into the hands and minds of the people who are to be protected from such assault. In Rochester, New York, a group using one of that town's famous Xerox machines reproduced pages from books with passages underlined and distributed them as slingers in the local shopping mall. After their request to have materials removed from a school library was turned down, a parents group in New Jersey printed leaflets with sample passages from *Grapes of Wrath* and *Catcher in the Rye* to continue their protest. They said they were forced to distribute the quotations that they disliked, "in order to safeguard their morals, their lives, and their souls," and noted further that the devil would blush to read those excerpts.[16] Yet these are the very constant and persistent clouds that hang over the head of the librarian. Certainly the learned explanation of Dr. Brain about our language taboos and the semantic example supplied by Dr. Hayakawa will neither disarm nor devastate the protesters. Instead, they may well bring down additional wrath aimed at the "pointy-head" and the "impracticality" of the education received by the librarian.

How does one cope with the fear of human sexuality that permeates much of society? The attacks on formal instruction about human sexuality, oblique and direct descriptions of sexual activity, discussions of homosexuality, and pictures, drawings, and symbolic representations of human genitalia are numerous, and consistent in their hysteria. The range of the attacks is wide: *Down These Mean Streets*, by Piri Thomas; *Time* and *Life* magazines; *How to Avoid Social Diseases: A Practical Handbook*, by Leslie Nicholas; *Girls and Sex*, by Wardell Pomeroy; *Flowers for Algernon*, by Daniel Keyes; *Laughing Boy*, by Oliver LaFarge and *Of Mice and Men*, by John Steinbeck have been recently attacked. The only consolation one might feel in looking at the list is that it seems to take the censors several years to catch up with what is on the market. Some librarians believe that more recent works could really give censors apoplexy.

Four of Alfred Hitchcock's best-known films were scheduled to be shown at a public library in Philadelphia: *The Birds, Psycho, Suspicion,* and *The Thirty-Nine Steps.* They were attacked as being "orgies of homicide and mutilation." The film of Shirley Jackson's story "The Lottery" is condemned because it is violent. The censors believe that if the discussion or depiction of sexual matters leads to sexual activity, the discussion or depiction of violence leads to orgies. Religious content is sometimes the basis for complaint, as in both the book and the made-for-TV version of *Dinky Hocker Shoots Smack. Abortion Eve* is a comic book that has been included in a few libraries' collections, with resultant theological attacks.

Discussions of politics and social conditions are frequently attacked by censors, who cite such materials as being "revolutionary," "too liberal," "permissive" and "socialistic." Among numerous recent examples are Galbraith's *Age of Influence,* Ebenstein's *Today's Ism's,* and Robert Lekachman's *Age of Keynes.*

In 1971 the Los Angeles Public Library staff was astounded to find itself under attack because of nineteen films being shown in special programs. The chief objection was that the films were "communistic." Some of the films were made in Poland and Czechoslovakia; in the mind of the censors, that was reason enough for suspicion. Other films questioned business ethics or discussed various religious practices. Significantly, the librarian who planned the programs said, "Being aware that I serve a conservative community, I made a conscious effort to avoid films which might be patently controversial."[17] She went on to note that she avoided subjects such as sex, civil rights, drugs, the draft, Vietnam, Hippie culture, abortion and witchcraft. This is an excellent example of how trying to avoid a protester is like picking your way through a mine field; if you step one way to avoid one, you find you've stepped on another and lost your leg anyway.

It should be apparent, then, that nothing is really immune from the library user's wrath. Obviously, no matter how reactionary or "conservative" the selections, the day will come when an objection is filed against them. Some of the most beloved books in recent times have been attacked: Arthur Miller's *Death of a Salesman* (for an attack on the family and salesmanship and a depiction of sexuality); Ernest Hemingway's *For Whom the Bell Tolls* (for its political content and sexuality) or *To Have and To Have Not* (for its immorality); John Steinbeck's *Grapes of Wrath* or *In Dubious Battle* (for their "dirty" words and political outlook), Robert Penn Warren's *All The King's Men* (for its anti-Americanism and sexuality) and Richard Wright's *Black Boy* (for its sexuality and racism). All of these titles have been in print for twenty years, but they are still being attacked today.

One can cite a wide assortment of other materials that upset censors. *Birth of a Nation*, a silent film classic by D. W. Griffiths, was shown in a public library program and attacked because the sixty-year-old film was "negative in regard to the black contribution to the birth of the nation." *How To Say No To a Rapist and Survive*, a film, has been attacked by various groups, including "Women Library Workers," as being offensive and containing misinformation. Several recent books about the religious sect Scientology have been attacked by that church as being libelous. *Catcher in the Rye* has been constantly under attack since its appearance, and although the character of a prostitute and the mild use of some four-letter words are often cited as the reason, it becomes apparent in many cases that the real "objection" to the work is the depiction of teenage rebellion against parental authority.

Sportspeople of the nation react to any material that suggests that the hunting and killing of animals is anything less than noble. They have been particularly upset by such films as *Say Goodbye* and *After the First*. On the other hand, *Daisy Summerfield's Style*, by M. B. Goffstein, has been objected to because the heroine stole something, enjoyed the act and got away with it. Antiabortion groups have attacked *About Sex* and other films produced to instruct the teenager.[18]

One might think that the Scopes trial over the right to teach the theory of evolution was ancient history, but a recent decision by a school board requires that the Biblical and the Darwinian theory of evolution receive equal attention in texts and the instructional program. A group in Georgia said that the current texts in use in the schools "promoted evolution and devil worship." In 1978 an organization sued the Smithsonian Institution because it mounted an exhibit on evolution.

While the scientific community often attacks astrology it does not hold an exclusive franchise on such attacks. After one library presented an astrology program, a letter-writer said that since astrology was unscientific, the library should not endorse it by

Freedom Denied   83

giving a platform to an astrologer. The correspondent did not object to books on astrology, but only to using the library to present a program on it.

Recordings have received their fair share of attacks in libraries. *Tales of Witches, Ghosts and Goblins Told by Vincent Price*[19] was the object of complaint because its violence scared a listener. The recording of *Jesus Christ Superstar* has received considerable flak for appearing in library collections. Recordings by the Beatles, the Village People and other popular artists have also been the object of complaint. In many libraries the inclusion of popular materials has been severely limited, and in many cases the collection consists only of recordings of classical music, probably in anticipation of complaints about more contemporary materials.

In addition to the materials themselves, libraries receive complaints about how the materials are promoted. The compilation of a bibliography or the laying out of an exhibit can bring its share of complaints. Libraries have not been successful in explaining that they are not endorsing a subject but simply making it accessible to the community. One of the authors once installed a window display of which he was very proud. He covered the floor and the backing for the display with black cloth. From the single light source he strung a hangman's noose. Directly under the light he placed a copy of *Dracula*, which had a vivid red cover. From a department store he borrowed a mannequin's arm, which he placed so that it protruded from under the cloth. Around the bottom of the window a hatchet, a knife, a bottle of poison and several horror and mystery books were placed. Two users of the library complained that the display was contributing to the delinquency of minors. There were no other reactions.

In its newly constructed exhibit facility, a library in North Carolina mounted a display of the history and paraphernalia of the Ku Klux Klan. Members of the community were not only startled by the sudden emergence of the library as a center of controversial ideas; they were also angry. The opening of the exhibit was marred by violence, and it had to be closed, leaving the reputation of the library damaged.

Too often librarians assume that because their institution has such a solid and comfortable air about it, they can do no wrong. What we must remember is that for most libraries, in particular public libraries, nowhere near a majority of the community even sets foot inside the door. The library is just not a part of most people's lives. As a result, for many the library is a place to find books, dust and quiet. You have to be not only literate, but *bookish*, to get any kicks out of the place.

As more and more libraries mount programs, add to collections of materials and arrange exhibits and programs that draw the nontraditional user in the door, the more likely is the library to run into controversy. Along with any program involving outreach and the development of community interests, there must be a coordinated public-information program that promotes the library as a community forum for ideas and a neutral ground for learning about oneself and the world.

Many complaints about library materials come from individuals who want to express their doubts about the wisdom of a selection or a program. They are indirectly asking for an explanation of how the library can be endorsing "flower gardening," "civil rights," "communism" and the "shamrock" on St. Paddy's Day. They may even think there are some vague, dark forces controlling the library. The story of another library display involving one of the authors illustrates this point. During the terrible civil strife of the late 1960s, when cities were being put to the torch, an exhibit was carefully mounted in the huge space used for such purposes, in the social-science section of the public library. Its logo was taken from James Baldwin's powerful essays *The Fire Next Time*, and materials were selected that discussed the history, sociology and moral problems created in the United States by its long history of racial bigotry and hatred. It was not long before a very irate gentleman appeared and asked to have the display removed. He declared that it was an open invitation to the racial minorities in the city to riot and pillage. A long discussion followed about the role of the library in the community and how this display was intended to convey to all who came into the library that there were materials at hand that could help the community understand and cope with the problems facing us all. The exhibit was also meant to convey the messsage that the library was not unaware of the powerful yearning of minorities to be free of oppression and discrimination. When he understood the library's mission, he relaxed and asked if he might read "that Baldwin fella." He never complained again.

Sometimes the complainant is not urging censorship but seeking a balanced collection, saying that certain material has proven offensive to that individual. Some guidance by the librarian will help such users steer clear of the types of materials bound to offend them. Those users don't mind if there are others who want materials that seem to them to be trash. They simply want respect and understanding for their particular interests.

Sometimes there is a real gap in a collection. Members of a public-library staff panicked when a self-proclaimed atheist began to complain loudly about the number of proreligious books on the shelves. A discussion with this man revealed that he did not object to religious material; rather, he felt that there should be more material discussing his point of view. When his cooperation and suggestions were solicited, several very good titles previously overlooked by the staff were brought to its attention. Of course, while all suggestions are welcome, the final responsibility for selection rests with the library staff. An explanation of the selection procedure and a copy of the library's policy often guarantees cooperation and appreciation from a complainant. In one library, a member of the John Birch Society, after having been given a thorough explanation of how materials were added and having seen it in practice, later rose to defend the library when it was attacked by another group.

Summary

Two facts clearly emerge from the foregoing discussion: Anyone—of any age, race, religion, occupation, educational level, economic status, political or social persuasion or level of intelligence—is likely to be a censor. And any item—no matter how innocuous it may seem—can be the object of a censorship attempt. While this has always been true, librarians cannot empty their shelves. And since it is obviously impossible to avoid occasional controversy, particularly when some citizens discover that the library is not quiet, sleepy and sedated, one must be prepared for it. The best preparation is to accept these conditions, and proceed from there. We must continually explain to the community how and why controversy sits on every shelf. And we must tell people how they can participate in maintaining a collection that fully reflects the diversity and challenges of life. But most of all, we must meet every challenge head on—not by being headstrong. Listen to people. React to them. If they are distressed, be ready to sympathize and work with them to alleviate their fear and distrust. You won't win all your battles, but you should be able to stay on the battlefield. And that, to us, is the sign of a good librarian and a well-run library.

NOTES

1. Other groups that have attacked materials in schools and libraries include Action Now, America's Future, Church Crusade, Citizens Against Pornography, Citizens for Decent Literature, Concerned Citizens, Concerned Parents, Conservative Citizens Council, Constitutional Heritage Club, Guardians of Traditional Education, John Birch Society, Morality and Media, Movement to Restore Decency Now, New Jersey's Policeman's Benevolent Association, Parents Who Care, Real Friends of the Public Library, and Save Our Schools. This is by no means a complete listing and is presented to provide insight into the words used to depict the group whose primary purpose is to control the publication and distribution of materials.
2. Office for Intellectual Freedom, American Library Association, *Intellectual Freedom Manual, ALA Chicago,* part 2 (Chicago, ALA, 1974), pp. 27–31.
3. *Variety,* April 28, 1976, p. 3.
4. An unpublished letter from William D. North, General Counsel to the American Library Association to John H. Davitt, Chief, Internal Security Section, Criminal Division of the U. S. Department of Justice, May 25, 1976.
5. *Variety,* February 27, 1980, p. 5.
6. *American Libraries* (March 1979): 131–32.
7. *Newsletter on Intellectual Freedom* (September 1975): 139.
8. *What Shall They Read; Should Underground Newspapers and Like Material Be Banned From the Public Library?* Pacifica Archive 024.
9. Marjorie Fiske, *Book Selection and Censorship* (Berkeley, Calif.: University of California Press, 1968), and Busha, Charles H., *Freedom vs. Suppression and Censorship* (Littleton, Colo.: Libraries Unlimited, 1972).
10. Michael Pope, *Sex and the Undecided Librarian* (Metuchen, N. J.: Scarecrow Press, 1974).
11. Don Roberts, "Report on Past and Present Censorship on Non-book Media in Public Libraries," published by the author, 1976.
12. Lester Asheim, "Not Censorship but Selection" (reprinted from *Wilson Library Bulletin* [September 1953]) *Building Library Collections,* ed. Mary Duncan Carter, et al., 4th ed. (Metuchen, N. J.: Scarecrow Press, 1974), pp. 366–67.

13. Anne L. Haight, *Banned Books: Information Notes on Some Books Banned for Various Reasons* (New York: R. R. Bowker, 1970).
14. John Lewton Brain, *The Last Taboo: Sex and the Fear of Death* (Garden City, N. Y.: Anchor Press, 1979), pp. 233-34.
15. S. I. Hayakawa, *Language in Thought and in Action* (New York: Harcourt, Brace & World, 1964), p. 33.
16. *Newsletter on Intellectual Freedom* (September 1975): 139.
17. Ron Sigler, "A Study in Censorship: the Los Angeles 19," *Film Library Quarterly* (Spring 1971): 36.
18. A school official, upon withdrawing the film *About Sex* from a showing, said: "to make certain that no one is offended, we voted to ban the showing of all sex films."
19. Caedmon TC 1393.

REFERENCES

Craig, Alec. *Suppressed Books. A History of the Conception of Literary Obscenity.* Cleveland, Ohio: World Publishing Co., 1963.

DeGrazia, Edward. *Censorship Landmarks.* New York: R. R. Bowker, 1969.

Lewis, Felice Flannery. *Literature, Obscenity & Law.* Carbondale, Ill.: Southern Illinois University Press, 1976.

National Council of Teachers of English. *Meeting Censorship in the Schools: A Series of Case Studies.* Champaign, Ill.: NCTE, 1969.

Chapter Five
Racism, Sexism and Other "Isms"

Segregating, subjugating and oppressing others are some of the oldest manifestations of the failure of many adults to progress beyond the adolescent state of self-hate, fear and peer grouping. The 1960s, a period of consciousness raising, made many librarians aware, along with other professional groups in the United States, of the numerous communications materials containing racist, sexist, ageist and other kinds of stereotyping based upon conditions beyond the control of those being discussed. As concern for minority rights, and human rights in general, began to take hold of the national consciousness, libraries found themselves receiving complaints from inside and outside the profession. Many of them concerned books that had become standard in library collections. Such titles as *Little Black Sambo, Huckleberry Finn, The Merchant of Venice, The Story of Doctor Doolittle, The Five Chinese Brothers, A Streetcar Named Desire, The Valachi Papers, The Fixer,* and *Laughing Boy* were attacked as racist. Some of these books are also respected, and the children's materials are particularly beloved and remembered as having endearing qualities. Those who remembered them with affection were, for the most part, individuals who felt that they had not been affected by the prejudices others had detected in them. But as the arguments continued and the materials were analyzed, many people discovered that racial stereotypes and prejudicial attitudes were indeed put forth in a good number of these works. Not everyone was convinced about every item, and the argument that racist charges seem exaggerated goes on.

As people became increasingly aware of stereotyping, objections were made to films and books considered antiethnic, sexist, ageist and stereotypical in the presentation of sexual mores and lifestyles. Books offensive to the handicapped are now being evaluated in terms of stereotyping. Sexist books are usually considered offensive to women, but recently one book thought of as being a solid contribution to the breaking down of sexual stereotyping, *Our Bodies, Ourselves*, an illustrated work on female sexuality, was attacked as being antimale. As we noted in the last chapter, it is possible to find something in libraries that is offensive to someone.

Of course, libraries have always contained materials that could offend almost anyone; sexual descriptions, the use of certain words, and various political and social opinions are offensive to those who feel threatened by, and consequently do not feel comfortable with, them. Mary K. Chelton, a noted librarian specializing in services to young adults, is not bothered by this state of affairs. In a recent speech she suggested that libraries adopt the following slogan: "Your Library Has Something to Offend Everyone." This is certainly the truth, although Ms. Chelton does not mean that libraries are necessarily insensitive to the content of materials in their collections. Stereotyping based upon racial or ethnic heritage, physical condition, sex and the choice of the object of human affection can be vicious. But perhaps even more damaging is the subtle and insidious conditioning to believe that such stereotyping is based on the truth, or is at most a charming conceit.

These prejudices are doubtless formed and reinforced by many elements: books, television, films, theatrical performances, advertising, the opinions of parents and the attitudes of peers are just a few. And librarians continue to agonize about whether they are perpetuating those stereotypes through their collections. It is easy to take a stand asserting that, in the name of freedom, we will defend everything we have on the shelves and will provide access to all who choose to see those materials. But this is an uncritical approach. The problem is a serious one, and we must continue to examine it, in the hope that we can understand and defend our reasons for selecting, rejecting or retaining materials that contain stereotypical representations of the human condition.

Let us look at the situation from the point of view of an

individual who finds some material offensive. Michael Dorris, chair of the Native Studies Department of Dartmouth College, author of *Native Americans: 500 Years After* and a descendant of the Modoc (native Americans), found himself caught up in a protest against the way in which a children's book was written, illustrated and distributed. *Michael Hendee*, by Cynthia Butler, was published in 1976 by the Regional Center for Educational Training, in Hanover, New Hampshire, as part of its Bicentennial Historiette Series. Aimed at a second- or third-grade readership, the story was a fictionalized account of an actual event that occurred during a conflict in 1780 in an area that later became Vermont.

According to the historical record, a little boy was captured by British and Mohawk troops and, after his mother appealed for his release, was returned to her unharmed.

Mr. Dorris explained that the book was based upon conjecture and depicted the boy as having been brutally and senselessly abducted, threatened with scalping, abused, tormented and terrified. The illustrations reinforced this. In the story's climax, the boy takes matters into his own hands and leads an escape of a number of prisoners.

In checking the primary-source material, Mr. Dorris found several changes had been made by the author. Instead of being abducted and dragged off by his hair (as illustrated), the boy was led away *by the hand*. The mother is depicted as trying to rescue her son at the camp, where he is tied to a tree (also illustrated), whereas the historical record notes that Mrs. Hendee went directly to the British and Mohawk headquarters and pleaded for her son's return. The British officer assured her that he would deliver the child to her as soon as the raiding party that had taken the child returned to the camp. Thus the boy was released, and there is no account of his being tied to a tree.

Mr. Dorris comments on what happened when he complained that public funds had been used to publish such a work and asked that it no longer be distributed:

> The furor which has arisen in response to my initial letter of objection to *Michael Hendee* is both unexpected in its intensity and disturbing in its implications. No one, certainly, expects to win a popularity contest by taking a critical stance on the work of others. But what has been surprising is that, with the exception of a single paragraph in Ms.

Butler's letter to me, no one—from the Regional Center to the faculty of Syracuse University—has made even the slightest attempt to deny the substantive objections to the book I initially raised . . .

Instead, it has been advanced by some that the book, regardless of problems it may have, should continue to be marketed because otherwise the Regional Center would lose money. Even more alarming than this apparent ethical myopia, however, is the nature of the reaction to the questions about the book I have raised. I have variously been personally accused of trying to ban the book from bookstores, of attempted censorship and of unprofessional conduct. It has been strongly suggested to my employer that I am unqualified to hold a faculty position, and I have been forced to defend myself and my position in writing and in person on numerous occasions.

Somehow the focus of the debate has been transferred from *Michael Hendee* to Michael Dorris, and the very right to protest the use of public funds for the publication of materials—which are at best ethnocentric and historically misleading and at worst racist and stereotypical—has come under fire. No individual (myself included) is at issue here; rather, the concern that *Michael Hendee* might in fact be a barrier to interracial and historical understanding for a second and third grade reading audience must either be effectively denied or attended to. . . . The issue is not one of censorship of material, but one of rights: of a minority population to a fair representation of its history, and of public school children to a fresh version of the world which is neither self-serving nor misrepresentative.[1]

Librarians are seldom confronted by such an eloquent and capable adversary, but such complaints may have the same result. The issue is pushed aside in favor of an attack on the individual as advocating that "ol' devil" censorship. For once, let us try to explore the issue. We must consider if materials such as this do any harm. Is there any psychic damage involved? Is that damage lasting? Is the effect limited to the individuals offended or does it extend to others exposed to the materials?

An article in the ALA children's services magazine, *Top Of The News*, cites three studies indicating that we really don't know what effect books will have on the reader.[2] These studies, although apparently admitting that books do have an effect, suggest that we don't know whether it is extensive or permanent. On the other hand, an editorial in *School Library Journal* discussing sexism asserts that "children's literature, from Mother Goose to history books... only aids in the sexual programming, setting into motion vicious, self-fulfilling cycles."[3] Ashley Montagu, a noted social biologist, remarks about the continued research on the conditioning of males and females:

> Many cases have been reported in the literature, in no way involving pre- or post-natal hormonal interference, in which sex-assignment of individuals from infancy has resulted in gender roles being completely reversed for the genetic sex with which they are usually associated. Thus, genetic males reared as females develop all the behavioral traits of femininity usually associated with females, while genetic females reared as males develop all the behavioral traits usually associated with males. While there can be no doubt that male and female hormones continue to play a role in the lives of these individuals, the influence of cultural conditioning in producing psychosexual differentiation is so great that, for all practical purposes, the influence of those hormones is held thoroughly under control by the role expectations of the reassigned gender.[4]

It would seem reasonable to conclude that the materials in a library contribute to conditioning an individual. It should be understood that the books, films, recordings and other materials available from the library are only part of this conditioning. But if these materials have no effect, why are we in business? And since we can assume that most librarians would not knowingly want to promote racism, sexism or any other harmful prejudice, we must consider what to do about the racist book or sexist film. If the characters in a novel are stereotypes or if a work of nonfiction betrays a certain prejudice, it can be assumed that those materials are flawed, and librarians frequently reject works because of their flaws. We do, after all, try to select the best materials for our collections, and children's and young-adult librarians have more leeway to do so (because they feel less pressure to purchase popular items) than those serving the adult. However, it must be borne in mind that a simple rejection of materials can become a method for ridding the library of works considered too "hot" to handle. In an interpretive document about the Library Bill of Rights, the ALA Intellectual Freedom Committee comments:

> The continuous review of library collections to remove physically deteriorated or obsolete materials is one means to maintain active library collections of current interest to the users. Continued reevalua-

tion is closely related to the goals and responsibilities of libraries and is a valuable tool of collection building. This procedure, however, is sometimes used as a convenient means to remove materials thought to be too controversial or disapproved of by segments of the community.[5]

The statement goes on to point out how such censorious action is in violation of the Library Bill of Rights, and recommends that libraries adopt guidelines and principles for evaluative procedures in library collection development.

This brings us to a second problem in confronting stereotyping in library materials: how does one decide whether or not a book is really sexist, racist and so on? If all the faces in a children's book are white, is the work racist? If a novel portrays a housewife singing while mopping the floor, is it sexist? If a film shows an old man as doddering, forgetful and cantankerous, is it ageist? For the moment we will look at the problem of literature for children, because that currently seems to be the area of greatest concern.

The Council on Interracial Books for Children analyzes books (for racism, sexism, and the like) in its *Bulletin* and has published two books: *Stereotypes, Distortions and Omissions in U.S. History Textbooks* and *Human- and Anti-Human Values in Children's Books*. In the second volume, books are examined for the following qualities: racism, sexism, elitism, materialism, individualism, ageism, conformism and escapism. Although one finds many of the comments helpful and valid, at other times the authors seem to be straining to find what they regard as bad qualities. Some of the "isms" listed above do not seem to be so bad to these authors. In discussing *Introducing Shirley Braverman*, by Hilma Wolitzer, the evaluators are generally pleased but give it bad marks for being racist by omission. *Dragonwings*, by Lawrence Yep, is given a very high rating in all respects, but it is criticized because oppression and racism are not "placed squarely on the economic system." In other examples, the children's-book authors were criticized for what they didn't do rather than for what they did. The council also seems to want children's books to be didactic. Perhaps its members should consider Emerson's comment that "life is rather a subject of wonder, than of didactics."

Masha Kabakow Rudman, in *Children's Literature: An Issues Approach* (Heath, 1976), suffers from the same problem; many of her remarks are useful, but, like those who are inclined to censor, she looks for the bad qualities rather than the good. In her analysis of *The Snowy Day,* by Ezra Jack Keats, which she generally praises, she says the black mother is too heavy and is dressed in gaudy clothes. The perpetuation of the "mammy" image is not desirable, but the illustrations show an overweight woman in quite ordinary dress. It seems to us that Ms. Rudman was trying too hard, in this case.

Lillian Gerhardt, in an editorial in *School Library Journal,* has parodied such analysis in a discussion of the *Tale of Peter Rabbit.* She suggests that Beatrix Potter's book could be called sexist because Peter is "actively naughty" and his sisters "placidly obedient." It also might be ageist because Mr. McGregor is "old, crotchety and violent." She does demonstrate how ridiculous such elaborate evaluations can be and sometimes are. But of course all reviews tend to be didactic and represent the bias of the author and the publication. Librarians must learn by experience, and by getting to know reviewers' biases, the value to be placed upon critical comments. All searching for stereotypes is not ridiculous. Some materials clearly do present stereotyped people and attitudes. In other works this is not as clear, and there are genuine differences of opinion. Most basic of all, librarians too are victims of social conditioning, and often are not as conscious as they might be of stereotypes and prejudices.

Ruby, by Rosa Guy, has been called anti-Semitic. It is a novel for teenagers, set mostly in a New York City high school. One of the teachers is named Mrs. Gottlieb, but is not otherwise identified. She is crippled in mind and body, and is one of the more unpleasant characters one is likely to meet, in or out of the world of fiction. Lillian Shapiro, librarian and educator, has stated that the book "contains so grotesque a portrayal of a N. Y. C. school teacher (with a slight odor of anti-Semitism) as to put to question the literary quality of the book."[6] The very same title appears, however, on the ALA Young Adult Services list "Best Books for Young Adults." It has also been reported that the teacher on whom the fictional character is based was not Jewish. There is an example of a difference of opinion about the book's quality and about its alleged anti-Semitism. In addition, not only the author's sensitivity but also her intention has been questioned. But whatever the author's intentions, it is the result that counts, and the book is perceived as anti-Semitic by many.

Summer of My German Soldier, by Bette Green, has also been called anti-Semitic. A twelve-year-old Jewish girl befriends a German prisoner of war during World War II. The girl's father is depicted as cruel and tyrannical, and the prisoner of war is presented as a fine man. At one point, the soldier compares the father to Hitler. It has been said that Jewish fathers don't treat their children in the manner portrayed in this story. The story has been described by reviewers as "powerful," "well written" and having a "positive effect." And although it has been attacked as anti-Semitic, some librarians of Jewish origin have told us they do not consider that to be the case.

Some of those same librarians, however, thought *Daddy Was a Numbers Runner,* by Louise Meriwether, to be anti-Semitic. The story is set in Harlem during the 1930s. It has been labeled "skillful," "poignant," and "important" by reviewers, and the author's skill has been called "exceptional." The complainants, however, said that all the white characters were Jewish and invariably unpleasant, although this is not, in fact, the case.

The Five Chinese Brothers, by Claire Biship and Kurt Wiese, is a book that for many years has been a popular part of most library collections. Frank Chin, a Chinese-American playwright, has this to say about it:

> Perhaps no single book has so insidiously stereotyped the Chinese as *The Five Chinese Brothers.* From this still popular "classic," published in 1938, generations of children have come to believe that Asian people and people of Asian descent are a putrid yellow, have slits for eyes, look exactly alike, and act the fool. *The Five Chinese Brothers* is an insult to Asian Americans the way *Little Black Sambo* is an insult to Black people.[7]

Other ethnic groups also feel offended by some library materials. A teacher recently filed a suit asking the court to ban from a library a number of books that he considered defamatory to Italian-Americans. In addition to the *Valachi Papers,* by Peter Maas, were such titles as *The Mafia and Politics,* by Michel Pantaleone, *The Secret Rulers,* by Fred J. Cook and *The Honored Society,* by Norman Lewis.

Such concern is not limited to books. We have seen a rise in attempts to thwart the making of films that are perceived to be based upon stereotypical characters and events. The filmed version of Mario Puzo's *The Godfather,* a depiction of the rise of a Mafia Don in the New York city area, was attacked prior to its filming. *Cruising,* based upon the novel by Gerald Walker, was the victim of a series of attacks in Greenwich Village during its filming, including attempts to spoil the sound track and interrupt the shooting schedule. The protesters charged that the depiction of the male homosexuals in the film was an invitation to murder and violence. More recently, court injunctions were unsuccessfully sought to halt the filming of a story about urban crime set in a police station in the Bronx nicknamed Fort Apache. It was contended that all of the Spanish-speaking and black residents of the area were being depicted as depraved and prone to violence.

Even completed and well-received films come in for their share of criticism. When The New York Public Library announced a showing of Louis Malle's highly acclaimed movie *Phantom India* (New Yorker Films), the Indian consulate objected. The Public Broadcasting System's decision to show a fictionalized documentary, *Death of a Princess,* in 1980 brought unprecedented pressure from the federal government, the Saudi Arabian government and the Mobil Oil Corporation (one of PBS's major contributors) to stop it, because the values of the Saudi Arabian society were alleged to have been denigrated by the story.

Are these materials prejudicial and stereotypical? One cannot judge entirely by complaints, any more than one can make a decision about the worth of materials by reading reviews. Yet we take them both seriously. We must take into account the problem of hypersensitivity, especially if we are members of the group in question. Librarians must search out and read significant books, reports and research evaluations and view significant films that describe or show the feelings and experiences of members of various groups afflicted by stereotyping. We must listen to members of those groups and try to see their point of view. Having done all of this, we can probably begin to make rational judgments.

If we do decide that some material is offensive, then our problems really begin, for we must consider the work's other qualities and decide whether there are conditions that might outweigh the flaw. Some materials become very popular and pose a conflict in terms of rights. Do library users have a right to ask the library to supply something they want, even if it is offensive to a particular group and felt to have few redeeming qualities?

Little Black Sambo and *The Five Chinese Brothers* fall into that category: they are favorites with adults, and children delight in the stories and continually ask for them. *I'm Glad I'm a Boy, I'm Glad I'm a Girl*, by Whitney Darrow, Jr. is very popular. One recently examined copy circulated twenty four times in two years from a school library. The book, delightfully illustrated by the author and noted *New Yorker* cartoonist, consists of pictures of girls and boys engaged in various occupations, with appropriate (or some might say inappropriate) captions: "Boys are Doctors, Girls are Nurses," "Boys fix things, Girls need things fixed," and so on. Showing the sexes in predetermined roles is offensive to many women and some men and seems to contribute to the perpetuation of stereotypical conditioning.

Although not quite so blatant but possibly even more popular and widely distributed is *Richard Scarry's Best Word Book Ever*. It pictures males and females in traditional roles, with no suggestion that any variation is possible. Mr. Scarry's books are liked by many adults, and their wide distribution, via supermarket and drugstore merchandising, has put them into the hands of many who consider them very useful in teaching their children.

For numerous adults, the Harlequin Romances provide considerable entertainment. They circulate tremendously in some public libraries and middle- and high-school library media centers. The list of these titles is lengthy, and they are consumed in great quantity; they obviously fill the needs of a considerable number of people. At the same time, others object to the stereotyped characterizations of the women in these books, who faint at the drop of a dire circumstance, lavish affection on and describe at length their trousseaus and enter into slavish bliss as they learn to cook for their new spouse on that cute little stove in the kitchen. Such books might be rejected because they are not well written, present stock characters and plots and so on, but they are in demand. Do their readers have rights too?

The Murder of Roger Ackroyd, by Agatha Christie, somewhat complicates the situation. Agatha Christie is perennially popular, and she generally writes well. In this title, the narrator, talking about some moneylenders who are preying on a woman with financial difficulties, suspects "a Semitic strain in their ancestry." Similar comments can be found in her other books. This prolific author has also been charged with what is termed a sexist attitude.

Perhaps a greater problem is posed by *One Flew Over The Cuckoo's Nest*, by Ken Kesey. Here is a work that has been tremendously popular in recent years, and it will probably continue to be so. It is well written and has interesting and important statements to make about our social condition. Yet the author seems to hate women, and it would be fair to call his work sexist. (Some librarians whose work we respect have had no hesitation in leveling this charge against the book.) The women in both the novel and the film are unpleasant in the extreme. Some of them have caused the male inhabitants of the state mental institution to be there, and the rest are probably preventing them from reentering society. The author seems to make the mental institution a symbol of society at large, and implies that women are causing many of its problems. Is the book to be rejected because of its sexist viewpoint?

Or consider the case of T. S. Eliot. No contemporary poet has enjoyed such great praise. His poems are to be found in most library collections, and there soon would be a public outcry if they were not. Consider, then, the following lines:

> My house is a decayed house,
> And the jew squats on the window sill, the owner
> Spawned in some estaminet of Antwerp.
> *Gerontion*

or

> The rats are underneath piles.
> The jew is underneath the lot.
> Money in furs.
> *Burbank with a Baedeker: Beistein with a Cigar.*

Even Eliot's references to Apeneck Sweeney who "spreads his knees/Letting his arms hang down to laugh," could be considered antiethnic. Other such passages can be discovered in his poems.

There are other such problems facing the librarian. Sometimes we need materials because they supply information that is not otherwise available or is not presented as well elsewhere. Morton Hunt's *Gay: What You Should Know About Homosexuality* has been called sexist, because it makes little mention of lesbians.

Furthermore, the author is said to have a bias against the gay lifestyle, because he favors a certain kind of homosexual activity. At the same time, reviewers have recommended the book and called it "generally informative."

It is the librarian's lot to have to decide what to do in the face of these conflicting evaluations and demands for "rights." Suppose we feel that a piece of material or even a part of it is racist, sexist or antiethnic. If we add it to the collection, we may feel that we are only contributing to the perpetuation of such prejudices. After all, many users of the library believe that by selecting certain materials, we are putting an official stamp of approval on it. And since we can't buy everything and we do reject materials all the time, why not reject that which is offensive? That would seem to be the simplest solution.

But is it? We have already agreed with Mary K. Chelton that the library contains something to offend everyone. And we do select materials for the collection that do not carry our personal seal of approval. Not many of us subscribe to the message in *Mein Kampf*, by Adolf Hitler, for example, yet we feel that it is a necessary part of most library collections. Or what about that wondrously sexist title, *The First Blast of the Trumpet Against the Monstrous Regiment of Women*, by John Knox? Would you hesitate to buy it if you felt it was needed in your library's collection? Probably not—especially if it has historical value because of the author's place in history or because it represents an important sociological movement, shows what people thought at the time and fits into your collection scheme; so you buy it, or keep it if you already have it. In the following quotation, Ashley Montagu is speaking about sexism as conditioning, but he could have well been discussing all the stereotypical prejudices that afflict our society:

> In the light of such evidence it becomes apparent that with respect to the mental differences between the sexes in any given society we are dealing not so much with the effects of biological factors, as with *cultural determinants*—cultural determinants which derive their force from a social heredity which we conventionally accept as if it were equivalent to what we understand by our organic or physical heredity. Traditional thinking here serves to preserve the practices and beliefs, the errors, the prejudices, and the injustices of primordial ages, and by its authority makes certain that whatever changes must take place in our thinking concerning the status of sexes shall take place slowly.[8]

It is these very cultural determinants that haunt the library collection. A good collection of materials will by necessity be holding a mirror up to the nature of human kind. Librarians cannot change that determinant any faster than does the society in which the collection exists. But they can, with diligence and by careful acquisition, try to find materials for the collection that will assist the individual user to see alternatives to prejudice. There have recently appeared versions of *Little Black Sambo* and *The Five Chinese Brothers* that have abandoned the racial stereotypes so long associated with those stories and placed them in their proper ethnic context, which includes new illustrations. It is now possible to find role-image materials for children that do not make doctors out of little boys or imply that the female is mechanically disinclined. We are not flooded with such materials, to be sure, but the alternatives are there.

Margaret Mead, one of the world's great anthropologists, tells a story that we quote to illustrate how libraries can assist in breaking the vicious cycle of racism. She tells of a small American boy, the dark-skinned child of a blond father and a brunette mother, the eldest "sibling of a family of three, who had two handsome, blond younger brothers."

> In the public school which he attended, he absorbed the prevailing attitudes of the white children toward black children and reacted with fury when his mother became interested in civil rights and took up the cause of black children. He became so unmanageable that his parents transferred him to a private school, only to be confronted on the first day of classes with the fact that his teacher was to be a tall, black, West African woman. But with all the pride West Africans carry with them, stately and assured, she took the angry little boy by the hand, and he, who blamed his rejection on his sallow dark skin, felt fully accepted for the first time in his school life.[9]

Certainly it is imperative to recruit minority-group members into the profession, for they can, from their own experience, help to balance not only the collection but the image of the library for the user. Librarians have a stake in their own development as well as that of the society served by the library.

If we decided that some very popular material was racist, we would probably (particularly in the public library) purchase it for the collection. If a small portion of the book were racist, and the work was widely acclaimed, one would also buy it. On the other hand, if the book were racist and did not have such redeeming qualities, it would be rejected. For films, this is also true. Many old movies are racist, some in the extreme. That many are sexist goes without saying. Yet these films are very popular, and libraries are busy buying them because they are an inexpensive way to build up their film collections. In addition to popularity they have, of course, other qualities: they are part of American and film history, some of them good examples of film art, some are acquired because of the director's importance, and so on. (Books are no different from films in this respect. There are some who hold that films have more impact than books—a subject we have discussed elsewhere—but we do not.) With some films, as with some books, the library might as well have one title as another; that is, a movie may be entertaining but have no other positive qualities. If that is the case and the item is in some way racist or contains other negative stereotypes, we would be likely to reject it.

Discarding long-lived classics, or what seem to be classics because they have always been on the shelves, is as big a problem for many librarians as acquisition. Too often librarians feel that, once selected, a piece of material assumes a special status. Some even go so far as to suggest that selecting is different from discarding because it adds to the cost, since the new material needs to be cataloged and readied for circulation. If the material is already in the collection, the argument goes, these costs have already been absorbed. This argument seems fallacious: if the material should not have been selected in the first place, why should it not be discarded now? The profit motive is not paramount in libraries.

At any rate, we discard materials all the time. We discard scientific materials that become dated unless our selection policy includes a historical perspective. We discard little-used books. We discard our misjudgments. And we discard sometimes just because we have no more room on the shelves. When it comes to unpopular or controversial materials, however, we have doubts. And in some cases we should have doubts. Although we know of libraries who have done so, we wouldn't discard *Huckleberry Finn, The Merchant of Venice* or the works of T. S. Eliot.

Now let us consider *The Story of Doctor Doolittle,* by Hugh Lofting. In this story, remembered and loved by generations, Prince Bumpo wants his skin to be made white and his eyes turned blue so that Sleeping Beauty will marry him. (She was horrified when she saw that he was black.) It is suggested in this work that all Africans are stupid and dirty. The Prince Bumpo story comprises only a small part of the book, although it is a crucial one. The book is imaginative, with good characterization. It is better than much that is currently being written, but it does strongly reflect the racist attitudes that were so common in Britain at the time of its publication. Many librarians have discarded it or moved it into the literature collection, for study by the more mature individual. Others continue to have copies in their children's collection.

Booth Tarkington is another author beloved by many for his stories of Penrod growing up in Indiana just prior to World War I. If one reads them today, however, one finds them racist. Some libraries have discarded these stories; and others have not. We recently reread them and found them rather boring and racist.

The Story of Epaminondas and His Auntie, while not as well known, is still available in some libraries. Racism infects the whole story; the stupidity of the child who never can and never will learn, the dialect, and the illustrations add up to racial stereotyping of the most blatant kind.

Then there is Lawrence Paul Dunbar, a black poet who wrote not only elegant examples of the classical style so popular around the turn of the century but also folk poems in the dialect he heard and lived with in his Dayton, Ohio home. For a considerable time his work was considered an embarrassment, and many libraries retired his work, while publishers let it go out of print. Recently, a young black woman discovered his works in the library, and felt they were an important part of her heritage. She gave a dramatic reading of the poems to the black community and received critical acclaim.

Decisions to add materials to or withdraw them from libraries must have equal weight. These decisions depend on the kind of collection and its place in the scheme of the community: if one is part of a large system, one can behave differently than if one works in the only library for miles around. However, complaints, real or anticipated, about the material should not be the deciding factor. The reason for selecting or withdrawing material must be based upon sound collection-development policies. If you know why you are making decisions, it is easier to defend them.

Summary

Racism, sexism, ageism and all the other "isms" that this nation carries on its cultural back cannot be solved by library service alone. But there is no reason not to expect that the profession should move with greater dispatch than the rest of society to reduce the pressures within its own house. Binnie Tate, one of the more articulate and realistic librarians in this nation, wrote ten years ago:

> We can't ignore or fear the separatism which still exists. Often, even where there is no institutional separatism, communities are divided by de facto segregation. Mental separatism is, of course, the most insistent and insidious. For example, a white librarian recently said, "I'm from the South but we never thought of having our library association meetings separate. Our white librarians have always met with the colored group." Yes, they met together, but in her mind there was still a "colored group."[10]

Today the American Library Association has its "colored" groups too—the Black Caucus, the Asian-Americans, the Hispanic-Americans and even its majority group felt it necessary to band together to bring the "rhetoric" of women's concerns to the attention of the profession. Such separatism is still with us. Yet we cannot go back even though we drag our feet as we proceed. It is fitting, perhaps, to finish with Margaret Mead's words:

> ...what we need most are ways of thinking and acting through which we will not be overwhelmed by increasing scale, nor driven to despair or cruel indifference by the magnitudes with which we must deal. This is the central problem for us who are conscious and sentient beings, living in the midst of an evolutionary process with a beginning on this planet which we can only guess at and a future for which we take responsibility without being able to know in what direction it may go. The importance of each daily act—rising in the morning to the day's tasks, spending an hour explaining to a sick child in a hospital how a caterpillar turns into a butterfly, sending a few dollars to relieve a family in another part of the world—have to be brought into relationship with our decisions to build more and more missiles or to consign a million tons of grain to one country instead of another. If we can see the Nigerian fisherman with his age-old nets, the Balinese farmer plowing his land for the planting of rice, and the hungry child

of India, all as parts of a whole of which we are not distant spectators, but a part; if we can see not only power-hungry manipulators, on the one hand, and oppressed and dying people, on the other, but both—and all—caught in the same moment of history, a moment when the whole future of life on earth, and even possibly life in the galaxy, or the universe, is at stake, the very vastness of the process can ennoble the smallest hope, deflate the most grandiose dream of world dominion, and reduce species-wide guilt to human scale, making possible action by human beings on behalf of human beings.[11]

NOTES

1. Michael Dorris, "Case History of a Conscience-Based Protest," *Inter-Racial Books for Children Bulletin*, 9, no. 2: 6. The article contains reproductions of the illustrations used in the book in question, as well as a description of supplementary materials included as a guide to teachers.
2. Pauline Gough, "Non-sexist Literature for Children: A Panacea?" *Top Of The News* (Summer 1977): 340.
3. Patricia Schuman, "Sugar and Spice," *School Library Journal* (January 15, 1977): 221.
4. Ashley Montagu, "Sex, Status, Gender, and Cultural Conditioning," *Culture and Human Development: Insights Into Growing Human*, ed. Ashley Montagu (Englewood Cliffs, N.J.: Prentice-Hall, 1974), p. 153. Dr. Montagu cited the following studies as a basis for his remarks: R. J. Stoller, *Sex and Gender* (Portola Valley, Calif.: Science House, 1968); John Money and Anke A. Ehrhardt, *Man and Woman, Boy and Girl*, (Baltimore, Md.: Johns Hopkins University Press, 1972); John Money and Joan G. and John L. Hampson, "Imprinting and the Establishment of Gender Role," *A.M.A. Archives of Neurology and Psychiatry* 77: 333–36.
5. American Library Association, Office for Intellectual Freedom, "Reevaluating Library Collections," *Intellectual Freedom Manual* (Chicago: ALA, 1974), p. 31.
6. Lillian Shapiro, "Best Books for Whom?" *Wilson Library Bulletin* (June 1977): 804.
7. Frank Chin, "Where I'm Coming From," *Bridge: An Asian-American Perspective* (July 1976): 28.
8. Montagu, *Sex, Status, Gender*, pp. 155–56.
9. Margaret Mead, *World Enough: Rethinking the Future* (Boston: Little, Brown, 1975), p. 97.

10. Binnie Tate, "Traffic on the Drawbridge," *The Black Librarian in America*, ed. E.J. Josey (Metuchen, N.J.: Scarecrow Press, 1970), pp. 124–25.
11. Mead, *World Enough*, pp. 214–15.

Chapter Six
Freedom in the Media

Newspaper and television journalists have pretty much run off with the term "media" as a popular short-form reference to their activities. In technological and educational circles, however, media is a term essentially applied to all mechanical systems designed to "transmit information without regard to the natural limits of space and time."[1] Basic to all technological media systems is written and printed language. Libraries came into existence having only to cope with written and, later, printed formats, but today and in the future, libraries must deal with an ever-increasing variety of media formats. Libraries able to add these new media to their collections discover that they can and should be put to a diversity of uses in their program design. However, most libraries are content merely to collect what amounts to examples of these other media so that people with the requisite equipment may borrow them for use either outside the library or in a library having such equipment.

Some libraries schedule film showings, present programs of recorded music, exhibit realia, produce or play host to live performances and, in some cases, broadcast radio or television programs. Some have undertaken to provide video programming and have gone so far as to have equipment that can be used by the community to tape its own programming, outside and inside the library. Video cassettes and discs containing a variety of programming material (often transcribed from the film medium) are only beginning to appear in libraries. However promising this rundown may seem, it must be borne in mind that nonprint media materials are not common items in library collections in general, and where they are available, they are handled differently from traditional materials by librarians.

Don Roberts, a librarian and film-company executive, pointed out in a recent report that there is considerable bias against non-print materials by the staffs of libraries, which has led to a slower utilization and provision of currently available media materials and concomitant services.[2] Such a bias is not surprising when one considers that there are differences among the media other than format. In the print medium, the reader must supply the images. In pictorial media, the image is supplied to the viewer (reader). In order to comprehend a printed format, the reader must go through a rather lengthy ritual of learning what each symbol and combination of symbols stands for and translate that into the equivalent of the spoken word and accompanying mental image, which is conditioned by experience. In the pictorial and audio media, the receiver does not need to be involved in such a lengthy ritual in order to begin to comprehend the message. If the pictorial medium has the added ability to create the illusion of motion by having one image rapidly succeed another, as in movies and television, then comprehension is enhanced while evaluation of the ideas is reduced. It is only at the end of the presentation that receivers can devote time to thinking about the images they have seen.

With print, however, one can think about the images created in the mind during the process of reading. The reader can stop or even go back and reread words or sentences to enhance the evaluative process. One can do the same with a filmstrip or slide-tape presentation if the viewer-reader is the operator of the equipment, but it is very difficult to do so with film and television, particularly when the rhythm of the images is also part of the experience. It is very difficult to take notes during nonprint media presentations without missing part of the message. As for print, experiments have shown that the mind, because of conditioning, supplies many images automatically. And those that are created differ much more from person to person than do the images in pictorial media. In viewing pictures, the mind need not do anything to construct the image and can simply react to the information provided and to the effect of the flow of image and sound, much as one does with the eye in experiencing "reality."

A look at the development of the human communications system reveals an interrelatedness that is not often articulated and could well be the basis for the apathy or bias that seems to stand in the way of the integration of other media formats into library collections. To give a very succinct and perhaps superficial summary, one should remember that for hundreds of years human beings depended upon written language as the means of transmitting a message from one person to another. The invention of movable type allowed for a faster and more efficient method of reproducing the message, so that it could reach a larger audience. Books became the primary device for the transmission of knowledge. Very quickly newspapers and magazines became an even faster method of transmitting information. Unlike books, which are devoted primarily to one subject, newspapers and magazines appear with greater frequency and deal with a variety of subjects. Early technological printing developments involved increasing the efficiency of production.

The invention of the halftone near the close of the nineteenth century marks the beginning of a long line of technological changes in communication formats. The halftone is a technique whereby a photograph is broken into a series of tiny dots that can be translated into the binary language of print. Print, it should be explained, is binary because it consists of or is characterized by two parts: the color of the paper and the color of the ink. With the halftone, if only half of the space is covered by dots that pick up the black ink, then the printed product appears as gray if the paper is white. The percentage of dots in a square inch used to pick up the ink produces a wide variety of shades, from white through the grays to black. Thus photographs were introduced into the binary language of print.

It is important that librarians understand this development in technology, which occurred a scant one hundred years ago, for we can then better appreciate the relation of technological development and the role of the library as collector of human-communication records. James Monaco, a respected educator and scholar of film language and theory, commented on the significance of the binary language in print:

> In its way, the concept of the halftone was as important as the recognition of the rise of the phenomenon of persistence of vision was in the development of motion pictures: both utilized basic physiological facts of perception in simple yet productive ways. Moreover, the concept that underlies the halftone process—the translation of a

continuous range of values into a discrete binary system—was to become one of the most significant and widely effective intellectual devices of the twentieth century: television, phototelegraphy, telemetry, and—most important—computer technology, all rest on this basic binary concept.[3]

If it is understood by librarians that all of the media formats have a common heritage in the print medium, then it is possible to begin to understand that the library, an institution designed to fulfill society's need for a repository of its records of communication, must provide access to the newly emerging formats. Admittedly the bias against other than print media in libraries has a basis in the inability of the library staff to develop a solid base of financial support. However, some believe that libraries' financial situations are often closely tied to the perception of the institutions by librarians, as well as by their users. If the library does not evidence a drive toward the inclusion of all communications formats in its collection, then it is only natural that society will turn to other methods or create other agencies to perform that service—and it does.

In turn, it must be allowed that the different types of media materials produced by technological developments serve the public in different ways and that those ways are deeply imbedded in the economic and political system. Books are economically controlled by their manufacturers and distributors. What is being sold is that one object, a book, and it can readily be made available through a broad variety of marketing channels, including the library. Because of the general availability of the book, once it is produced, it is fairly accessible. The user can consume all of its content or extract only part of it at any time and place; there is no need to adjust one's schedule or change location to use the product. The same can be said for magazines and newspapers, except for the added economic consideration that advertisers pay for the product as much as, and usually more than, do the users. Therefore the product is tailored to advertiser needs and marketed to audiences that have been carefully defined. Books, magazines and newspapers are the staples of library collections today. The design of the buildings that house them, and the system that acquires, circulates and maintains them, caters to those print formats.

Film has a different economic base. It is primarily a communal experience for the viewer. Because special equipment and a particular environment are needed, the user must arrange to be in the right place at the right time to experience the message. As a result, access is currently far more limited than with the print medium. It is true that you need not sit through an entire film presentation if you don't want to, but if you want access to the message, you probably must see it through. It is not possible to skim a film, as one can with the print media. Film in libraries has primarily been limited to the educational, documentary and shorter entertainment types, produced for use outside the general commercial production and distribution system used for mass-entertainment products. Libraries, because of their building design and distribution system, have a tendency to treat films as separate items in their collections, often with separate collection policies, circulation and storage systems.

Radio is economically based in the selling of advertising space, much in the manner of magazines and newspapers. Access is limited by the number of stations broadcasting, the number of channels available and the number of receiving sets available to the user. Programming may be on a twenty-four-hour basis, but the user cannot be very selective about listening to what is broadcast and the message being received. The use of radio in libraries has been limited to a few instances of regular programming, and a few libraries have had broadcasting facilities of their own. The programming is usually of the book-talk or classical-music variety. It would be interesting to see what might happen if libraries were to move into the radio programming by presenting samples from their audio collection, broadcasting meetings in their public rooms and interviews with an oral-history orientation and even answering reference questions, much like the once-popular "Mr. Answer Man" of earlier radio days. It should be noted that the most interactive of all radio activity is the citizen's band (CB), which has not yet produced noteworthy examples of library involvement. Calling the library for information on CB equipment could become a valuable method of expanding community service.

Audio discs are similar to books, in that they usually are single-subject items; however, like film, they require special equipment. Experiencing the message need not be as communal and does not require as special an environment as film. Unlike print, the audio and film experience does not require a high level of literacy. Access is good because of the success of the producers and distributors of the product in marketing the relatively unsophisticated device needed to use the discs. In libraries, discs have become more accepted as part of the collection than other nonprint media, but in most instances discs also require special facilities, selection policies and circulation systems.

Audio tapes are extensions of the disc technology, and the portability of the equipment needed has made the environment for listening less crucial than for discs. In libraries the tapes have been slower to appear, and are generally disliked because their pocket-sized packaging allows for easy theft from a building designed for the distribution of books.

The economic base for television is very similar to radio, and the broadcast limitations are much the same, thus making access a problem. It is true that new technologies are about to change this, by providing more channels and, possibly, random user-demand programming by combining television and computer capabilities, but special equipment will be needed, and it will be several years before the equipment costs little enough for the general public to afford it. Television is a more closed medium than print. It is difficult for an individual to give a message on television, since programming is paid for by advertisers and is thus very expensive.

Television has appeared in libraries on a very limited basis, but librarians seem to show more interest in it than in radio. Special equipment and a higher degree of sophistication is needed for the operation of broadcasting equipment. Video-tape players are used in some libraries, but not as much as one would assume (particularly in school library media centers) from casually perusing the literature. Library-building design is not conducive to video technology. We have heard of such facilities being designed in a very few new buildings, but this has not caused any breakthrough in the use of video in terms of increased access.

Libraries faced with these differing media formats and facilities have for the most part stayed with the print format because there is little or no need for special equipment other than literacy. Librarians, where they have added other formats, have felt compelled to create separate enclaves within the print collection to house them. There have been attempts to integrate these media, but the experiments have been doomed from the start because the librarians found themselves trying to pound round pegs into square holes. They have had to try to adapt book shelving, journal bins, and magazine racks to accommodate nonprint materials.

One can hope for improved library access to these newer formats, but we cannot join those wailing over the death of print. Librarians are right in their recognition that the more specific coding of print remains the most efficient method for communicating abstract information. Computers will undoubtedly serve some of the needs supplied by traditional forms of printed materials. But that change is not imminent, nor is it likely to occur overnight. The data-transmission capabilities of the computer already sound the death knell for many types of books, magazines, journals and newspapers, because computers will be able to provide the user with better control of the time and place of access (the home, the car, and so on) or, as it is called, "real-time" access. However, such services sold to the home user will, of necessity, be packaged in the manner of books, and the service supplied will be but one possible data source. Libraries traditionally seek multiple sources of information so the user will have a choice. It is this seemingly very elementary service concept that demands that libraries face the responsibility of providing access to a multiplicity of formats, much in the manner once reserved for special collections, vertical files and pamphlet collections.

Impact on the User

Mark Slade, in his discussion of media called *Language of Change*, points out that we have access to two languages that will bring about unparalleled social and political change. He contends that it is only through a full appreciation of this fact that the individual will be able to navigate through life. "Traditionally," he says, "we think of a medium as a means to express experience. It is a go-between that makes appearances important. Now, however, media constitute a very big chunk of everyone's experience. Media are experience. The go-between of discourse becomes the coming together of intercourse. That makes structure important—far more important than appearances."[4]

Mr. Slade is speaking of the language of motion. It operates in two systems. One is data in motion and the other is image in motion. These two systems have the capacity to speed the process to the point where it will be almost immediately assimilable. And it also opens the door to almost undreamed-of control and manipulation. At its base is information. Data and image in motion is the language of control because it is thoroughly manageable and can be learned by anyone. Slade points out:

> Our most crucial task is the reorganization of existing information. The language of change does not collect; it transposes, translates and transforms. Besides, it could be argued that the gathering of information, like the production of goods, is no longer a pressing concern. We have mastered these processes. We know how to produce any quantity of anything. But we don't always know what to do with what we produce or how best to use the information we gather. From being something so precious that it was locked away in priests' manuscripts, information is now the cheapest commodity of all, available to everyone.[5]

Although information comes in a variety of formats, any librarian who has worked at the service desk for the past twenty-five years will tell you that the problem is finding it in the right format for the right person. Even more complex is the problem of being able to deliver the information already gathered, regardless of format. Charles Bernier and A. Neil Yerkey, information scientists, speak of what they term "functional obsolescence": "Because of the inability to read all of the relevant material in even a narrow subject field, people's knowledge, including that of professionals, becomes obsolescent..."[6] Add to that the inability to have access to the variety of media in which information is packaged, and we further reduce the chances for using that information. If we learn faster through data or image in motion, how better to combat functional obsolescence than to make information available in that way?

There is a discernible difference in impact among the various media. A sampling of recent research can point up what the librarian faces as an information-transfer agent. One experiment indicated that film presentations yield superior recall over verbal presentations or a single pictorial representation, and even over a sequence of pictures.[7] There are also indications that the response from reading is different than the one from viewing a filmed version of the same material. The difference seems to be one of involvement. Those who observe the image in motion on film are more involved in the action, while those reading the material are more likely to have interpretive reactions to it. It would also seem that seeing the film and then reading the story or vice versa is not as positive an experience as we might expect. Those who view and read the two versions are sometimes troubled by the discrepancies between them and may feel that their own interpretation of the experience was somehow wrong.[8] Certainly this would tend to support Slade's contention that media are experience.

Other studies indicate that recall rates of those involved with print and film are very similar, but that the text-based recall deteriorates faster.[9] Film seems to be able to inspire greater verbalizing in terms of recall, particularly in relating story action and describing an environment or giving other peripheral information. Verbalization in recalling the print medium produces a higher rate of figurative language, description of textural content and repetition of vocabulary.[10] These samplings of research are indicative of the problems inherent in exposure to only one of the media or of a reliance on the print media alone. Imagery and data in motion are part of our experience, and the longer we have such experience, the greater our preference for extracting information from a variety of media. These facts indicate that those librarians who have been advocating the multi-media approach to library service have been much more cognizant of the issue of access than those clinging to their stacks of print materials.

Sound recordings differ from other media too. Listening to a recording may conjure up an image, but one's response to what one hears is usually emotional. Print and film produce emotional responses, too, but in an entirely different way. We know what the tone of voice can do independently of the words we hear. Every kind of sound causes a different response in the listener, whether it be the beat of the jackhammer, the lilt of the humpback whale or the insistence of the synthesizer.

Given these differences, any medium might have any effect. Printed words can make the reader angry, sexually aroused or sad, and cause any number of emotional reactions, not the least of which may be boredom. Photographs, paintings, sculpture, films, recordings, and a lot of very surprising things—such as shoes, gloves, scarves (as Krafft-Ebing reported)—may produce reactions. The effect of such exposure may be instantaneous, unexpected and lasting. In a study made for the Commission on Obscenity and

Pornography, there was little discernible difference in measurable reaction to either print or photographic stimuli, as compared to what happened when the subject was asked merely to think about certain topics.[11] In that same study it was found that less explicit material tended to create a stronger reaction than the more explicit type. The age-old notion of mind over matter seems to be true.

Unfortunately we have yet to devise a method for recording exactly what goes on in the mind. Instead we rely on introspection and verbalization by research subjects as to how they interpret the reaction(s) they have to certain stimuli. We have cited some studies comparing reactions to different media. Some of these studies used electronic-monitoring devices to gauge subjects' reactions, but most used observation and questionnaires. Mary Corde Lorang, in her report on her doctoral research, conducted in 1944 and repeated again in 1967, concluded that "there is indisputable evidence that actions, attitudes, thoughts are conditioned by reading material, and some of the conditioning leads to anti-social acts and crimes, even homicide."[12] She encountered no difficulties in terms of response with her original questionnaire. However, in 1968, she reported, she met resistance on the part of superintendents, parents, teachers and principals. "They told me the questionnaire was suggestive, an invasion of privacy, an instrument which would rile parents; a chance for a nasty splash by the John Birch Society."[13] She admits that her sample became skewed because she had to add schools in Hawaii, the Philippines, Africa and Guatemala to arrive at a second group comparable to her first sample. She claims, nevertheless, that the results of her second study are the same as those of the first.

Librarians should be interested in the rating system devised for this study. Some of the books rated as having 100 percent "bad effects" included *Adding Machine: Three Plays About Business; Alfred Hitchcock Ghost Stories; Amboy Dukes*, by Irving Shulman; *Andersonville*, by MacKinlay Kantor and John McElroy; *Ape and Essence*, by Aldous Huxley; *Awake and Sing*, by Clifford Odets; *Buchenwald*, by W. Poller; *Civil Rights*, by Peter Goldman; and *Conscience of a Conservative*, by Barry Goldwater. The list goes on to include works by Tennessee Williams, Dante, Norman Mailer, Ernest Hemingway, Robert Frost, Morris West and Cervantes, all of these lumped together with the John Birch Society's *Fearful Master*.[14]

Another study asserts that, while communications media do

affect individuals, one medium is no more powerful than another. According to the authors, the students surveyed "did not react differently to the written and filmed versions of *The Lottery;* they responded favorably to both."[15] The investigators reported that in watching the film, "significant attitude change did occur in this sample of high school viewers. Generally, students reported more negative feelings toward 'violence,' 'tradition,' 'cohesion' and 'community' and more positive feelings toward 'parents,' 'mother' and 'love.' There was no evidence of attitude change toward the concept 'god.' "[16]

The most likely conclusion to this discussion of the extent of media impact on users is that it varies from person to person. Depending on our background, some of us are powerfully moved by print and not by film. For others, the reverse is true. And for some there is little or no difference between the two. It would seem that film librarians, however, do have a case when they contend that more people are affected by the visual media than by print.

There may be, however, a common perception about these media that has nothing to do with reality. And what people perceive as their reality must of necessity become a reality for librarians. The author of one study suggests that

> violence is found much more objectionable in films than in books. Objections to films *because of their ideas* (italics ours) seem to appear more often than is true for books. Are people more willing to accept the notion that the function of a library is to present a wide range of ideas in books than they are to accept a similar philosophy in films? It should be remembered too that national policy does support legal constraints on films and television. Many cities and states have film censorship laws or agencies; very few such laws or agencies exist for the print media.[17]

Attacks on Nonprint Media

Let us cite some other incidents that demonstrate the belief that films are more in need of censoring than books. When the Board of Education in Prince George County, Maryland, banned the film version of *The Lottery* from schools, it did not ban the short story on which the film was based, in spite of the fact that the film very closely followed the details of the story. It has also been pointed out that *Catch-22* was not widely attacked until after the film version appeared.[18] In Westchester County, New York, in late 1980, an announcement by the library that the film of Mario Puzo's novel *The Godfather* would be shown, unleashed a storm of protest from the local Italian community. Ironically, the film had been extremely successful and had been shown twice on national television. Members of the Italian community seemed to feel that although they could not stop the film from being shown nationally, they could make it difficult for the local library to provide access to the film. Oddly enough, they were not pressuring for the novel to be removed from the library. Could it be because one has to be "literate" to read it?

Films and television programs based on books are likely to be seen by many more people than will read the book. The impact of television can be enormous. It is estimated, for instance, that some seventy million people tuned in to the "Dallas" series one night in November 1980 in order to find out "who shot" one of the characters. Nevertheless, it is books that continue to draw most of the fire from critics. A listing recently showed that in educational institutions, over a ten-year period, sixteen books were mentioned in censorship cases more than any film. Furthermore, the books *Catcher in the Rye* (mentioned twice as often as any other title), *The Grapes of Wrath*, *Of Mice and Men*, and *To Kill a Mockingbird* were among the top ten titles under attack.[19] You can draw any conclusion from that list that you like. But for the librarian, it all comes down to this: you choose an item—regardless of the medium—because it fits into the collection, will meet a community need as defined in your selection policy and because you can and will defend that choice.

After a librarian acquires an item, the decision about user access must be made. It is here that labeling occurs—an eight-letter word that is considered twice as bad as any four-letter word by the defenders of intellectual freedom. And those defenders are right, of course. The practice of labeling films, either in the theater or in advisory warnings given out prior to television broadcast, has proven (when such advisories alert the audience to erotic or violent content) to attract larger publics than those films bearing no qualifying statements or symbols.[20] If library users are to be influenced by being told, one way or another, that the ideas contained in materials may be dangerous to their health, or by being given irrelevant details about an author's life, then, the librarian has performed badly. With books, this is rarely a problem. Any reader can look through a book, and, if it seems unsuitable, decide not to read it.

The same is not true for films. One must make preparations in order to view a film, and the viewer will probably sit through the entire movie. Previewing films is desirable, and film librarians encourage the user to do so. Relatively few do, however. Film reviews are not as widely available as book reviews, particularly for the type of film collected by most libraries. For this reason extensive annotations are necessary. The trick is to decide what those annotations should include. Since a film is usually seen by a group of people, it must be acceptable to the entire group. Obviously, the annotation should be a full one. A detailed description of the contents, an indication of the style of photography and editing and a suggested age level would seem appropriate and necessary. Adults wouldn't want to see a film for preschoolers or a comedy, when they were expecting a serious study. Confusion about what to include in the annotation arises when the film contains something that may be controversial—a nude, for instance. If the annotation is precise and factual, a note about nudity might be included. But such a note should be included only if it is necessary in describing the film. A film on the history of painting and sculpture would be likely to include nudes, and it would be redundant for the annotation to say so.

Unusually violent action in a film might also be worth mentioning in an annotation. Such scenes can be described factually, without resorting to subjective words. Any feelings evoked by the film can usually be brought up in the annotation, which may be desirable if a group is not prepared for the emotions it may stir up.

Do details about the director or producer's political, social, religious or economic background constitute labeling? Yes—when they are not needed to establish the film's credentials. Certainly the viewer selecting a film on economics would want to know if the presenters of the thesis were qualified in some way. But unnecessary or irrelevant details about the director, the producers and the performers can often only end up as fodder for a censorious attack.

Problems in Programming

If a librarian produces a program, mounts an exhibit, or publishes some material, does it bear the imprimatur of the library? Is the library promoting an idea by allowing a program, an exhibit or a publication to appear under its sponsorship? We feel it is not, any more than the acquisition of an item in the collection does, provided the activity is in conformity with library policy. If a film is presented, it should be because the librarian feels there is community interest in the subject, not because the library is endorsing its point of view. This is true of public performances, an exhibit of crafts and arts, the publishing of a magazine for teens or a list of books for children.

There are problems inherent in any such activity, and librarians, for the most part, seem to recognize them and go to considerable lengths to avoid controversy. Public performances, where allowed, are often carefully monitored to insure that the content will not disrupt library "decorum." Exhibits of the arts are usually screened to avoid controversial nudes or avant-garde styles. Publications for teenagers have suddenly disappeared from library programs when the content has become too controversial, although often such publications are so bland that they disappear because of the intended audience's disinterest. Lists of materials published by many libraries are carefully selected recent acquisitions or small bibliographies, often on "safe" subjects such as gardening, beauty hints, vacations, rare books and classics.

Major issues facing the community served by the library are seldom presented in the library's exhibit facilities. Most exhibits are inside the library, although some buildings have display window space available. Libraries have exhibited in shopping centers, local store windows, street fairs and at agricultural/industrial fairs. Once again, these exhibits seldom attempt to explain the diversity of ideas in the library collection. Instead, they tend to reinforce the "image" of the library by featuring noncontroversial materials. Complaints about these displays are seldom heard (although the authors have encountered a few during their careers), because they are almost always so innocuous that the only complaints concern poor construction or sloppy design rather than ideas.

Complaints about displays in libraries include the usual concern about the content of library materials, with obscenity usually the major worry. It is amazing to us that one can hang up a picture of a horse, and no one will complain, but if the picture is a study of a nude human figure, one is "forcing" people to view obscenity! In California, a man was arrested for having an offensive word on his jacket. He was in a courthouse corridor at the time, and there were children present as well as "ladies." Thus, the atmosphere was similar to that of a library (a public building), where anyone has a right to be and people of all ages are often found. Justice Harlan, speaking for the Supreme Court, which upheld the right of the defendant to wear the jacket, said: "Those in the Los Angeles courthouse could effectively avoid bombardment of their sensibilities by averting their eyes."[21] It would seem possible to apply the same principle in a library situation. Art has a place in the library collection, and its display is consistent with that policy. Libraries should not have to limit their exhibits to pictures of horses.

A more difficult situation, involving a library display, recently received nationwide publicity. The incident never went to court, although it could have made an interesting case. The public library of Winston-Salem, North Carolina, inaugurated its new exhibit space and recently adopted the Library Bill of Rights by allowing the Ku Klux Klan to design and present its organization's history and paraphernalia. The result of the grand opening was unusual for a library exhibit, although many librarians who have dealt with knife-wielders, gun-wavers, belligerent drunks and fistfights would have taken it in stride, as did those in Winston-Salem. Shortly after the exhibit was in place, representatives of a group described as "leftist" appeared, leaped on chairs and yelled, "Let's tear it down." As Klansmen were advancing on this group, four uniformed Nazis kicked open the door to the display area. Black picketers, meanwhile, were outside the building, chanting, "Ku Klux Klan, Scum of the Land." At this point police escorted everyone out of the area and the library closed the exhibit.[22]

Most librarians would agree that in the interest of public safety, the exhibit should come down. But should the library have allowed the exhibit in the first place? The assistant director's answer has some validity. Any group, he said, that offered material of interest to the public was allowed to use the display space. "We look at it," he continued, "as akin to London's Hyde

Park—to express concerns and interests on as liberal a base as possible." He said something else that should give librarians pause: "The board has had hundreds of calls, all negative. The public doesn't understand that we don't endorse the Klan—we endorse free expression."[23]

One can't fault this philosophy, and certainly, in Winston-Salem, there are many who think about the library differently now. It is just such experiences, however, that offer librarians an excuse to stick to their "safe" programming. And, for the inexperienced librarian, it is often the initial excitement of working with the Library Bill of Rights that inspires virtuous crusades and wounded retreats. It is necessary for a library to design a program to inform and educate, not only the general public but community leaders as well, about its attitude toward freedom of expression. In one day to lose a reputation as a nice, quiet place for children and retirees, because of an exhibit on something as volatile as the Ku Klux Klan, is traumatic for the community as well as the library staff and the board. No one is ever so prepared for confrontation as to be blasé about it, and the effects of this case are probably so far-reaching that it may be a long time before the Winston-Salem library mounts a controversial exhibit again. One hopes this is not the case. Perhaps, now that the shock has passed, the librarians will build a better base, so that the community comes to understand that the library is expected to stand for and endorse free expression.

A library—and in particular the public library—should be the agency people look to, not only for recreational reading, but for stimulation and inspiration. Part of such a program should involve a direct exchange between people, through the medium of the live performance. Libraries should have within their physical facilities the space to allow for discussion, speakers, concerts, play and poetry productions, seminars and community forums. These activities may be produced by the library; others may be presented in cooperation with other organizations. In some cases the library provides the space and, under certain conditions, spelled out in a policy statement, allows community groups to create their own programs. Some of these activities will be classified as controversial and generate complaints. Library policy should state whether a speaker or program is any different from a book using the same words, and whether the library has the right to allow the use of its platform in the same manner as it allows the use of its shelves for the book.

It should be remembered that the Supreme Court has determined that public places are public forums. This includes the streets, parks, transportation terminals and, specifically, public libraries. The case of Brown v. Louisiana, 383 U. S. 131 (1966), concerned a sit-in attempting to end segregation in a library. The sit-in was, ironically, a silent one, and there was no disturbance of any kind. The court determined that although the nature of the place might shape the range of conduct permissible within it, officials were not allowed to let one group use the facilities and not another. Thus, a library with meeting-room facilities for the public must make them available to anyone. The library may determine what conduct in the rooms would interfere with normal library functions, and so proscribe such activity. But it may not deny access to the room by those who agree to meet those conditions. To so deny is to open the library to legal action.

Radio and television programs under library sponsorship have generated complaints. In many cases, when an original program is involved, the library functions like any part of the press and is subject to the same restrictions. One library, for example, broadcast a documentary about two alleged bank robbers. An attorney general said the broadcast might prejudice the trial. The issue has not been resolved at this writing but is being watched in journalistic as well as library circles.

A complaint was filed against a library that ran a television show produced by another agency, a puppet show with a religious orientation. The protester said that the show constituted an illegal use of public funds for the establishment of a religion. The authors are not aware of many such complaints about library radio and television programs—there are too few of these programs, and they are likely to assume the traditional, innocuous mode. Since listeners or viewers can control their reception, the burden is on them to do so. In any case, such a library program would be subject to the regulations of the Federal Communications Commission, and that should be restriction enough for anyone.

Conclusion

If the library is to be understood and accepted by the public in our evolving society, it could well take to heart the comments of R. Kathleen Molz:

> The "library," then, and that word will have many connotations, both loses and gains from our changing concepts about print. In part, it loses its identity as physical plant and institution, for its location will be impermanent and its resources ever changing. Yet, it will gain in adaptability, since its clientele will become no longer readers but an audience, an audience of younger people attuned not only to reading but also to listening and watching.[24]

NOTES

1. James Monaco, *The Art, Technology, Language, History and Theory of Film and Media* (New York: Oxford University Press, 1977), p. 337.
2. Don Roberts, "Report on Past and Present Censorship on Non-book Media in Public Libraries," published by the author, 1976.
3. Monaco, *Film and Media*, p. 338.
4. Mark Slade, *Language of Change: Moving Images of Man* (Toronto: Holt, Rinehart and Winston, 1970), p. 103.
5. Ibid., p. 5.
6. Charles Bernier and A. Neil Yerkey, *Cogent Communication* (Westport, Conn.: Greenfield, 1979), p. 25.
7. Michel Denis and Pierrette de Ponqueville, "Realism of figuration and memory for concrete actions," *Bulletin de Psychologie* 30 (March–April 1977): 543-50.
8. Janet Kay Evans Worthington, "A Comparison of Responses of Selected Eleventh-Graders to Written and Filmed Versions of Selected Short Stories," *Dissertation Abstracts* 38-A.
9. Patricia Merkle Baggett, "The Formation and Recall of Structurally Equivalent Stories in Movie and Text" (Ph.D. dissertation, University of Colorado-Boulder, 1977).
10. Laurene Carol Krasny Meringoff, "A Story, A Story: The Influence of the Medium on Children's Apprehension of Stories," (Ph.D. dissertation, Harvard University, 1978).
11. United States Commission on Obscenity and Pornography, *The Report of the Commission* (Washington, D. C.: U. S. Government Printing Office, September 1970), p. 7192.
12. Mary Corde Lorang, *Burning Ice: The Moral and Emotional Effects of Reading* (New York: Scribners, 1968), p. 122.
13. Ibid., p. 12.
14. Ibid., pp. 192-270.

15. Kathleen Jamison and Vicki S. Freimuth, "The Banning of 'The Lottery'; Implications for Censorship in Schools," *Sightlines* (Fall 1977): 14.
16. Ibid.
17. Lee Burress, "A Brief Report of the 1977 NCTE Censorship Survey," *Dealing With Censorship* ed. James E. Davis (Urbana, Ill.: National Council of Teachers of English, 1979), p. 32.
18. L. B. Woods, "The Most Censored Materials in the U. S.," *Library Journal* 103 (November 1, 1978): 2,171.
19. Ibid., pp. 2,172–73.
20. Ginnette Herman and Jacques-Philippe Leyens, "Rating Films in TV," *Journal of Communication* 27 (April 1977): 48–53.
21. Cohen v. California, 403 U. S. 15 (1971).
22. *New York Times*, February 27, 1979, p. A12.
23. Ibid.
24. Kathleen Molz, "The Changing Capacities of Print and the Varying Utilities of Libraries," *Background Readings in Building Library Collections*, 2nd ed., ed. Phyliss Can Orden and B. Phillips (Metuchen, N. J.: Scarecrow Press, 1979), p. 59.

Chapter Seven
Confronting the Complainant

One day, when all preparations have been made, your heart is in the right place, your philosophical base feels firm, and you are nodding on the barricades, suddenly the censor will come to call and, perching there like the raven, will cry, "Nevermore." You will find that your heartbeat has increased and your knees are quaking. You are, in spite of all your preparations, caught unawares. You begin to feel that all of your advance preparation may have been for naught. Yet your chance of avoiding the one great potential pitfall—panic—is greatest, because you have thought about why the library's materials were selected. We feel that such preparation is the most important part of collection development, to insure freedom of access for users. As a librarian you must know in advance how you handle stressful situations. You must know what steps are necessary to insure that you will be able to roll with the punches aimed at you personally and professionally.

Therefore, it is important to decide who will handle complaints. They are often made to the first person the complainant sees upon entering the library. That person is often the clerk at the circulation desk, who should not be expected to be able to field complaints; nor should such a responsibility be placed upon an employee at that level. Staff policy should be always to refer complaints to the first supervisory level above the clerk's—usually the librarian who works in the collection-development area, especially when the complaint has to do with an item in the collection. In small libraries, where one or two professionals usually share the load, the person in charge should be consulted. Each library will differ in its staffing pattern, and as a result, so will the procedure. It is most important, however, that there be a procedure, and that it be reviewed with the staff on a regular basis. It should be mentioned here that for the administrators of the library, it is important to develop feelings of trust among members of the staff, in order to insure their willingness to refer complaints to supervisors. After all, not all complaints are about the content of library materials. They may be about staff conduct, the library environment, other library users and so forth. Those on the staff must feel that, should any of the complaints concern them personally, the administration will neither publicly embarrass the staff nor take the side of the user without making a careful investigation. Once such mutual trust is established, administrators will find the staff only too happy to refer all difficult complaints for settlement.

Of course, when a complaint starts, the first person within earshot will have to hear it out, and that may be the end of it. Fortunately, it usually is. Most would-be censors seem satisfied to let off steam. Having done that, they will probably pursue their peeve no further.

But should the complainant demand an answer, or "satisfaction," as some will have it, then an answer must be supplied. And some answers are obviously better than others. They are often influenced by the attitudes of the complainants, since attitudes often are more telling than words. Those who are complaining about the content of some library material are often visibly upset. They have come in contact with a word or an idea that they feel should not be available in such a public place. The complainants may often be parents concerned about the damage they feel will be inflicted on their children, or someone else's children, by the material they have discovered. The librarian can share their concern, to some extent at least, and perhaps be able to establish a more tranquil atmosphere in which to discuss the possible solution to their complaint.

Some people, however, will start a nonstop tirade that may seem to go on for an eternity. They do not want to be interrupted and probably can't be. Once started, they do not want to listen to anyone but themselves. It is important to allow the tirade to continue while carefully removing the person from center stage, into an anteroom or an office where the door can be closed. Often a diminished audience decreases the dramatic value of the confrontation, and complainants begin to lower their voices and even to pause. Such a pause is a good time to make some conciliatory statements. In any case, do not expect to resolve the complaint instantly. Time will work in your favor, provided the complainant is certain that you are listening.

Then there are those complainants who can be as cool as streetwise hustlers while they calmly tell you with whom they have connections and how their tax-paying status gives them the power of life or death over your future. And it requires the patience of Job for the librarian to stay calm.

In all situations, however, it is important that the person receiving the complaint remain calm and listen intently to the complainant. Every workshop you attend throughout your professional career that concerns this problem will stress the importance of calm. It is not easy to achieve, especially if someone is shouting at you in front of the staff and other library users. When your job security is threatened, your ancestry and your morals questioned, it is difficult to summon up more than a pale imitation of a smile. With experience you will find that you are able to maintain your calm. It becomes easier not to become excited after some experience demonstrates that, given a little patience and time, the pressure will ease or disappear.

One way to accelerate that learning process is through staff workshops employing role-playing. The staff will enjoy the experience and profit from learning in a nonthreatening atmosphere. Always include in those workshops verbal descriptions of why and how the library selects as it does and what the effect on the community would be if the library responded to every request for the removal of materials. Remember not to put yourself on the defensive.

It is the potential censors who must suddenly find themselves on the defensive. One technique for achieving this is to find out what types of materials the complainant feels *should* be in the collection. Calmly substantiate that such materials are there. Ask quietly what the complainant would want the library to do if someone came in and demanded that *those* materials be removed. Who should be the one member of the community to decide what is or is not to be in the library?

We have stressed calm and reasonableness, but we would be unrealistic if we were to suggest that these are always effective. One librarian managed to calm down a complainant and then wrote a reasonable letter as a follow-up to their conversation. The complainant fired back a letter to the librarian's supervisor, demanding to know why that person should not be fired for such conduct. Fortunately, incidents of this type are infrequent. If you are successful in getting the complainant into an office setting, make little comment as you allow the story to run its course. An occasional interjection of "yes" or "I see" will assure the speaker that you are listening. Do not interrupt, even though it may be difficult to resist, especially when incorrect statements are being made; but remember that your purpose is to ride out the storm. Make notes as a further indication that you are taking the complaint seriously. These notes will not only help you in the subsequent framing of your answer; they will also be important if you find you must report the incident to your colleagues, your supervisor or the governing body of the library.

Once the conversational ball is in your hands, you will find that there are a number of possible answers to a complaint, and must be very careful to select the most effective. If you say that the object of complaint never hurt anybody, you are on shaky ground. First of all, the material in question has obviously upset or hurt the complainant, and to say this is not so may well be taken as either an insult or an indication that you are a fool. Such a stance can also backfire if you have been known to say that books and other materials can have a salutary effect on the individual: if this is so, then, you may be asked, may the opposite not be true too? Your response cannot help but be weak.

If you say that the material under discussion has literary or creative value, you will be telling the complainant that he or she is too stupid not to have taken this into account. The complainant then has no choice but to rebut your claim. If you begin to list the authorities who have responded favorably to the material, the complainant will dismiss all such unreliable authorities. You might, in the course of the conversation, mention the material's merits and its generally positive reception by others, but do not use these as primary arguments or expect them to stand as satisfactory answers.

You should, as a professional, know why the item was added to the collection and understand that the complainant has a right to know the reason for the way the collection is developed. You are not expected to remember every purchase and the reason for its selection. It is not unusual, as new materials are processed into the collection, for their selector to look at them and wonder why they were chosen.

Some recommend that a review file be kept on potentially controversial materials. This seems to us a hopeless task particularly since, as we have noted before, all materials are potentially controversial. Take, for instance, the case of some librarians in a midwestern city who were taken to task for expending taxpayers' monies on a book on the fishes of New Zealand. While there is no harm in keeping a list of controversial materials, the investment in terms of staff time is a costly one, with little potential return. It is better to spot materials you feel may be controversial and keep abreast of what is causing problems in other libraries. The *Newsletter on Intellectual Freedom*, published by the American Library Association's Office for Intellectual Freedom, is currently the only nationally published source of such information. It even provides a monthly listing of titles covered in that issue, thus providing a handy index. This newsletter is a much more cost-conscious way of keeping abreast of potential problem materials than maintaining an extensive review list of your own.

One kind of remark that complainants often make can provide you with a rather telling response. The complainant will, either directly or by innuendo, state that the community does not want or need the material in question. We recall a confrontation concerning a book about a religious sect, which had disturbed a complainant, who insisted that there were no people from that sect in the community. We pulled out census information for that community and pointed out the listing for that religious sect and the number of individuals in the community who had been counted as members by census-takers. The complainant was silent for a moment and then reluctantly complimented the library for doing its job. Of course, such tactics do not always work, for there are those who will not admit that any minority should have rights. Such people feel that books selected for libraries should serve only the interests of the "majority," as represented by the individual seated before you. That a certain subject is in demand is often a good defense. In one case, in which a slang dictionary was being attacked, the complainant fell silent when told that it was often used by the police and clergy in the course of their professional duties. It is often helpful to be able to demonstrate that there are many people who want a particular item or that it is heavily borrowed.

A defense of the freedom to read may be useful, but the idea is an abstract one. It is often better to express it by saying that an item is wanted by members of the community, and that the community is composed of individuals. The usual response to this argument is that while it is all right for adults to have access to the materials, what about young people? "Surely," the complainant might say, "you don't think kids should have the right to read this." Well, do you? We have discussed this problem in an earlier chapter. The argument about the age of the individual seeking access is the one most often faced by the school and public librarian. There have even been recent indications that some community-college libraries may find themselves under fire because of the materials on their shelves, as organized censors broaden their scope of attack.

Dr. Dorothy Broderick, children's-services specialist, author and editor, has suggested an approach to complaints of any kind.[1] The process, while admittedly difficult, also may well be the most rewarding. She says that complaints should be answered immediately. This, of course, assumes that you are well-informed and can think quickly. Dr. Broderick cites a series of complaints about the novel for teenagers, *The Summer of My German Soldier*. The majority of the complainants said that "Jews don't abuse their children."

Dr. Broderick answered this way: "The whole question of child abuse in our society is very misunderstood, primarily because for so long nobody was willing to talk about it openly. We are now acquiring a good bit of information, and here are some of the best articles on the subject. Perhaps you'd like to read them and then we can talk about the subject. Why don't we see if we can get a group together?"

As Broderick[1] says, this method shows that you respect the complainant and you know the issue is a complex and disturbing one, and demonstrates that it is being taken seriously by others. Most important, it immediately demonstrates that the library is concerned about the same things as the complainant. Instead of being adversaries, we are suddenly allies. And by inviting discussion and suggesting further reading, there is a solid indication to the complainant that the librarian has not mounted a soapbox or taken a superior stance but is willing to sit down and work out the problem.

It often seems that the minds of would-be censors are permanently closed, but this may well be because such censors have a long history of taking adversarial positions. A method such as that proposed by Broderick does not mean that minds will be changed, but it does seem to defuse certain potentially volatile situations. Such an approach worked such wonders on some John Birch Society members that they wrote a letter to the local newspaper defending the library's attempts to make available materials on both sides of important questions facing the world and the community.

Unfortunately, not all of us are prepared to respond as Dr. Broderick suggests. If you are unprepared, try to gain time by stating that you will investigate and call back, write a letter or whatever. Such a delay can allow you to inform yourself about the facts and respond within a few hours, which should keep complainants from feeling that they are being put off. One librarian who used the letter-writing tactic stated that he was able to gather a number of useful facts about a controversial film, pointing out that it had circulated over 100 times without complaint. He listed the awards it had won and the favorable reviews it had received. He mentioned the names of various local organizations that had borrowed the film. Finally, he sent copies of his response to the advisory group listed on the letterhead of the complainant's letter, for he had noted that it contained several locally prominent individuals who might well have been unaware of the complaint being filed on their behalf. Although the complainant had threatened future action by his organization, nothing further was heard. Although we can conclude that the answer was successful, we do not know why.

The main point of the foregoing discussion is that, if you are the only source of contact for the complainant, it is incumbent upon you to avoid fruitless argument. It is not at all difficult to get so incensed that you make statements that can later be used against you and your library. Regretfully, we must point out that because librarianship is a profession with a large percentage of women, including its leaders, it is often felt that these practitioners are easy to intimidate. Of course there are those who will go to any lengths to avoid unpleasant situations. But it should be pointed out that successful defenses against intimidation have been conducted by male and female librarians. Therefore, librarians should remain firm in the face of complaints. There are those who will attempt to intimidate by using threats; if you refuse to take the bait, the threat evaporates in the face of your cool. Do not try to defend the content of any item in your collection, its artistic style, the intent of the creator or publisher or the format. Instead base your defense on the fact that the library's purpose is to meet the needs of the community and that others have the right to have access to the materials.

Sometimes you will be asked to add materials to the collection rather than remove them. Requesters will want to place materials in the collection either to substitute for those they consider offensive or as a counteractive agent to something already in the collection.

In some cases you may have already considered the item and decided that it was not needed. In that case, you could say that the material does not meet the library's collection standards. However, this is a dangerous position, because doubtless there are other materials in the collection that don't meet those standards, either, and the complainant may point this out, to your embarrassment.

If someone demands the acquisition of certain materials, you can say that there has been no demand for it. This ploy may work if you have the kind of system that indicates how often items circulate. We have used the demand statement when we were able to show that, although we had a couple of books in a particular subject area, they had circulated very little or not at all. Some of the automated circulation systems in libraries today are able to produce impressive printouts showing how a particular subject class is doing in terms of use. In such cases you can demonstrate that precious dollars must be used to meet demonstrated demand areas. If, however, you are using demand as an excuse to avoid the acquisition of a particular work, you are on doubtful ground, and your sins will find you out.

You may decide to say that the cost of processing a certain work does not justify its acquisition. This can backfire in much the same manner as the demand argument. The complainant can point to some materials already acquired and ask about the justification of their processing costs. You are again on shaky ground. If you are quick-witted, you can say that the material can be obtained via interlibrary loan (which is another form of censorship used by librarians). Or if you belong to a system that has a central or subject library collection with its logo on the endpapers, you can say with a certain smugness that it is a system problem and does not belong in your library. All of these ploys work sometimes, but when they backfire, the blast usually carries away any hope of credibility from the librarian making the statement. The best response is to have a sound selection policy, a good reason for acquisitions and the conviction of your decisions.

Devising a System for Handling Complaints

If you establish a system of handling complaints, it might include the following guidelines:

1. The person who initially receives a complaint should be coached to hear out the complaint and to be sympathetic to the distress of the complainant but not express an opinion on its merits. Once the smoke has cleared, it may be best for this person to suggest that the complainant meet with someone who can give more details and offer some assistance in resolving the matter. The library contact then uses a well-tested interpersonal communications device, saying, for instance, "As I understand it, your concern (request) is . . ." and then offering a brief paraphrase of the problem and the solution the complainant is seeking. Wait for confirmation or modification of the statement and then thank the complainant. This process helps complainants to review what is being asked for and strengthens the feeling that they are being given the attention they sought.

If the complainant has already been escorted into an office area that has a phone, then you may proceed. If there is no phone, have that person accompany you to one, so that you can contact the next level of library official who will be brought into the complaint. Let the complainant listen to your call, as you repeat the complaint and ask the library official for a follow-up.

2. If the complainant is to be taken to another librarian's office, do it yourself—do not send that person off with a stranger. Explain where you are going. You might say something to explain your actions, such as "I am sure you will find that he/she will be able to help resolve the questions you have raised." It is important to remember that in conducting people into bureaucratic situations you are arousing their suspicion. Many people who are unafraid to speak out when they are upset have had disastrous experiences

with bureaucratic run-arounds. If they feel they are being placed in another one, they will begin to build an additional set of grievances. On the other hand, if they sense your concern and realize that you are seeing to it that they will be listened to, they will relax and believe they are making progress. It is only the most insensitive individuals who will maintain their dudgeon in the face of warm and gracious consideration of their needs.

3. Be certain to formally introduce your superiors, including his or her title. It is wise to remind the library official of the telephone conversation and to present an even briefer paraphrase of the basis for the visit. Then excuse yourself, saying how happy you are to have met the individual and adding that you will be glad to offer further assistance if necessary.

4. Now complainants should once more be permitted to explain their concern. This will help to determine if they are feeling more tractable and will give the librarian additional time to plan strategy. Often, when complainants are satisfied with the response they have received, they will be conciliatory and may even invite you to offer some interpretations or comments. If you are the final arbitrator, be prepared to discuss the situation without bringing up the merits of the material. One librarian we know of takes the complainant on a tour of the library, dramatizing what the library is doing and how it goes about it. These tours are very successful, perhaps because, for the first time, the complainant begins to understand how a library works and has a sense that its basis is professional. Complainants may lose the feeling that the library is a toy enabling the staff to indulge its whims in a shopping spree in the garden of media delights.

If negotiations need to proceed beyond the time allotted for the complaint, it is important to set a date convenient for the complainant. One librarian used to tell all complainants that they had to meet with the library board at eight or nine in the evening on the first Tuesday of the next month. She got away with it for several years, until one person went to court, on the grounds of the denial of due process, and won a judgment against the library.

In summary, you may have already noticed that the "golden rule" is the prime base for sound interpersonal communication in these cases. The majority of those who have enough courage of their convictions to approach the librarian to express concern about the collection deserve respect for that act alone. Too many people today suffer their anger in silence or feel rueful resignation. If library users who speak up are met with compassion, understanding and respect, they will usually return the compliment. From there, it is possible to keep many potential problems from expanding into community-wide confrontations that profit no one, especially the library.

Group Action and the Media

Group action, actual or threatened, often does not allow for the one-to-one interaction discussed in the preceding pages. When a group is represented by a single complainant or several complainants, it is important to obtain the full, formal title of the organization, including the names of its officers. Groups sometimes do not make their complaint to the library staff but will go directly to the trustees, the school board or other community agency. Whenever a complaining group is identified, the staff should notify the director of the library. The staff should read the local newspapers to see if articles or letters to the editor having reference to the library appear, and should do the same with local television news broadcasts or radio talk shows. As soon as the director or chief librarian is aware that a group has instigated an action against the library, the trustees or any other governing unit should be immediately notified. One might be tempted to wait to see if the complaint or potential confrontation blows over, in order to refrain from "bothering" the governing unit. We do not recommend such action. If you call the governing unit's attention to a situation and say that you and your staff are ready to handle it, then the stage is set to keep the problem in house. If a member of the governing unit is confronted by a member of the hostile group or a media reporter, he or she may not know what to say and may be angry about having been placed in such a situation. At the same time, referring minor problems to members of the governing group must be avoided, and the chief librarian must constantly remind that group to refer any direct contact back to the library administration whenever possible.

In their dealings with the media, librarians learn to be wary. We know of one librarian who, upon receiving a visit in his office from a group concerned about an item in the library, called the local television station and reported an attempt to censor materials in the library. By the time the six-o'clock news came on the air, the librarian found himself being quoted out of context, implying that the group members "were a bunch of nuts." Photos of the allegedly offensive periodical were flashed on the screen, along with some man-on-the-street interviews asking if people thought the publication should be in the library. By nine the next morning, the mayor and several city counselors had entered the fray, demanding the removal of the material. The librarian had a full-blown cause célèbre on his hands within twenty-four hours. The outcome was the removal of the material and, eventually, the chief librarian.

If the media appear on your doorstep, do not shoot from the hip. If you have a procedure for dealing with complaints, be willing to explain it. Do not attempt to discuss the merits of the material under attack. Explain that you will respond to a formal complaint, but only after you have ascertained its exact nature. Refuse to deal with hearsay. We are not trying to portray the media as villains, but merely pointing out that, in their drive for attention-getting news, they will emphasize the sensational, and because of tight deadlines and time and space restrictions, the news can be distorted.

The press can be a good friend to the library in time of distress, but this requires an ongoing relationship that involves knowing the reporters assigned to cover your institution. In addition, you must show news editors that you understand their needs and will provide them with straightforward answers. In other words, if you wait for library news to be generated by a complainant, you will not be known by members of the press.

The Complaint Form

Another procedural aspect of your operation is the review form, called, in some libraries, the complaint form. In the library literature and in workshops we have attended, it is suggested that the complainant should be requested to fill out a complaint form. There are a variety of such forms. Many were designed years ago and have continued to be used, unrevised. They should not be used uncritically. The use of the complaint form at all has been questioned from time to time. Edward N. Howard, for instance, former director of the Vigo County Public Library, in Terre Haute, would have only a suggestion form in his library. He stoutly maintained that to use a complaint form created a negative feeling in the individual seeking change. Dr. Broderick, in an article in *Top of The News,* said she thinks we make enemies of those whom we ask to fill out such forms. She also observed that librarians usually have already decided not to remove the item in question when they give the form to a complainant, no matter how good a case is subsequently made for the removal of the material. The complainants soon learn this.[2] If we delight in intimidating such users, as Broderick claims, we are in the wrong. If we have decided beforehand that we will do nothing, regardless of circumstances, we can be certain that our attitude is quickly communicated to the complainant.

On the other hand, proponents of the complaint form believe that it is an excellent cooling-off device. Some point out that many people do not like to put their complaints in writing. As soon as the librarian hands such complainants a form, they walk away; a few will grimly fill it out. Some library users have been known to wad the form into a ball and deftly bounce it off the nose of the one who offered it.

Complaint forms can be useful, but they must be properly placed in the sequence of complaint negotiation. If the one-to-one negotiations are getting nowhere, it can help if the librarian assists the complainant in filling out and signing the form, so that a proper review can take place. (People who are particularly obstreperous do not seem, as a rule, to want to sign anything; asking them to use a complaint form may serve as a way of getting them to back off.) Going over the form with the complainant may be another way of paraphrasing the concern, as discussed earlier. The process will make complainants rethink their stand; at this juncture, some feel their point has been made and will withdraw their complaint.

If they do persevere, assisting them to fill out the form insures that both of you are in agreement as to the nature of the complaint. In addition, complainants do not feel they are simply being handed a form in order to get them out of the way. And the completed form can provide the starting place for a formal review, to be undertaken by others. For those so inclined, a file can be built up for referral and identification of chronic complainants.

Let us now discuss specific aspects of the review form. Most ask for similar information: author, title, form of the material; name, address, telephone number of the complainant; and specific parts of the material to which the complainant objects. As you will note in the examples provided, there are some significant variations on this theme. One noticeable difference is the name of the form itself. One of the more common titles is "Citizen's Request for Reconsideration of Library Materials." A more subtle version is "Request for Review of Material." Others are called "Book Selection Inquiry" and "Patron Comment on Library Materials." Some of these titles indicate to the user that the request stands a good chance of succeeding. Others are more noncommittal. One of the forms asks the complainant to suggest an alternative piece of material to replace the one under question. This seems to imply that the user can play a direct part in the selection of materials for the library. Since, in most cases, this is not so, raising the expectation of the reader seems not only undesirable but eventually damaging to the image of the library and its staff.

If a form is to be used, it should be part of the library's policy and should include a statement of its selection principles, indicating, too, that from time to time materials selected do not seem to have a place in the collection. The form should note that the staff is willing to review a specific item upon the request of the user and will supply a response if it decides to retain the material. In those rare instances where the material is determined to be no longer useful to the collection, the staff will withdraw the material and notify the user who questioned it. The exact wording of the form is crucial, and should be worked out in the context of existing library policies and procedures. What is most important about such a form is that it should be used as a communication device. Any attempt to use it as a weapon against anyone daring to protest is eventually going to be challenged by a sophisticated user or user group.

Some forms are designed by those so eager to be intimidating that they read like a final exam for a freshman English-literature course. For instance, they may ask: what is the theme of the work? What is the author's intention? This is not to say that questions are not helpful. Asking the complainant if the entire work has been read or viewed can make possible a discussion of the problems involved in taking words or passages out of context, or talking about why particular words or passages fit the author's intention.

Confronting the Complainant 139

Admittedly, this type of question is particularly infuriating to the complainant who does not care about content or intention. If such a user finds a word, a description, a scene or passage objectionable, he or she will have no interest in the integrity of the work.

Asking the complainants to state what harm may result from the use of the objectionable material may force them to think it through. Asking, conversely, what they find valuable about the material may also help them to see its positive side. Most forms ask objectors if they are aware of critical opinion about the work in question, although that is not something that impresses many would-be censors. Often the actions of such individuals are based in traditional anti-intellectualism, so to offer intellectual arguments may only confirm their opinion about the wrongheadedness of the establishment. However, citing the use of critical opinion as part of your selection policy and subsequently making a statement about the worth of the challenged item can only confirm the statement that selection is not based upon personal whim.

Asking complainants if they are willing to meet with the review committee is an act of intimidation. If the normal review procedure calls for a meeting with the review committee, then it should be so stated on the complaint form. However, it should also be noted that if the complainant does not wish to meet with the review committee, that will in no way lessen the seriousness with which the complaint is reviewed.

We generally feel that using a form is a delicate process. It smacks of cold bureaucracy. However, for some it may be the only way a certain type of complaint can be expedited. In any case, the form should be simple, clear and to the point. It should be a record-keeping and communications device, not a barrier between the user and the library staff.

If you use one, there are further considerations involved. When the form is completed, you will have to do something with it—the challenged material will have to be reviewed. In some school libraries it is a matter of policy to declare the material guilty until proven innocent. The material is removed from circulation until it has passed through the review process. In public libraries the review committee may be composed of staff members. In a few cases a subcommittee of the library board meets with a staff committee for a joint review, before reporting to the entire board, which makes the final determination. In school libraries the final review authority is the school board, but it often has a select committee, composed of teachers, librarians, community leaders and local experts, that acts as a screening agency. We have been unable to determine whether college and academic libraries have such a review procedure. Indeed, it would seem that in most such cases it is the librarians who have the primary responsibility for the selection of materials, with the exception of a few institutions where the faculty retains that responsibility. We are concerned about public-funded institutions of higher education, where challenges about materials have for the most part been internal. However, recent events indicate that successful censors are beginning to question the type of materials found in local community colleges. If that is the case, can college and university libraries be far behind?

The use of advisory boards can be dangerous in the selection or deselection process. Regardless of the make-up of these groups (we knew of one such group composed of the spouses of the members of the school board), if they are intended to be a rubber stamp for preconceived decisions, the group may resent being manipulated and the community may resent the implications of such a transparent activity. On the other hand, if the policy makers do not honor the advisory board's decision, how does the library appear? There have been cases of advisory-committee decisions being ignored or violently denounced by the governing body. It is our opinion that, once the responsibility to build a library collection is delegated to the professional library staff, such justification as is needed by the governing body should be sought only from those responsible. If the board does not feel that the authority was properly exercised, it should be willing to so state in its review of the professional staff. The use of advisory boards has not proven profitable to either side when library materials have been challenged, and should no longer be used to resolve these issues.

The Effects of Complaints

When the *Underground Dictionary* was challenged by some parents concerned about its possible harm to the young, it had been circulated from a bookmobile. Upon investigation, it was found that the majority of the users of the bookmobile were children of elementary-school age, who were primarily interested in recreational reading. The collection ran to about 2,000 volumes. It was agreed, after a review by the staff, that the book contained potentially dangerous information; most of it, particularly about drugs, was available in a more appropriate format for the age group being served. The review group decided that the title would better function as a reference work in one of the larger branch libraries, which had a substantial information service.

Reference librarians had stated that they had found the work useful and that it contained information not readily available elsewhere. The work was thus removed from the bookmobile and made available to users as a part of a collection more suited to the work's purpose. Everyone seemed to be content with the decision.

A complaint involving the notorious work by Henry Ford, *The International Jew,* proved to be much more complex. This 230-page book can be charitably described as virulent anti-Semitism. It sells for about thirty-five dollars and is still in print (1982). The foreword, written in 1948, supports the stand taken by the author over a decade earlier. In this case, it was purchased, "after a couple of requests," by a small public library serving a community of 35,000. It did not take long for a complaint to be lodged against the book. A staff committee meeting was called and the decision to include the book in the collection debated. The committee members decided that the work should be available to those interested. However, they decided to reclassify the work. Originally put in the class devoted to works about racial, ethnic and religious groups, it was moved into a class on "control and development of public opinion." It was felt by the committee that this was a more appropriate classification. It is not known if the complainant was satisfied, but it is obvious that the staff felt it had solved the problem. We cannot help but wonder how that same committee would deal with the problem of the labeling of materials.

Up to this point we have been discussing the run-of-the-mill complaint, wherein a response is made and complainants feel their point has been made, while the staff feels it has defended the challenged material through the prescribed methods. However, when complainants are not satisfied with the way their demands have been met, the situation can have serious consequences for both the librarian and the library. In some instances, budgetary cuts result. There have been examples of librarians withstanding a challenge and being fired or so harassed that they had to leave their positions. As you can see, it is necessary for any librarian to approach challenges to the library collection and its procedures for developing it with the utmost gravity. Those librarians who continually evaluate their community's strengths and weaknesses and have an understanding of what constitutes the political and social power base in the community, the attitudes of the press toward the library and the strength and weakness of the governing body of the library, are best able to analyze and cope with the opposition in a difficult situation.

If there is any indication that a demand for the removal of materials from the library comes from anything more than a concerned individual, librarians must be alert to the possibility that they will suddenly be involved in a crisis of major proportions, complete with angry board meetings, press coverage, peer interrogation or withdrawal of support or abandonment by the library's governing group. Many librarians are not familiar enough with their community to know where to turn for support from the strongest elements in the community. Those librarians often are the ones who, at the first hint of a complaint, either direct or indirect, quietly remove the material from the collection and pull the cards out of the catalog.

Other librarians feel that they have a moral responsibility to the community to defend the right of the library to collect materials and to provide access to them, regardless of the vocal opposition of a few. However, they do not know how to conduct their defense. They are uncertain about where to turn for support and how much it will be forthcoming. This uncertainty shows in their conduct after the initial complaint is lodged, and, like a hunting dog on the scent, the opposition steps up the pressure. It is only then, in great confusion and personal agony, that the librarian quietly removes the materials and pulls the cards from the catalog.

In recent years a growing number of librarians entered into exhausting, expensive and harrowing battles with those who would censor materials in a library. Some of these individuals set off on their course armed with little more than their convictions, not knowing where to turn for support; nor were they aware of how much pummeling they would have to withstand. Many such librarians have been damaged in the process, both professionally

Confronting the Complainant 143

and personally. They have been left disillusioned and bitter, standing on the sidelines of the profession, confused as to why they have been punished for having taken a stand supporting intellectual freedom in libraries.

Yet there are also librarians who have made it their business to fully understand the ramifications of actively supporting the right of a community to sustain free and open access to the information available in libraries. These librarians are well aware of the noble sentiments involved, but they are also prepared to deal with the less-than-noble tactics that can be used when resistance to censorship appears. How do these librarians develop such sophistication? The following ways, in differing combinations, have been suggested by those who have gone into the fire and returned comparatively unscathed.

1. They constantly read the literature of librarianship as it recounts cases where library collections have been challenged. They know that one can profit from the experience of others.
2. They have made it a point to become involved in local and state groups concerned with matters of intellectual freedom. Usually these include a chapter of the American Library Association, which has a committee and round-table discussions devoted to the subject.
3. They have discussed the way in which library collections are developed with authoritative figures and groups in the community. These discussions are conducted well in advance of any attack on a specific piece of material. This allows the discussion to focus on the concept of a variety of ideas being housed in the collection and avoids the emotionalism often associated with a specific title or subject.
4. They have been willing to go into the lion's den. They have appeared before parent's groups, the Kiwanians, the Toastmasters, church discussion groups, senior citizens' and youth groups, to discuss the problems of censorship, the role of the library in the community and how a strong program can enrich a community.
5. They have been among the first to support, through letters to the editor, calling in to radio talk shows, or appearing on local TV public-affairs programs, a free press, open

communications, freedom of information and public involvement in the affairs of the nation and the community. As a result they are considered more than custodians of books.
6. They have gone to considerable lengths to use the library's community rooms as a public forum. Indeed, they brag about it.
7. They have assisted community groups and individuals interested in local issues by publishing bibliographies, arranging discussion programs supplemented with library materials; they have used portapack video tape to help develop community pride and interest in local history; they have developed provocative displays; they have arranged for community leaders to appear in the library in special programs designed to make the community aware of special issues.
8. They have constantly promoted the library as an active part of the community, thus changing its image as a passive member of an otherwise dynamic community. They have been able to sell the idea that the community has—and needs—what Kathleeen Molz so deftly described as a "house of ideas."
9. They know what their options are. They know how much financial support they can or cannot expect, should they need legal help. They know just what the state library association can and cannot do. They know what to expect from the American Library Association and its legal arm, the Freedom to Read Foundation. They have long ago developed solid contacts with the nearest chapter of the American Civil Liberties Union (to which they are often modest contributors) and they know how much support to expect from it, should it be needed.
10. They are very much aware of their personal strengths and weaknesses. They know in which areas they can be effective and which areas it is best for them to avoid. If they are public performers, they perform. If they are good at organizing behind the scenes, they act accordingly. If they are motivators, they follow that path. What this adds up to is knowing whether or not they can withstand threats to their family and home, vicious rumors about their morals and

private affairs, late-night telephone calls and so on. That is, they know just how far they can go in supporting their personal and professional convictions.

If all of this has a familiar ring to it, it is because such action is so closely tied into all aspects of normal library programming that it sounds as if we were repeating the obvious. And yet our experience has been that many people working as professionals have, either through oversight or fear, ignored that vital connection. Facing the censor is as much a part of librarianship as is facing the satisfied user at the reference or circulation desk. If you do your homework; if you refuse to be lulled into the fanciful dream that it will never happen to you; if you accept the fact that it is as logical to have professional insurance as it is to have health insurance; then, by preparing for the day when—as you nod on the barricades in the sunshine of your library career—censors come knocking at your door, you will be ready to meet them.

NOTES

1. Dorothy M. Broderick, "Racism, Sexism, Intellectual Freedom and Youth Libraries," *Top of the News* (Summer 1977): 331.
2. Ibid., pp. 323-32.

Chapter Eight
Freedom Attacked:
A Case Study

Caledonia is a small agricultural community nestled among rolling hills, just far enough from Metropolis to be able to retain its rural qualities. A growing number of professionals from Metropolis have moved into the area to restore its old houses and establish their versions of farms, living out the romance of the "return to the land." The school district serves the town, whose population is about 9,000, and the nearby farm families. The yellow school-buses can be seen bouncing around the narrow roads and homing in on the campuslike "Central," with its separate buildings for the elementary and the secondary levels, which share a gymnasium/auditorium along with an athletic field that boasts it is the home of the Cougars. The quality of education is considered high enough to place its graduates into the state university system or the county's two-year college. Minority groups are so small as to be easily absorbed, if not overlooked. The drug culture has primarily surfaced in the secondary level and is limited to "pot" and amphetamines.

In 1968 there was a brief flurry of concern when the board of the Caledonia Central School District received a complaint from a parent disturbed to find that Lillian Smith's *Strange Fruit* was in the secondary-school collection. The board was caught unaware; it had no selection policy or procedure for processing such complaints. At the recommendation of the librarian's supervisor, the board appointed a committee of teachers to review the novel and its use in the school. The evaluation was favorable, and the complainant dropped the request for its removal.

In 1971 the Caledonia board adopted a materials-selection policy, modeled on recommendations by the American Association of School Librarians, a division of the American Library Association. The policy included an endorsement of the ALA Library Bill of Rights. The board was nervous about the document, but after carefully reviewing it with the superintendent and the librarian, agreed that it was better to have a written policy, in case of another complaint about the materials being used in the school.

The board did not have long to wait. In 1972 parents of a child in secondary school objected to his coming home with a book called *Thumb Tripping*, by Don Mitchell. The procedures outlined in the selection policy were followed, and the review committee recommended that the book be withdrawn. It disappeared from the collection. The following year, *Addict in the Streets* disturbed a parent. This time the review committee recommended retention, and the title stayed on the shelves. There were no complaints in 1974.

In January of 1975 Mrs. Alice O'Brian appeared before the board at its regular meeting and requested that her newly formed group, Parental Involvement in Education (PIE), be placed on the agenda for the next meeting. She stated that, as head of the group, she would make a presentation indicating the depth of degradation depicted in the materials used by the school system and offer a proposal on how the "offensive" materials could be removed from the school's libraries. The board granted her request and directed the superintendent to send a copy of the selection policy to Mrs. O'Brian.

The following weekend found Mrs. O'Brian and several members of her group in front of the Farmer's Grange Memorial Community Center. They had set up two card tables and laid out a display featuring some of the following titles: *The Godfather, Across 110th Street, Go Ask Alice, Comix, Loophole, Soul On Ice,* and *A Clockwork Orange*. All of the books had been checked out of the secondary-school library at Caledonia Central. Tabs had been attached to certain pages and color-coded for blasphemy, obscenity, anti-Americanism, anti-Christianity, and antifamily-ism. The offending passages were underlined in a matching color. In addition, photocopies of pages from dictionaries were available, with words considered offensive and improper for a school library underlined. There were also copies of reviews taken from

School Library Journal and *Booklist* that proposed using these titles. The group worked most of that Saturday, a day when many people came into town to do their weekly shopping. The group interested many, and a fair number were upset enough to sign a petition addressed to the school board calling for the removal of these titles and supporting PIE in its demand for parental review of all materials in the library. Not all were receptive to the position of PIE, and several letters appeared in the Caledonia *Gazette* the following week, supporting both sides of the issue. In particular, one high-school student objected to not being allowed by the PIE group to inspect the materials; nor would its members discuss with him their purpose in making the proposal. The student felt that because he and his peers would be affected by PIE's actions, the group should be willing to listen to the students discuss their needs and their attitudes toward such materials.

The following week PIE appeared before the school board, along with about one hundred observers. The president of the board, Carl Bell, was obviously nervous. As the session began, he reminded the members of the board that, with 1,200 enrolled in the Caledonia Central School District, there were bound to be divergent points of view and levels of interest in the children's education. He emphasized that the board was elected to represent all of the interests in the community and not to seek a majority consensus. "Every individual parent," he concluded, "should have the right to decide what his child shall read but not necessarily what other people's children should read." He called Mrs. O'Brian to the podium.

She thanked the president of the board and began in slow, deliberate and temperate tones to point out that PIE was present in order to make "positive, constructive suggestions to see if there is something we can do about the unwholesome literature available in the school library." She did not list titles or offer examples at this point. Instead she addressed the logic of establishing a parents' advisory council that would devote its time to reviewing books for the library. The council would start by reviewing the existing collection, having the power, to be delegated by the board, to remove any materials found to be "patently offensive." Such titles removed would then be turned over to the superintendent, who would designate a committee of teachers to review the materials. If there was any disagreement between the council and the teachers' review, then the materials would be sent to the board for final review. At the conclusion of her presentation, Mrs. O'Brian provided the board with the petitions and photocopies of all "offensive" materials that had been on display the previous week.

The board opened the floor to discussion. Officers and members of PIE were vocal in support of the proposal. Some parents recounted their shock at viewing the examples presented to them by PIE. Other parents did not agree with PIE's contention that parents should be trying to evaluate materials, and some went so far as to label the action censorship. Mrs. O'Brian returned to the podium and pointed out that PIE was opposed to censorship. She said that society had to develop rules of conduct, such as traffic regulations, which allowed everyone to know what level or standard of conduct was expected, in the interest of the majority. One of the final speakers was a young woman, who took pains to establish that she was a farmer's wife and had come from a family of farmers, where the realities of life were an everyday occurrence. She objected to the PIE proposal, on the grounds that it attempted to shelter the young from the harsh realities of life, leaving them defenseless when they went out on their own.

"If you do a good job at home," she said quietly, "your children will learn to evaluate and handle whatever they are confronted with." She concluded by observing that those children who were sheltered from reality seemed to have the greater difficulty maturing into healthy and responsible adults. The room was quiet. Mrs. O'Brian rose and moved to the podium. She was slightly flushed, and her words had a sharper edge than they had in her earlier presentations.

"PIE is seeking to support community standards by removing smut. Removing smut is not censorship!" As she returned to her seat, there was a smattering of applause, then silence. The discussion seemed to be over.

Board President Bell thanked all who had taken the time to come in and address the board. He pointed out that the books taken from the district's library by PIE should be returned. He reviewed the selection policy and asked that those titles the group sought to bring a complaint against be listed and the form provided by the district for such action be filled out, so that the machinery could be put in motion for a review. Mrs. O'Brian called out that the form was only designed to "harass" those who objected to school policy. Mr. Bell gaveled the meeting to a close.

The meeting of the board was fully reported in the *Gazette*, along with a flurry of letters. One writer commented that

> a frightening thing is happening in our community.... I do not believe that the biological ability to reproduce gives us divine insight. The well-prepared child is capable of judging, discarding and ignoring offensive materials. The parent who feels that he is failing in his home may feel censorship is the answer, but why should the child of a successful parent then be forced to lose freedom of choice and evaluation?

Others felt differently. "PIE is proposing a way in which parents and the school could work together to solve problems. We hope much good will be accomplished for all. Schools should *help* build good moral standards ... rather than destroy them." Another commentator took that position that "if you want your child to read this kind of material, go buy it; but when it's our tax money in our school, that's our business." Another offered the rights of students as a base for comment: "Students have a right to select their own material for reading ... it is up to the student to demonstrate that they have not abused their privilege to read what they want."

On February twelfth, accompanied by considerable publicity, PIE staged a meeting in the hall of the community center. Mrs. Luella Klieb, chair of the statewide PIE organization, was invited to speak. This was the first time many in the community realized that the local group had statewide connections. Mrs. Klieb assured the group of support not only from the state group but from the Heritage Foundation, headquartered in Washington, D. C. There was a buzz in the audience as this revelation of national affiliation was made. Mrs. Klieb waited for the reaction to die down and then proceeded to tell them that they had real support and therefore should not be "afraid, and to speak out at every opportunity" against the forces that were undermining community values. She explained that there was some financial support available and that the Heritage Foundation had considerable "experience" in such cases. She explained how the organization had sprung to the defense of beleaguered parents in West Virginia who were under attack from the "liberal establishment." Mrs. Klieb announced that in addition to the books taken from their very own library she had brought along examples of other materials found in her travels around the country. She labeled education as "humanistic" and designed to promote "interference in family relationships." She claimed that even such an innocent thing as school registration forms and show-and-tell sessions at the elementary level were solid evidence of the invasion of the privacy of the home and child-parent relationships. And as for censorship being the charge placed against PIE, she snapped, "Librarians and schoolteachers practice censorship when they select materials. We concerned parents have a responsibility to react when we find the moral fiber of our nation being destroyed by our schools."

Mrs. Klieb concluded her remarks with a warning that the media would be against PIE and hold it up to ridicule as it tried to rid the schools of undesirable materials. She said that the news media in Metropolis had refused to cover the story or even announce that the meeting was being held. The only way the parents could fight this, she claimed, was to start a letter-writing campaign aimed at the state legislature, the U.S. Office of Education and federal legislators. She told people to go out into their neighborhoods and canvas door to door, alerting parents by demonstrating the kind of materials their children were being exposed to in the school system. And, most importantly, PIE members should pack the Board of Education meetings and force the board to let the parents decide what materials were suitable for their children.

For many who attended, it was an exciting session. Materials were copied, and door-to-door as well as telephone campaigning began the next week. The *Gazette* gave a detailed account of the PIE meeting. By the time the board held its meeting the following week, the room was jammed with observers. The president, Carl Bell, read a statement, which said in part:

> We feel very strongly that our policy does take into account both your feelings [he nods to the PIE group, seated in one section of the room] as well as the many other differing opinions which must be treated fairly to serve a school district of this considerable size. The Board of Education has decided to maintain its present library policy. We believe our policy is broad enough to permit parents to restrict their own student's reading if they wish, and yet not infringe on the rights of

other parents who want their students to have the opportunity to read on a more liberal basis.

He concluded by urging PIE to return the materials taken from the school library and fill out the complaint forms so that a proper review could be undertaken. He urged that everyone go home and begin to honor the policy and procedure developed by the board. The meeting was adjourned.

The *Gazette* provided a complete account of the board session and an editorial in support of its decision. Several letters were printed that accused the paper of being biased against PIE and the concern of the parents. Alice Harriet, owner and editor of the weekly paper, replied in a strongly worded statement indicative of her style:

> We are not against PIE nor any concerned parents in the District. Unless they can prove beyond a certainty of a doubt that they represent all parents in the District, then they must be willing to let both sides be heard. Our objection lies in bringing in outsiders. The net result is to frighten and destroy faith in our school, its Board of Education, administrators, and teachers.... PIE needs strong, alert leadership to insure that its real goals are not clouded by issues that have no relation to our schools...

PIE staged another meeting in the community center and presented as main speaker a member of the Board of Education for an adjoining district, Cuba City. Mr. Earl Carson was a past president of the board but made it clear that he was not present as its representative. Having heard of the conflict, he felt that, as a concerned parent, he had a duty to appear in support of the campaign being conducted by PIE. He was critical of the policy as adopted by the Caledonia district and said that Cuba City would not allow such a policy to exist in its district. He recommended that the group get involved in a letter-writing campaign similar to that proposed previously by Mrs. Klieb. The *Gazette* covered the meeting, and a brief editorial questioned why the community needed an "outside" expert to offer advice.

At the next board meeting PIE was again asked to bring back the books and file a formal request for review. PIE's counter-proposal was that it be billed for the cost of the books. The board took that offer under advisement and in a subsequent communication denied PIE the right to purchase the books. It again urged the filing of a complaint form and the return of the materials. The board reminded PIE that once a complaint was filed, materials were removed from library circulation until the review was completed. The *Gazette* continued to receive and print letters about the issue, and the teacher's union sent a long statement in support of the board's approach.

PIE finally relented, and in March returned the materials and sent in the complaint forms. The review committee (composed of faculty members in the district) went to work. It moved quickly and in little over a week turned in the following recommendations to the board:

To be removed from the collection: *A Clockwork Orange, Comix* and *Soul on Ice.*

To be returned to the shelves: *Go Ask Alice, The Godfather* and *Loophole.*

Across 110th Street was so badly marked up that the review committee requested a new copy so as to make as fair a review as possible. Subsequently approval was recommended.

At the same time that the review process was going on, PIE formally requested that the Pledge of Allegiance be made in classes on a daily basis. The board responded that the Student Council had decided in 1970 that such flag salutes were to be conducted only at the beginning of assembly meetings. PIE resubmitted its request at all board meetings for the remainder of the school session. It received the same answer—that it was the prerogative of the students and the teachers.

The pressure continued to mount. The members of the board received angry phone calls, letters and an occasional catcall as they moved about the community. They talked among themselves and decided to take action. On April fourteenth they called a special meeting of the board and announced that they were closing the library. They had appointed a subcommittee of the board to work with the two librarians (although the elementary-school library had not been under attack, the board involved both librarians in their plan), to search out all possible objectionable materials in the library collection. The board said that it felt a stalemate had been reached and the effectiveness of the administrators and teachers was declining in the current climate. The continued clamor by PIE for a parental-review council had created doubts in the community. When the board asked for a listing of other materials being questioned by PIE, it was refused. The board said that if the list were produced, the library would be kept open, and only those materials subject to review would be removed. PIE again refused, stating that the group wanted a written assurance from the board that a parental advisory council would be established, before it would reveal other titles it considered objectionable. Mrs. O'Brian admitted within the hearing of Alice Harriet, *Gazette* editor, that the Heritage Foundation had recommended this tactic. The statement was reported in the next edition of the newspaper.

Members of the board expressed their frustration with the liberal guidelines on materials selection suggested by the American Library Association and that organization's state chapter. They were particularly upset because the State Department of Education had only recently produced similar guidelines and was recommending their adoption by school boards across the state. Several members stated that they felt caught in the middle, trying to support the professional library staff and at the same time finding themselves under fire from members of the community, with little evidence of support from those who had elected them. Finally, deciding it had no other recourse, the board voted to close the library and begin the search for "objectionable" materials.

Shock waves rippled through the community. Those who had been supporting the board's resistance to the demands of PIE felt that they had been betrayed and the cause was lost. Some of the more concerned parents met and formed a new group, calling themselves Parental Action for Student Rights (PARS). They announced in a letter to the *Gazette* that they welcomed members, as well as support from those who believed that "we as parents . . . object to any interference with established policies by unqualified individuals."

Kelly Watts, the high-school librarian, and Emily Glass, the elementary-school librarian, were under orders from the superintendent's office to draw up a list of materials in the school library that were being attacked, in other libraries around the nation, as "objectionable." The librarians spent hours poring over professional literature, and they received lists of materials under attack, compiled by the National Library Association. They also obtained materials from the American Library Association containing the titles of materials considered "objectionable." They talked to both public librarians in the immediate area and to some in the larger system in Metropolis. They were also able to collect the names of a few authors whose background had been questioned in terms of whether it was "suitable" for students to be exposed to their writings.

Finally, the librarians produced a list of 147 titles in their school libraries that had at some time or another been under attack in other school libraries. The board accepted the list and had all titles removed from the shelves before reopening the library. The list was made public, and this time the media outside of Caledonia took notice. Soon the wire services were telling the nation that this small community had banned 147 titles from its schools. Television stations sent out reporters. Mrs. O'Brian appeared on a cable talk show, and brought along some samples of the materials that had been in the collection. News of little else appeared in the *Gazette*. The list of titles withdrawn follows:

Fiction

    Abe, Kobo. *Inter Ice*
    Algren, Nelson. *The Man With the Golden Arm*
    Allen, Richard. *No Enemy But Winter*
    Andrews, Matthew. *The Black Palace*
    Ansell, Richard. *Summer*
    Arden, William. *Die to a Distant Drum*
    Atwood, Margaret Eleanor. *Surfacing*
    Baker, Peter. *A Killing Affair*
    Baldwin, James. *Go Tell It On the Mountain*
    Ball, John. *In the Heat of the Night*
    Bankowski, Richard. *The Barbarians at the Gates*
    Bass, Milton. *Jory*
    Beare, George. *The Bloody Sun at Noon*
    Bechko, P. A. *Night of the Flaming Guns*
    Becker, Stephen. *Dog Tags*
    Benchley, Peter. *Jaws*
    Benton, John. *Carmen*
    Benton, Kenneth. *Twenty-fourth Level*

Burke, Howard. *The Sun Grows Cold*
Bodelsen, Anders. *Freezing Down*
Brodeur, Paul. *The Stunt Man*
Brown, J. E. *Incident at 125th Street*
Burgess, Anthony. *A Clockwork Orange*
Burke, J. F. *Location Shots*
Bush, Christopher. *The Case of the Prodigal Daughter*
Butterworth, W. E. *The Narc*
Cain, George. *Blueschild Baby*
Chaver, M. S. *The Acid Nightmare*
Childress, Alice. *A Hero Ain't Nothin' But a Sandwich*
Coles, Robert. *Riding Free*
Colver, Alice Ross. *Say Yes to Life*
Condon, Richard. *Winter Kills*
Connolly, Edward. *Deer Run*
Cordell, Alexander. *If You Believe the Soldiers*
Craig, Margaret Maze. *It Could Happen to Anyone*
Curtis, Jack. *Banjo*
Davies, L. P. *Genesis Two*
Davis, Mildred. *Three Minutes to Midnight*
Davis, Russell. *Anything for a Friend*
Delman, David. *He Who Digs a Grave*
Dennis, Patrick. *Paradise*
Donis, Miles. *Falling Up*
Dutton, Mary. *Thorpe*
Elliot, Janice. *The Kindling*
Ellison, Ralph. *The Invisible Man*
Emmett, Martha Wiley. *I Love the Person You Were Meant To Be*
Eyerley, Jeannette. *Bonnie Jo, Go Home*
Fair, Ronald. *We Can't Breathe*
Fairbairn, Anne. *Five Smooth Stones*
Falkirk, Richard. *The Chill Factor*
Forrest, Maryann. *Here*
Freeman, Gilliam. *The Alabaster Egg*
Garfield, Brian. *Death Wish*
Garfield, Brian. *The Hit*
Gerson, Noel B. *The Sunday Heroes*
Godey, John. *The Taking of Pelham One Two Three*
Hamilton, Virginia. *The Planet of Junior Brown*
Hebden, Mark. *Mask of Violence*

Heinlein, Robert A. *Stranger in a Strange Land*
Hentoff, Nat. *I'm Really Dragged But Nothing Gets Me Down*
Herbert, Frank. *Soul Catcher*
Hesse, Hermann. *Siddhartha*
Johnson, Annabel. *Count Me Gone* (2 copies)
Johnson, E. Richard. *Cage Five is Going to Break*
Johnston, William. *A Little Grass on the Side*
Jones, James. *A Touch of Danger*
Kellogg, Marjorie. *Tell Me That You Love Me, Junie Moon* (6 copies)
Kerr, M. E. *Dinky Hocker Shoots Smack*
Kesey, Ken. *One Flew Over the Cuckoo's Nest*
King, Stephen. *Carrie*
Kingman, Lee. *Peter Pan Bag*
Krantz, Hazel. *A Pad of Your Own*
Levin, Ira. *This Perfect Day*
Lilley, Tom. *The Officer From Special Branch*
Lowery, Bruce. *Werewolf*
Lynne, James Broon. *Collision*
McAfee, Thomas. *Rover Youngblood*
Mailer, Norman. *The Armies of the Night*
Malamud, Bernard. *The Fixer*
Markstein, George. *The Cooker*
Miller, Warren. *The Cool World*
Mills, James. *The Panic in Needle Park* (2 copies)
Motley, Williard. *Knock on Any Door*
Neufeld, John. *Edgar Allan*
Neufeld, John. *For All the Wrong Reasons*
Nourse, Alan. *The Bladerunner*
Parker, Claire. *The Rookies*
Ponicson, Darryl. *The 1st Detail*
Quartermain, James. *The Diamond Book*
Rendell, Ruth. *Some Lie and Some Die*
Rodman, Maia. *Tuned Out*
Segal, Erich. *Love Story*
Sherburne, Zoe. *Too Bad About the Haines Girl*
Smith, Lillian Eugenia. *Strange Fruit*
Steinbeck, John. *In Dubious Battle*
Swarthout, Glendon. *Bless the Beasts and the Children*
Townsend, John Rowe. *Good Night, Prof. Deer*
Trumbo, Dalton. *Johnny Got His Gun* (2 copies)

Vonnegut, Kurt. *Breakfast of Champions*
Vonnegut, Kurt. *Cat's Cradle*
Vonnegut, Kurt. *The Sirens of Titan: An Original Novel*
Vonnegut, Kurt. *Slaughterhouse Five*
Walker, Alice. *In Love and Trouble: Stories of Black Women*
Wambaugh, Joseph. *The Blue Knight*
Wambaugh, Joseph. *The New Centurions*
Warner, Peter. *Loose Ends*
Watson, Colin. *Kissing Covens*
Wersba, Barbara. *Run Softly, Go Fast*
Wertenbaker, Lael. *Unbidden Guests*
Wilson, Jacqueline. *Hide and Seek*
Wohl, Burton. *That Certain Summer*
Wright, Richard. *Native Son* (2 copies)
Zamyatin, Yevgeny. *We*
Zindel, Paul. *My Darling, My Hamburger* (3 copies)
Zindel, Paul. *The Pigman* (2 copies)

Nonfiction, by Dewey Classification

Lyons, Arthur. *The Second Coming: Satanism in America* 133.4
Tallant, Robert. *Voodoo in New Orleans* 133.4
Pomeroy, Wardell. *Girls and Sex* 176
Sex Instruction and Education Council of the U. S. *Sexuality and Man* 176
Toffler, Alvin. *Future Shock* 301.2
Wolfe, Tom. *The Electric Kool-Aid Acid Test* (2 copies) 301.2
Friedan, Betty. *The Feminine Mystique* (2 copies) 301.41
Greer, Germaine. *The Female Eunuch* 301.41
Baldwin, James. *No Name in the Streets* 301.45
Cole, Larry. *Street Kids* 309.1
Connections: Notes From the Heroin World 362.2
Wambaugh, Joseph. *The Onion Field* 364.1
Moore, Robin. *The French Connection: the World's Most Crucial Narcotics Investigation* 364.15 (2 copies)
Morris, Desmond. *The Naked Ape* 599.9
Bohannan, Paul. *Love, Sex and Being Human: A Book About the Human Condition for Young Adults* 612.6
Guttmacher, Alan F. *Understanding Sex: A Young Person's Guide* 612.6

Larner, Jeremy. *The Addict in the Streets* 616.86
Landau, Deborah. *Janis Joplin, Her Life and Times* 784.092

The community was stunned by the number of titles removed. Members of PIE made such comments as "This is only the tip of the iceberg." No one could understand the criteria for removing the titles or why the titles had been acquired in the first place. In both informal and formal situations, the board tried to explain the pressures under which it had been operating during the past months. The PIE complaints had gone all the way to the desk of the Governor, who in turn sent them to the head of the State Education Department. It was the suggestion of that department that had led the board to close the library and search for all controversial titles, according to President Cole. He said that the state had advised that the next step be to select a broad-based community group to review all of the titles removed.

Students wrote letters and expressed their shock as well as concern that their education was being damaged by being denied access to so many titles. In a letter to the *Gazette*, a teacher who had visited the American Civil Liberties Union office in Metropolis said that the group had expressed considerable interest in investigating the removal of the titles, in order to determine whether the students' and teachers' First Amendment rights had been violated. Some members of the community, including the editor of the *Gazette*, stated that they did not want "outside" interference.

PIE continued to agitate. It announced a meeting open only to members. There the PIE members were introduced to William McKenna, legal counselor from the Heritage Foundation. He offered financial support and to set up an office in the community to assist the PIE group in its efforts to establish a parental review system. The effect was not quite what Mrs. O'Brian and Mrs. Klieb could have expected. Some fourteen members of PIE, including the vice-president, publicly resigned, stating that they were not happy with the "outside" influences brought into the group. They formed their own group, the Alliance of Parents and Taxpayers (APT). They avowed in the *Gazette* that there would "be no secrecy in our activities and we believe we should not be seeking outside help but should be working within the community."

Editor Harriet had a similar comment: "The PIE made a strong attempt to bring in the kind of outside pressure that was brought into West Virginia, the kind that stirs up violence and dissension. Our community didn't buy it . . . it appears that a fair number of PIE's own membership didn't buy it and last week organized their own group . . ." She continued her editorial by offering an explanation of the board's dilemma:

> We think it is unfortunate that firm support from those who opposed any attempt to remove the books from the library was not forthcoming. Meanwhile the PIE was making constant demands on the time of the Board, most of it in requests for private sessions; any reasonable offers the Board made were constantly refused, a threat was made to enter the library by force, if necessary. And finally a request was made to withdraw all the books on which they had filed complaints and which were already being reviewed by the teacher committees. With little or no evidence of public support from the other side, the Board felt that action of some kind must be taken to make certain the entire school district became involved.

The board moved ahead, with the formation of a Citizens Library Advisory Committee. All churches, fraternal, social and service organizations in the district were asked to send one member to be on the committee. In addition, all board members chose a representative from each of their geographic areas, and PARS sent a representative. The committee was charged to address the following four questions:

1. What should be the role of the High School Library in the educational process?
2. What kinds of material does the school community find acceptable for use in the library by students in an age range of 12 to 18?
3. What changes, if any, in book selection policy are needed to foster selection of materials acceptable for this age group?
4. What revisions are needed in the review procedures for books already in the library and books which might be objectionable to some parents in the future?

The advisory committee was reminded by the board that "of top priority will be some decision as to how the committee will approach the problem of the books currently being withheld from the library."

As the committee began its work, the letters to the *Gazette* continued. The newly formed APT group announced that "we wish to inform the public that we are united in our effort to rid the school of unwholesome literature . . . we feel that our children can be prepared for the outside world without resorting to explicit violence, greatly detailed sex and books containing anti-American philosophy . . ." One letter-writer was upset about the titles that had been withdrawn, and in particular about *Siddhartha*, by Hermann Hesse. "It says so much of what I believe in," she said, and quoted Hesse on the importance of love. With books like this being withdrawn she could only conclude "that something dreadfully wrong is being done."

The thirty-three-member advisory committee elected Kenneth Dorrence, an engineer on the staff of a branch of a national manufacturing firm, to be chair. Mr. Dorrence was a native of the area, had obtained his degree out of state and had returned to spend his entire work life at one firm. The group was divided, by random selection, into five discussion groups. Each group was to take one of the four questions, and the fifth group was to ponder the fate of the 147 titles.

As the meetings proceeded, some questions were raised and materials consulted as the members wrestled with their problem. They investigated the budget for the library and wanted to know if the materials in question had a high circulation rate. This was difficult to measure. Could books be returned after purchase if found undesirable? Under the current jobber contract, only if they were damaged. The group received review summaries of Victor Cline's *Where Do We Draw The Line?*, an attack on the rise of explicit sexuality and anti-American philosophies in recent books; *Foolish Fig Leaves*, by Richard Kuh, a liberal historian's look at censorship; and the conclusions of the *Commission Report on Obscenity and Pornography*. The group also had access to the U. S. Commissioner of Education's paper, "School, Parents, and Textbooks."

Outside the meeting room, all was not peaceful. Mrs. O'Brian sent letters to the *Gazette* attacking the cooperative services between school districts as further evidence that parental influence was being ignored in the schools. She again urged parents to conduct a letter-writing campaign. The PIE, fishing for other issues, attacked the high-school English classes for conducting exercises in value clarification. The exercises were characterized as invasions of home and family privacy. PARS announced that it would cease to agitate and would assume a watchdog position, to insure that outside "agitators" did not move into the community to cause trouble, adding that it had engaged the services of an ACLU lawyer, should they be needed.

Mrs. Klieb took to the mails as state chairperson of PIE, and papered the community with an attack that shocked many and amused those who sat around the Bun and Burger restaurant every morning gathering in the "news." Editor Harriet was not amused:

> Our reaction to the mass mailing sent into our School District from PIE through its state chairman, Luella Klieb, is one of anger.... Mrs. Klieb is determined to try and use her influence here, and that of the state level group and the national group, the Heritage Foundation. This despite the fact that the community as a whole made it clear that they wish our present controversy to be settled locally. We object strongly to the quotes of objectionable language in her mailings. Granted it does state that those books are part of the Caledonia School District Library but the implication is there.... We also object to the *gossip* type of propaganda ... which is pure sensationalism, has nothing to do with Caledonia specifically and only serves to try and poison the minds of parents about all teachers.... Caledonia is one community that prefers to solve its problems without outside interference and believes it can.

As the advisory committee continued its work, its members were given a report by the district's social-studies faculty explaining its goals and philosophy and how these were coordinated by utilizing the library collection. Reading lists from the social studies and English programs were supplied. The committee reviewed policy statements from other districts and heard a report from the English faculty. Its members were provided with newspaper editorials on school censorship, a statement on conservative views of morality and a long list of books that have been censored in the United States. The advisory committee felt that the book-selection policy should be included in the student handbook. And, after much discussion, took the following action:

1. Passed a motion that all of the 147 titles should be returned to

the shelves, subject to the revised review procedure.
2. The "Basic Principles of Book and Printed Materials Selection" of the current policy statement were accepted unchanged.
3. The Selection Policy procedures were revised and approved.

The advisory committee was pleased with its work. One of the members was moved to write to the board:

> If we wish to show reverence for our Constitution, all possible weight and bearing must be placed on upholding that Constitution which guarantees free expression through books, speech and the media. These may be tempered by one's own conscience, and, in the case of the school library, parental authority which does not have the authority to abridge the rights of others. I feel our Committee conclusively reaffirmed the school board's policies.

This member went on to comment that she felt no need for an advisory committee to continue to operate. "I trust and respect your decisions, urging you always to have the courage of your own convictions." Her wish was granted, and the committee was disbanded.

It wasn't until September that the board formally accepted the advisory committee's report. The board was particularly interested in the proposed changes in the selection procedure which required the use of book lists and reviews in addition to the general recommendations of the American Library Association. In addition it required that all accession lists be published in an official newspaper, to be designated by the board. The report observed that review services seemed to be solely oriented to ALA lists and standards, and added that those lists do not seem to include books from religious publishing houses or review fiction that is wholesome and interesting without preaching or being doctrinaire. The committee wondered if these lists did not betray a bias that violated the ALA's own Library Bill of Rights, and recommended that the board study this on a cooperative basis with other boards and school administrations.

Albert Reedy, the newly appointed board president, proposed four amendments to the committee's recommendations. One was to label the books under a coding system to be devised by administration. The board directed the administration to investigate and return with a proposal for a coding system that could be applied to certain titles. Such a system was devised, by the high-school librarian, and subsequently adopted by the board. The 147 titles and all subsequently purchased materials are labeled on the spine with 7-9 or 10-12, to indicate the level of maturity. In addition an RA is placed on the spine and the book's card pocket for those books whose circulation is restricted. The checkout card for RA books is of a different color, in order to insure the staff's attention and that the individual is allowed the material. In order for RA materials to circulate, students must have a signed waiver from their parents. The PIE, now down to nine members, tried to protest the decision and again arouse the community, but to no avail. As Editor Harriet proudly wrote of the decision:

> By this action they [the board] reaffirmed the fact that education in general and books in particular cannot be limited by the opinions, beliefs, or prejudices of any group or group of individuals. . . . We can be proud of our Board of Education which proposed the plan, proud of our committee which worked it out so successfully, and proud of our community that urged this kind of solution by our own people.

In the five years since that decision, Kelly Watts, the high-school librarian, sits in his workroom, designating books as 7-9 and 10-12 and occasionally as RA. He isn't happy, but perhaps he is a little wiser. As he will explain to anyone who wishes to ask, the story didn't end the way he thought it would.

"I had this feeling all along that right would win out," he says.

> It was inconceivable to me that once the Committee understood the what, the why, and the how of library materials in the education process that all would not come out right. Well, it didn't. As a matter of fact I have never felt so alone in my life. Not one area librarian came to the defense of the library, its collection or its policy. About a year after it was all over, a small group in the next county sent a written notice of support. I don't think the Board even acknowledged receiving it.

"In talking to others," he continued, "I found out that many of the school districts used that damned list to pull titles off their shelves as insurance against a similar attack. And the irony is that the students don't bother to get the waiver. They don't check out the RA titles. And we have had only one minor complaint from a parent in the five years since."

Note

Although the names in this study have been changed, it was not done to protect the innocent but to allow readers to clearly evaluate events and identify issues. We felt that would be more easily achieved if readers were not involved in attempting to recognize actual personalities or identify a geographic area. Also, we felt that it would serve no purpose to hold the school district, the students and the staff up for inspection at this late date. While the experience is not unique to any program under fire for materials in its library or curriculum, this particular case gives a good picture of the human struggle for understanding and freedom from anarchy. The failures that all flesh is heir to are too often sensationalized or used to teach a moral. We are offering readers the opportunity to draw their own conclusions.

Chapter Nine
Freedom Defended

It is important to bear in mind that the library profession is not unified in its approach to freedom of access to the materials housed in libraries. One need only visit a library to find restrictive rules and regulations posted. They may be based upon the class of individual, such as student versus faculty or resident versus nonresident taxpayer. Interlibrary loans seek an indication of one's seriousness of purpose in asking for a particular item. The list could go on. Instead let us discuss the moral stance often assumed by librarians concerned with control of access and acquisition of materials. One of the quotes frequently cited from Marjorie Fiske's famous 1959 study illustrates this position, which we heard paraphrased as recently as 1981. "We haven't been censoring but we have been 'conservative.' After all, this is a conservative community, and that is how the parents here want it to be."[1]

When faced with such an attitude by professionals, what is the sense in trying to establish policies that will enhance the freedom of access to materials and strengthen the library's ability to practice those policies? The answer is a practical one. If there is a censorship problem, it will neither remain invisible nor disappear through neglect or faulty rationalization. Studies of personality characteristics of practicing librarians have not been well documented, but the data that have been collected are disturbing: they point to passivity, submissiveness and a lack of self-assurance as frequent characteristics of that group.[2] If there is any hope for a library to develop a workable and effective program that will assure even a modicum of ability to withstand pressures from internal and external sources, assurance and aggressiveness must be carefully nurtured in the staff. Assurance is not developed when pressure on the staff is strong. That is not the time to learn to take an effective stance.

Where does one begin? Begin with yourself, of course. Take some time to reflect, read and evaluate yourself, in order to discover a basis for self-assurance. Lester Asheim's distinction between censorship and selection, made in 1953, is still as valid a starting place as any. "The selector says, if there is anything good in this book let us try and keep it; the censor says, if there is anything bad in this book, let us reject it."[3] It is in this classic statement that one can find some answers to the following types of statements, which often come hurtling out of confrontations to land at your feet: "If they want to read it, let them buy it," or "The taxpayer has a right to demand that taxes not be expended on material repugnant to any member of the community." Asheim also places in perspective the overused shibboleths of "standards," "intent of the author" or "anticipated problem materials."

We recommend that you search through the literature for articles that deal with intellectual freedom, censorship, collection development and policy making for materials selection. This will help you to develop a rationale for the creation of a selection policy, which will assist the library staff in maintaining its equilibrium when challenged. Howard D. White, in his report on library censorship, puts the permanent dilemma facing librarians into the following refreshing context:

> Some fair number of their customers want and expect materials with explicit sexual content to be in the collection. But if librarians supply such materials, they risk controversies, or worse, with the large majority of tax-paying citizens who want the collections sexually innocuous. On the other hand, if they try to please the majority, a very large fraction of whom never visit the library, they may disappoint their actual users, who include vocal advocates of the liberal point of view.[4]

This quote contains the nucleus for establishing a clearly defined policy and program for the selection and maintenance of a library collection.

LeRoy C. Merritt, in commenting on selection, was aware of the actual user in the collection-building process when he wrote, in 1970, that acting in good conscience and without fear of intimidation, the librarian must select each book as being in fact a positive contribution to the collection and of potential benefit or usefulness to some portion of the library's clientele ... a book is selected because of its usefulness to a group of readers, even though it may not be useful to others, or may even be distasteful, repugnant, or objectionable to them.[5]

The creation of a policy should gain its impetus from the need of the library staff to clarify its goals and procedures in order to insure that its selection program is in the interest of the library user. Although it is easy to think of the policy as a device to protect the staff in the event of challenges to the selection of materials, a well-drawn policy statement is in fact the most reliable way to insure support of the staff by users of the library. As White pointed out, many of the people who would expect and desire the library to function as a censorship agency are not its users. Studies of library users indicate that as a group they have a high level of education, are noticeably active politically and are heavy users of all the communications media.[6] It is that reader-user group who, if it is aware of how the library builds its collection and why (or can be provided with evidence that the process is indeed orderly and rational), would be most likely to rise to the protection of the collection if it were to come under attack, particularly from citizen groups not generally known to be users of the library.

One observation culled from conversations with several librarians who found their collections under attack seems worth interjecting at this point. Often when the attackers' use of sensationalism is first reported in the media, regular library users do not respond, because, as far as they know, the materials may be suspect. Others feel that the basis for attack is so witless that it will laugh itself out of the community ... so why bother to respond to it? In any case, it often takes those users of the library who might be articulate and politically effective considerable time to begin to respond to attempts either to remove materials or to prevent them from appearing in a library collection. In the case history recounted in the previous chapter, the librarian felt that the attack was so opposed to the community's views that, as tempers cooled, all would come out right. A group opposing the aims of the attacking group did appear, late in the process, but it was never able to organize into a strong force. The head of the school board lamented that little or no support for his stance was forthcoming. Other cases indicate that generating a response to an appeal for help in maintaining the *status quo* is difficult. It is easier to generate a response for change, be it negative or positive. Thus we are suggesting that an informed user group is likely to react strongly if its support is sought to fight those who would censor or control their access to materials in the library.

DEVELOPING A MATERIALS-SELECTION POLICY

We assume that those involved with all kinds of libraries will understand the process that must be undertaken to bring a policy statement into being. But although this is probably an accurate assumption, school and public libraries are often considered the only kinds of libraries that need a materials selection policy. We recommend that academic, research and private-sector libraries also draw up similar documents. The selection-policy statement is an excellent way to communicate the reasons for the development of a collection, and can serve to ward off criticisms of library staff similar to those often heard in the school- and public-library arenas. In addition, those academic libraries supported by public taxes can often find themselves under attack, although admittedly not with the frequency and depth recently evidenced in school and public libraries. It is amazing, for example, how often the offspring of a legislator or "influential" taxpayer will complain about the materials they find in their local community college or state university library. If you have been following our advice and reading the literature on materials-selection policy, you must have been struck by the almost unanimous support coming from the articulate members of the library profession in support of policy development.

The following ideas are intended to help develop a policy statement. Regardless of the type of institution involved, it is important to plan the process well, allowing time for deliberation and the development of consensus and enthusiasm.

1. The concept of developing a materials-selection policy should be introduced to the professional staff for discussion, and the potential usefulness of such a policy outlined. Most staffs would react coolly or with indifference if they

were simply given a draft of such document, on the assumption that the project was to be undertaken without their assistance and input.
2. A brief but well-documented report should be prepared by a special committee of staff members that will summarize the place of the materials-selection policy in the operation of the library. Its benefits and format could be suggested. This report, when accepted by the staff, can then be used to introduce the concept to the governing body of the library. The report should be available for study before it is placed on the agenda of the governing group, although such bodies are not generally given to reading reports in advance. The purpose of such a report is only to provide information. After it is presented, immediate authorization to act on it should not be expected or requested. Instead, an opportunity to discuss it in detail should be provided. A slide-tape presentation of its salient points will expedite its introduction.
3. Allow a reasonable amount of time to elapse before placing an authorization to work on a policy statement on the agenda of the governing body. Bringing it up in an almost casual manner provides a nonthreatening atmosphere in which to make the decision. The authorization should be worded so that it is clear to the governing body that it is neither endorsing a materials-selection policy or committed to adopting one. Instead they have approved the writing of a draft document, for evaluation and possible adoption. The governing body should consider whether a materials-selection policy will provide support for the library and its staff.
4. The governing body should be informed that an ad hoc committee will develop a draft of a policy statement. This group might represent the professional staff, professionals in the community, educators and users of the library. Specific members need not be designated at this time, but it is important to seek recommendations from the governing body for the committee members. Some battle-scarred veterans of policy-drafting battles have told us that there are governing groups who are so skittish about controversy that they do not want the world to know they are considering a

materials-selection policy, for fear of creating controversy. If the initial report was well done, it should have made clear to the governing group that community awareness and understanding of this document is important.
5. Once the drafting committee is put together, it should be clearly established that the document will consist of positive statements about the kinds of materials to be selected for the library; it will not list reasons for rejection. Examples of selection policies should be collected and examined. It should be established whether there is to be a single document, which includes both policy and procedure, or two separate documents—one that outlines goals and policies and another that addresses itself to procedures. The proposed document(s) should be outlined and the work divided among the committee members.
6. There may have to be several meetings to discuss and edit the various sections of the document as they evolve, to assure consensus. All available staff should be involved in examining them and making recommendations for changes. We are of the firm conviction that work by committee on a policy statement is possible only if, during the final stage, one person is assigned to bring the parts together into a document that is cohesive in style and language.
7. Once the ad hoc committee is satisfied with the draft document, it should be distributed to the governing body. A special session could be called, to encourage discussion, suggestions and possible additions or deletions. Members of the ad hoc committee could be invited to the session if the governing body wished to know reasons for specific recommendations.
8. In some situations the governing body may want to designate a subcommittee, composed of its members, to study the document before the full body considers it. At this meeting, too, ad hoc committee members could act as elucidators.
9. If the governing body feels the document is workable, it may wish to proceed with its adoption. However, in recent years it has become politic to seek further support for the policy by distributing the draft document to a variety of community groups having an interest in the goals of the library.

This practice has been used primarily in the public-library sector.

10. It is important for the governing body to know how the policy is to be implemented and its contents disseminated to the community. A plan for so doing should be presented prior to final adoption of the policy. It is important to establish in the minds of the governing body that a materials-selection policy is not a static statement, doomed to be filed away in the policy book and whipped out only in an emergency. It is a positive statement on how the library plans to select materials needed by the community it serves. It should be used daily by the staff in developing the collection and making decisions about the withdrawal of materials already in it. The document must also be flexible enough to react to change in the community. For this reason we recommend that, in the procedural statement, provision be made for regularly scheduled reviews, in order to amend and revise the policy as necessary, so that it can remain active, influential and effective.

What Should Be Included in a Materials-Selection Policy
Policy statements may use a variety of formats, but they should include the following points, to ensure clarity and comprehensiveness:

1. A statement establishing the governing body as legally responsible for the selection of materials for the library collection.
2. A statement of how delegation of that responsibility to library personnel is made. Often such statements list as responsible only the chief administrator, who in turn has delegative authority that need not be spelled out in this document.
3. A statement of the philosophy or goals upon which selection of materials is based, along with the objectives of the selection policy. The rights of library constituencies can be defined, and examples of those constituencies given. It is here that a clear statement of principles can best assist when potentially controversial materials are to be considered for addition to the collection.

4. A statement clearly identifying the materials to which the policy is to apply. This refers primarily to their formats.
5. Specific criteria for the evaluation and selection of categories of materials should be supplied to ensure that any special problems or exceptions are clarified; e.g., gifts, textbooks, curriculum and supplementary materials, media other than print, free materials, local history, annual reports.
6. A statement that delineates the criteria to be used when considering the selection of materials the community may feel are sensitive or controversial.

   A point needs to be made here about the American Library Association's Library Bill of Rights as an advisory document and a statement of principle. Rather than attempting to draw up specific statements of principles about the role of the library and its collection in a community of diverse values and goals, the designers of library policies have often felt it was sufficient to state that they endorsed the Library Bill of Rights. As a single statement of policy, we do not object to such an action, and we would tend to consider as responsible any governing body that did so. But when such an endorsement of the Library Bill of Rights is made without carefully reviewing its contents and evaluating what it means to the library for which the policy statement is designed, then we would advise against summarily adopting it. It is important in developing a policy statement on materials selection to review the Library Bill of Rights and all of its interpretive documents, in order to select those components that specifically apply to the agency adopting the policy. The Library Bill of Rights has without question proven to be an excellent tool for libraries preparing to ensure that access to their materials and services is as open and equitable as possible, including such vital policy matters as the labeling or expurgation of materials or the age of users. The Library Bill of Rights should not be used as an excuse to avoid making clear statements of policy as designated by the governing body. To do so is an abdication of authority. It is important, in the day-to-day operations of the library, that the materials-selection policy be specifically tailored to the community it serves.
7. A statement establishing the rights of individuals to make

suggestions about the selection of materials for the collection. At this point, there is no need to develop a procedural document about this issue. It is more important to establish that an orderly and effective procedure will be followed, to ensure that recommendation for the selection of materials receive careful consideration.

*Developing The Content
of a Selection Policy*

In the library literature, there are numerous sources of statements about and guidelines for achieving specific objectives, as well as for deciding on criteria for a selection policy or procedure. Such statements, relevant to the specific policy, should be collected from a reliable source, such as a state library, state association or an appropriate national association. At the risk of repeating ourselves, we must point out that these resources can be most helpful in the development of a draft document, but it may be discovered that many of the statements of objectives and criteria for selection, when applied to local needs, are not specific enough, especially in terms of potentially sensitive areas.

In the process of bringing together various issues for consideration in a selection policy, some advice offered by the ALA Office for Intellectual Freedom should be considered: "A strong collection and intellectual freedom go hand in hand. It is less likely that problems will remain unresolved if the collection reflects the logical, coherent, and explicit statement from which it grows. In developing a materials selection statement four basic factors must be considered: 1) service policy, 2) environmental characteristics, 3) collection specifications, and 4) current selection needs."[7] Some of the criteria to be considered for inclusion in the policy statement are as follows:

1. Materials shall be chosen that foster respect and understanding for ethnic and minority social groups, with an appreciation for the pluralistic character and culture of our society.
2. Intergroup tensions and conflicts should be represented in the collection, offering insight and analysis, with an emphasis on resolving the social and economic stresses of modern society.

3. Materials should be selected to reflect the various levels of maturity and comprehension within the community served by the library.
4. Materials selected should allow for the diversity of interests within the community served.
5. Materials selected should reflect the problems, aspirations, attitudes and ideals of our society and be supportive to individuals seeking to make intelligent choices in their daily lives.
6. Materials should reflect a reasonable balance, collectively, in presenting opposing sides of issues and should seek to foster critical thinking.
7. Materials shall be selected without regard to the race, nationality, political or religious views of the creator or manufacturer.
8. Biased or slanted materials are to be selected when it is necessary to meet the criteria of balance or to reflect the sources of intergroup tensions or social problems.
9. The value of material selected is determined by an evaluation of its entire statement, as presented by the creative artist or producer.
10. Materials about religious thought and denominations should be provided as representative of the community served, and where needed to meet the foregoing criteria.
11. Materials on human sexuality should be selected, also based upon the foregoing criteria. The presentation of sexual incidents and the use of vernacular or slang words are to be considered in context and evaluated by the foregoing criteria.
12. Materials selected may be labeled to designate a format or genre and, in special situations, their location. Such labeling should be applied most carefully, to ensure that the process does not limit circulation or use by the library community or place the material in conflict with the foregoing criteria.

In conclusion, it is important to view the formation of a materials-selection policy as a positive project that will improve library operations. Too often have we witnessed the encouraging beginning of such projects quickly followed by a backing away from possible controversy. Such evidence of despair communicates itself to each participant, and the result is a document that is weak with compromise when it should be strong with the spirit of providing improved and consistent service to users.

Battles Lost and Won

No one wants to be caught up in the stinging gust of publicity and media hype that goes along with the battle cry of the hounders of library collections. Perhaps we would say that *most* librarians do not welcome such attention. We have observed a few instances in which the librarian may well have been interested in stimulating conflict. Yet we feel that one of the reasons many more librarians do not fight off the would-be censor is because such a battle is primarily a venture into the unknown. It is the librarian's twilight zone.

In searching through the literature, we find that there are scant accounts of successful, or even unsuccessful, battles with those who would attempt to remove materials from library collections. One of the reasons is surely because merely an encounter with a would-be censor carries with it a hint of failure. There have been plenty of comments in the literature suggesting that anyone encountering a censorship problem is not doing a proper job as a librarian. Another reason for the lack of accounts is undoubtedly that the experience is not pleasurable. It is nerve-racking to suddenly find yourself being characterized as deviant and to be submitted to untold pressures. Once the experience is over, regardless of the outcome, it is easier to let it sink into the past. The result has been a void, which needs to be filled. All librarians could profit from the experiences of others.

Take the example of Kathy Russell, at twenty-three, director of the Washington County Public Library, in Abingdon, Virginia. She was fortunate to capture the attention of *Village Voice* columnist and First Amendment defender Nat Hentoff. He wrote of her experience in late 1981. A local politician lined up with a local Baptist minister to cleanse the local library of "destructive, perverted filth." Here Hentoff sets the scene: "The Reverend Williams busied himself rounding up other fundamentalist preachers in the jihad against the library while Bobby Solores [the politician] said he was going to use his power on the Board of Supervisors to get funds for the library cut off if it did not clear its shelves of pornography."[8]

The politician also charged that the librarian was unqualified for her position and should be fired. A quick check showed that she held an accredited M.L.S. from the University of Tennessee. Hentoff continues his account by observing that "Kathy Russell could have been Athena, sprung from the head of Tom Jefferson, for all the good it would have done her in the Abingdon library war if she had not developed cool, clear logistics. And implemented them in an open, forthright style." He goes on to recount her refusal to be placed on the defensive; her tactics included well written and telling letters to the editor, in which she pointed out that the only things the so-called pornographic books were guilty of was having been on *The New York Times* best-seller list. And, as Hentoff summarizes, "it was Kathy Russell's own self-possession, steady courage, counterpunching skills, and absolute belief in a *free* library that won the war." And she is quoted in evaluating the situation after it was over: "You know these times, when you're by yourself, and you do really wonder what's going to happen. But I did what I had to do. As a librarian, I had no choice."[9]

Elizabeth G. Whaley, librarian in a private school, had no choice when she left her position after losing her battle to keep the collection, and the students' right to know, intact. She could not continue her professional career after an order from the headmaster that included the following statement: "Books that are presently being used are to be reviewed and those that would be deemed 'Dirty Books' by the majority of the parents in the community which the Academy serves, are to be taken out of circulation." In writing of the experience some two years later, Elizabeth Whaley wryly commented that she had no idea how much the "incident had to do with my failure to find another position, but I suspect that it was a contributing factor. I managed to get a little feedback from two of the ten interviews I had and this convinced me that [the incident] was a negative feature."[10]

An account in *North Carolina Libraries* that is particularly introspective is well worth reading in its entirety, but for the moment let us be content with a quote, which makes its point with a power seldom found in such narratives.

> As the days go by, you ponder over and over and over again the questions of, how do you cope with people who would destroy one of our most precious liberties? How can you prevent yourself from getting

mired down in hatred against them? They call us atheists, communists, perverts, dope addicts and intellectuals with a tone of scorn. Will you in turn call them ignorant, prudish, zealots? You know in your heart that name-calling only adds to the problem. Yet, the temptation is so very, very hard to resist.... Since many of these individuals are *tithers*, the movement is "loaded" financially. To be frank, the leadership we have encountered has been unscrupulous, noisy, tough, uncompromising, unsmiling and untiring. Clothed in garments of self-righteousness, some will stoop to a low level along the road of their holy crusade.[11]

Daniel Gore, in accounting for his reactions to a censorship case in Texas, found that all was not always sunny in the groves of academe. "In retrospect," he said,

I find it difficult to conceive of an academic library situation more likely to provoke a censorship episode when the library's director [Gore] happens to be neither fundamentalist in religion nor conservative in politics. Yet, at the time the issue first surfaced at McMurry, it took me totally by surprise and caught me rather poorly prepared to deal with it properly. What surprised me was not that a reader had been offended by something he had read in the library, but that the administration and some of the faculty in a liberal arts college should feel that what is offensive should be suppressed, when I had expected them to feel that it should be studied, analyzed, reflected upon, debated about, retained in any event as a provocative illustration of the power of some publications to stir men up.[12]

One other thing that shocked Gore during the course of the problem he had at McMurry was finding that librarians are not in a very solid financial position when it comes to defending themselves, particularly when they lose their position and have to fend for themselves. As was mentioned in the North Carolina case, the opposition, be it a public group or a governmental agency, has funds it can use against the librarian. Yet most publicly funded libraries do not have access to the kind of money that allows them to use the media to fight back.

John Forsman recollects, from his experience in Riverside, California, that

Financial strength allows you to utilize all the forces of modern communications, the press, radio and television. This is primarily because you will have to take your case to the people if you expect to win. The public must know what all the fuss is about. It takes time and money to explain why the removal of even one magazine from the library, *no* matter how *personally* repugnant it may be, is the institution of censorship in the library.[13]

Having the virtue of hindsight and not being on the firing line, we can use Mr. Forsman's observation to repeat an important message: prepare for censorship incidents long before they occur. While is nice to be able to counteract the censors with a media blitz, and we would approve of funds being available in the library budget for such a purpose, we know from the experience of others that is it easier to fight the good fight when no one is taken by surprise or saddled with an uninformed public. Let us examine the case of the Tulsa public library, as told by Allie Beth Martin.

An attack that contained all of the classic elements was made on its collection. What may not have been classic was the Board of Library Commissioners' firm procedural conduct and final refusal to bow to censorship. In looking back over the situation to determine the origin of the strength to stand firm, Mrs. Martin observed that it was "the image of the library in the community." In assessing the situation prior to the decisive commission meeting, its chairman said:

> The best thing we have going for us is a tremendous reservoir of community goodwill. The library has demonstrated that it is indeed an "open forum" where widely diverging points of views are expressed in collections, in the many programs conducted regularly in the libraries throughout the system. From the John Birch Society to the New Left, all are welcome.[14]

Support in a censorship battle is difficult to find, and in many cases has been particularly elusive once the first volley is fired. A survey conducted nearly a decade ago is indicative of the feeling among practicing professionals. They believe that existing organizations should play a more active role in supporting libraries and librarians when censorship enters the scene. Those surveyed felt particularly strongly that the profession needs an agency to give it financial, legal and moral support when censorship problems arise.[15] The appearance of the Freedom to Read Foundation as a legal agency affiliated with the American Library Association has not changed the situation, for they concentrate on seeking legal precedents that could in the aggregate establish rights for libraries whose collections are challenged. The LeRoy C. Merritt Memorial Fund is a nontax-exempt organization founded by a few members and housed in the ALA offices. But it has received scant loving care from the ALA, which seems to be embarrassed by its presence. Its funds are so few that it is usually able to offer no more than $500 to help a librarian in trouble. Recently, the Office for Intellectual Freedom, which acts as a secretariat for the Freedom to Read Foundation as well as for ALA's Intellectual Freedom Committee, passed the hat for the expenses incurred by Jeanne Layton, in a censorship battle in Utah. Why this sudden burst of concern occurred is not clear, but even though considerable money was raised, the issue of undertaking such fund-raising as a regular activity of the Merritt Fund was not.

Another problem that has not been extensively dealt with in the literature is the ability of librarians to clear their names and professional status after a censorship battle. As mentioned previously, it is often the case that librarians standing up for freedom of expression can lose their jobs. Left on their own, with only out-of-pocket resources to rely upon, they cannot fight the entrenched and "respected" library governance group, which is busy covering its tracks. The case of Joan Bodger in Missouri in 1969 is a very complicated one, and can only be sketched here. As a result of speaking out in support of the freedom of access to materials, she was dismissed from her position on the state library staff. Not content merely to dismiss her without due process, the State Library Commission sent out its only professional-librarian member (who was not a witness to the process) to present a fabricated justification for its actions to the concerned members of the Missouri Library Association, which in effect smeared Mrs. Bodger's reputation. This was the first major, public examination of such a situation by the American Library Association, which attempted to provide some sort of support and, possibly, redress to the librarians (or libraries) under attack because of the issue of intellectual freedom. It is certainly a historic investigation. But the ALA report is also, in our opinion, the prime reason why subsequent investigations have not served to protect beleaguered librarians: (1) The printing of the report had no visible effect on the Missouri situation. Mrs. Bodger was neither reinstated nor compensated for her loss of income; nor was an official apology made for the attack on her conduct as a professional. (2) The report was curiously circumspect in detailing the role of the state librarian in the case. (3) The report did not offer any censorious recommendations to the American Library Association although it could have done so.

The result of the activities of the ALA Staff Committee on Mediation, Arbitration, and Inquiry has been, at best, interesting, as an attempt to meet the needs of librarians. It seems that the only institutions ripe for censure by the profession for being "naughty" are small public libraries. No such attempt was made when the Library of Congress received what constituted an unfavorable review on its treatment of minority employees. There is an obvious need for some source of protective support with fiscal sufficiency to sustain a battle with those who can and often do "tithe" themselves into formidable political and legal juggernauts.

The best accounting of a censorship battle we have found is written by Duane H. Meyers, an associate director of the Oklahoma County Libraries. His is a case history that leaves the names unchanged. We recommend it to all who would know what the ordeal can be like and how it can become ensnarled in community politics. The accounting reveals that when a library's governing body is not familiar with its own policies, it has a tendency to go off on its own.[17] And it demonstrates that policy decisions that can affect freedom of access must be considered within that context, or they may come back to haunt subsequent attempts to use policy as a basis for taking a stand. Here again we are indulging in hindsight, for Mr. Meyers's article makes clear that he and his colleagues learned just such lessons the hard way. In his summation of the incident, Mr. Meyers says that he supposed "we all realized that the struggle was just part of our job; in fact, I think the job description of everyone who works in a library should include simple language listing the defense of intellectual freedom as one of the everyday duties to be done."[18]

Defending the freedom of access to materials is not something that occurs just once in a career. It is a daily and all-pervasive activity, which requires as much planning and thought as does providing a collection of materials for the use of the clientele. Defense of intellectual freedom is not always confined to the defense of materials. It is more than that, as Ms. Zoia Horn demonstrated to a confused and perplexed profession when she refused to testify, under subpoena and a grant of immunity from prosecution, in a federal grand-jury investigation into a 1971 "conspiracy" case known popularly as the Harrisburg Seven. She took her stand because the federal government had sent an undercover agent into her library and her home in an attempt to gather evidence against the litigants. She maintained that the use of such covert activity undermined the freedom of thought, association and speech inherent in the U.S. Constitution. She was found guilty of contempt and sentenced to jail. She had great difficulty in gaining the support of the ALA establishment, such as its Executive Board and the Intellectual Freedom Committee. However, after an extensive review of the case, her action was later declared to be a noble act.[19] This pronouncement in no way detracted from Ms. Horn's nobility and perseverance. The ALA now has a policy statement on its books about the use of government agencies and the judicial process to intimidate the free flow of thought in society and libraries. Being a professional librarian carries responsibilities little dreamed of by most practitioners. The actions of just a few, who have the strength to face financial, personal and professional loss to seek to redress a wrong, have dignified our claim to be seeking freedom of access to collections in libraries.

NOTES

1. Marjorie Fiske, *Book Selection and Censorship: A Study of School and Public Libraries in California* (Berkeley: University of California Press, 1959, 1968), p. 62.
2. Ellen Altman, "The Administrator: Characteristics and Skills," *Local Public Library Administration,* 2nd ed. (Chicago: American Library Association, 1980), p. 65.
3. Lester Asheim, "Not Censorship but Selection," *Wilson Library Bulletin* 28 (September 1953): 65.
4. Howard D. White, "Library Censorship and the Permissive Minority," *Library Quarterly* 51, no. 2: 204.
5. LeRoy C. Merritt, *Book Selection and Intellectual Freedom* (New York: H.W. Wilson, 1970), p. 12.
6. White, "Censorship."
7. *Intellectual Freedom Manual,* part 4 (Chicago: American Library Association, 1974), p. 6.

8. Nat Hentoff, "Armageddon in the Library—Starring Kathy Russell," *Village Voice*, February 18-24, 1981, p. 8.
9. Nat Hentoff, "'God Forbid That Sodomites Control This Country,'" *Village Voice*, February 11-17, 1981, p. 8.
10. E. G. Whaley, "What Happens When You Put the Manchild in the Promised Land?" *Newsletter on Intellectual Freedom* 23 (November 1974): 141-42+.
11. A. A. Whitman, "Buncombe County Case: What it Feels Like to be Involved in the Censorship Movement," *North Carolina Libraries* 31, no. 4 (1973): 17-18.
12. Daniel Gore, "Skirmish With the Censors," *ALA Bulletin* 63 (February 1969): 195.
13. John Forsman, "Dangers of Being Honest With Yourself," *Virginia Librarian* 16, no. 4 (Winter 1969): 6.
14. Allie Beth Martin, "Decision in Tulsa: an issue of censorship," *American Libraries* 2 (April 1971): 374.
15. S. J. Leon, "A Survey of the Handling of Certain Controversial Adult Materials," *Pennsylvania Library Association Bulletin* 27 (July 1972): 205.
16. "Report of the Staff Committee on Mediation, Arbitration and Inquiry..." *American Libraries* 1 (July-August 1970): 700-701.
17. Duane H. Meyers, "Boys and Girls and Sex and Libraries. The Chronicle of One Library's Fight for Intellectual Freedom," *Library Journal* 102 (February 15, 1977): 459.
18. Ibid, p. 463.
19. "Documenting Zoia Horn's Protest," *Library Journal* 97 (June 15, 1972): 2,152.

Chapter Ten
Freedom and the Library- and Information-Professional

"Professional librarians as a group are hardly known as flaming radicals. As civil servants, they find themselves in the delicate position of being guardians of much that is controversial, while their place on the totem pole of authority gives them very little power to defend their professional opinions and their personal security."[1] That statement, from *The New York Times* editorial page, marked an important change in the understanding of the vulnerable position faced by those involved in the nation's libraries, dedicated—as Jesse Shera has pointed out—to maximize the social utility of graphic records. Certainly it is true that not all library and information professionals are civil servants, but that fact seems to make little difference when it comes to measuring their location on the "totem pole of authority."

Not being radical in their approach to social change, the self-conception of librarians has also been slow to evolve, as has translating that feeling into a statement of ethics. Over the past few decades, librarians, through the American Library Association, have adopted a series of ethical statements that were little more than oaths of fidelity to those institutions that housed them. Yet in the past decade librarians have begun to perceive themselves as individuals operating from a base that has little to do with an institutional affiliation. This shift can best be illustrated in the Statement of Professional Ethics, adopted by the ALA in 1981. In the introductory statement to that document, there is an indication of an emerging philosophy of personal professional ethics, in the following statement: "This latest revision of the Code of Ethics

Freedom and the Professional 185

reflects changes in the nature of the profession and its social and institutional environment." Having set the tone with that, the document goes on to make a strong statement on the role of the professional in library and information services.

> Librarians significantly influence or control the selection, organization, preservation, and dissemination of information. In a political system grounded in an informed citizenry, librarians are members of a profession explicitly committed to intellectual freedom and the freedom of access to information. We have a special obligation to ensure the free flow of information and ideas to present and future generations.[2]

Anyone involved in this profession can recognize that librarians are called to account for their abilities to select, organize, preserve and disseminate information taken from the graphic records. As a practicing professional it is possible to be involved in one or more of those activities, in varying combinations, either within an institutional setting or as an entrepreneurial figure. Regardless of where the practice is carried out, librarians are "explicitly committed to intellectual freedom and the freedom of access to information." With that in mind, let us examine the six points that now make up the Code of Ethics:

1. Librarians must provide the highest level of service through appropriate and usefully organized collections, fair and equitable circulation and service policies, and skillful, accurate, unbiased, and courteous responses to all requests for assistance.
2. Librarians must resist all efforts by groups or individuals to censor library materials.
3. Librarians must protect each user's right to privacy with respect to information sought or received, and materials consulted, borrowed, or acquired.
4. Librarians must adhere to the principles of due process and the equality of opportunity in peer relationships and personnel actions.
5. Librarians must distinguish clearly in their actions and statements between their personal philosophies and attitudes and those of an institution or professional body.

6. Librarians must avoid situations in which personal interests might be served or financial benefits gained at the expense of library users, colleagues, or the employing institution.[3]

There is in that statement considerable support for the contention that the general perception of the library professional is changing. Personal dedication must be considerable, when saddled with such descriptors as "accurate, unbiased, and courteous" or "protect each user's right to privacy." In addition, the admonition not to use the information gained for a client for "personal interests" or "financial benefits" begins to acknowledge not only the librarian's role as mediator between the user and the graphic record, but to give moral weight to that practice.

The Library Bill of Rights began to evolve in 1939 as a statement of principles that placed the institution on record as being dedicated to the intellectually free, to all who would seek that freedom, and opposed to those who would deny that freedom to others. The first code of ethics appeared almost at the same time, at the ALA Midwinter Meeting in 1939. It contained an exhaustive list of twenty-eight numbered statements. A few examples from that list should suffice to indicate its tone and content.

4. The Librarian should perform his duties with realization of the fact that final jurisdiction over administration of the library rests in the officially constituted governing authority. This authority may be vested in a designated individual, or in a group such as a committee or a board.
11. The librarian should try to protect library property and to inculcate in users a sense of their responsibility for its preservation.
16. Acceptance of a position in a library incurs an obligation to remain long enough to repay the library for the expense incident to adjustment. A contract signed, or agreement made, should be adhered to faithfully until it expires or is dissolved by mutual consent.
21. In view of the importance of the ability and personality traits in library work, a librarian should encourage only those persons with suitable aptitudes to enter the profession and should discourage the continuance in service of the unfit.[4]

There is a naive wistfulness in the profession's view of itself over forty years ago. One should remember that the concept of a fifth-year degree in library and information service was just emerging, and that the attempts by the University of Chicago to make librarianship a discipline patterned on the emerging social sciences was causing snorts of indignation from the "practical practitioners." Nowhere in that 1939 document will you find evidence that the free flow of information was considered a problem, and access to the collection was at best negatively viewed.

The adoption of the more definitive Library Bill of Rights ten years later, the trauma of the McCarthy era and the impact of the Chief Justice Earl Warren "Court," with its emphasis on safeguarding the rights of the individual, all created a climate wherein librarians began to accept the idea of "intellectual freedom." Borrowing the term from the academics, who used it for a while before they settled upon the term "academic freedom," librarians began to think of themselves as the custodians of the information warehouse, with its problems of acquisition, organization and dissemination. At the same time librarians were moving toward a basic credo that no caretaker activities were worthwhile without having a commitment to open access to the graphic records stored there. It should be comparatively easy to understand that such a shift in thinking is difficult to make when one has been involved in an institutional setting wherein the professional has not been making professional decisions, but instead administering rules and regulations designed "to protect property" and to "inculcate users." Those who have long been in the field or are intimate with the history of librarianship are well aware that such a recently arrived-at credo has not been accepted by a majority of professionals. Studies have indicated that, although understood in principle, intellectual freedom is more agreed-with than practiced. Such wariness has been the cause of some hand-wringing and condemnation of professional librarians as hypocrites and closet censors. Such lamentation may be premature and lacking in understanding of the place that mythology plays in the development of social practice.

> When functioning properly, myth provides social control and encourages activity. It moves political systems to heights of achievement and beneficence. Wherever there is human civilization, no matter

how invisible or intangible, myth inevitably accompanies it. This happens because people require myths, not only as an "escape from reality," but to give meaning and direction to reality.[4]

And it is just such a myth-creating process that can be discerned in the emergence of the concept of intellectual freedom and the demand that the library and information professional be committed to that concept. In reading the essays of Everett T. Moore in the late fifties and the sixties or reading accounts of the activities of the ALA's Intellectual Freedom Committee since its inception in 1940, one can gain insight into the "purist" First Amendment approach developed through publications, workshops and conference programs. Librarians were being asked to change their attitude about the control of materials in their collections; they were being told censorship was not acceptable, regardless of whether denial of access was imposed by the librarian, a community member or the policy-setting authority.

The new mythology made of the librarian a "neutral" in the sea of controversy that surrounds society. The ideal was a librarian dedicated to only one idea, freedom of access to controversy, presiding over a diversity of ideas. For a considerable period of time, the Library Bill of Rights referred to the library as an "institution of education for democratic living." Librarians, library trustees, users of libraries adopting this new mythology were extolled by the profession. The document was illuminated and framed to hang on library walls. The mythical figure of the librarian standing in the doorway to the collection and warding off those who would prevent the mind from roaming freely through the ideas contained therein is an appealing one. It hints of potential martyrdom and even sainthood. One can understand how this myth can be used to exert social control over the profession and encourage responsive activity. The myth helps us escape from reality; but even more important, it helps us to understand reality. And so it is that we begin to find more and more accounts of librarians who have accepted the myth as reality and have stood in the doorway.

Some are amazed to find that they are, to a degree, successful, but many must retreat and/or face personal loss. Among the newly hatched "professionals," we find a deep concern as to how they will react when the first censorship salvo is unleashed across their bow. Like the green recruit fearful of showing cowardice in combat, new librarians fear they cannot face up to the reality entailed in practicing intellectual freedom.

And what is that reality? It is professionals employed in institutions controlled by individuals and committees or boards who do not have sympathy for, or understanding of, the librarian's ethic, intellectual freedom.

The following is extracted from a deposition taken in a recent case, in which a library director was fired for resisting efforts by the governing body to remove certain materials from the collection. The interrogator is taking the public-library board member through the Library Bill of Rights. The board member had acknowledged that he was unfamiliar with the document and so had been given a few minutes to read it before the questioning resumed.

Q. Now, let's go through this paragraph by paragraph. Is there anything in paragraph one of that document that you would disagree with?

A. Well, where you get to the book selection which should be chosen for values of interest, information and enlightenment of all people in the community, I think that's perhaps true. I think I would agree with that, except for the word enlightenment, and I'm not sure what that word enlightenment would entail.

Q. What do you understand the word to mean?

A. Well, enlightenment should be something that I would say would be uplifting or something that would benefit a community or an individual.

Q. What about just depressing books—are they appropriate for a public library?

A. They are not very enlightening. I guess they may be appropriate, but they are not enlightenment.

Q. Well, isn't enlightenment another definition for something that teaches me something I didn't know before—that is, casting light in an area of my mind that was black before that?

A. I guess you could read that into it.

Q. What about the last sentence, do you agree with that? ["Materials should not be excluded because of the origin, background, or views of those contributing to their creation."—ed.] Paragraph one, the last sentence.

A. I think I could agree to that.

Q. Okay, I gather you are in general agreement with paragraph one?

A. Pretty much so, yes, sir.

Q. How about paragraph two? Do you have anything in there you disagree with?

A. I think I could agree with that one.

Q. All right, what about paragraph three? ["Libraries should challenge censorship in the fulfillment of their responsibility to provide information and enlightenment."—ed.]

A. Again, enlightenment would be the one thing that I would question. Other than that, I would agree to that.

Q. You are not against enlightenment?

A. No. I'm not against enlightenment. I'm against—I question what the word enlightenment means in that particular situation.

Q. You believe it means something that's uplifting?

A. I think so, yes.

Q. Could a mathematics textbook be enlightening?

A. If you understood it, I presume it could.

Q. Okay, what about paragraph four—do you agree with that? [Libraries should cooperate with all persons and groups concerned with resisting abridgment of free expression and free access to ideas. —ed.]

A. Well, again to a degree I agree with it, but when you say "free access to ideas," what kind of ideas?

Q. All ideas.

A. No, I don't believe that.

Q. You believe there ought to be some restrictions in access to certain ideas?

A. I think there's time when a child could read a book that would give him some ideas that wouldn't be for the betterment of him or the family or the public.

Q. We will get into that in a little more detail, but I remind you, Mr. Swapp, we are not talking about school libraries now. We are talking about public libraries.

A. I'm talking about public libraries.

Q. Okay now, what about paragraph number five?

A. I think that's true.

Q. Now, let's get back to this idea of free access to ideas. I gather you think there are certain ideas that might be detrimental to certain groups of people. Is that right?

A. Yes, I think there is.

Q. Let me try a few examples here. Do you believe that books relating to and favoring abortion are appropriate for a public library?

A. I presume there are people who would be interested in abortion, who would like to know more about abortion, and I would not have any reason to believe that they shouldn't have access to knowledge of it.

Q. So you think that type of book would be appropriate for a public library?

A. Yes.

Q. How about a book favoring planned parenthood? Is it appropriate to have those in a public library?

A. It depends on what you are talking about when you are talking about planned parenthood.

Q. Generally, birth control.

A. Well, there are a lot of different factions when you come to talking about birth control, and just let me tell you what I mean. When a planned parenthood organization wants to go into a high school and proselyte [sic] 15, 16, 17-year-old girls to come to their headquarters for pills, no. I don't agree with that. I do agree that there are methods of planned parenthood that could be perhaps a help to a community or to a nation, but there are methods by which planned parenthood work that I don't agree.

Q. Well, that's not quite my question. My question to you is do you believe it would be appropriate for the Davis County Public Library to have available books which would, let's say, for example, instruct teenage children in how to use artificial birth control, including pills?

A. No, I don't. I think it would be all right if the parent came and got the book and read it, but I don't think it's all right for the kids to come and get and read it. If the parent and the child want to read it together, or the parents want to read it and discuss it with the child—

Q. What is your definition of a child, for that purpose?

A. Oh, perhaps anyone under 18 years old—until we become of age.

The questioning proceeds, investigating such topics as atheism and communism, until the board member balks at using "taxpayers' money" to add a book "advocating the violent overthrow of our government." Following that line of questioning, the interrogator establishes that the board member generally doesn't object to certain subjects being in the collection, provided the materials were donated, and not purchased with tax monies.

Q. Now, all of these various things that you say you would oppose buying with taxpayer's money, assuming those books were donated, would it be appropriate to include those in the library?

A. I couldn't help it. I presume if they were—if the people wanted to donate them to the library, and you had them in there, it would be a Library Board's prerogative to determine that.

Q. But, they don't stock every book because it's donated, do they?

A. Oh, no.

Q. A library has certain standards in the selection of books. Isn't that right?

A. That's right.

Q. So I guess my question is you are drawing a distinction here between books that are purchased with taxpayer's money and books that are donated. If I wished to donate to the public library the book *The Joy of Wine*, would that be appropriate for the library then to carry it? [The board member had previously said he would not spend money to purchase this title. —ed.]

A. I would presume that there could be a section of donated books concerning this, this, and this, that could be indicated that they were donated, and adult books, and people could come in and read them.

Q. How about me donating books advocating the violent overthrow of our government?

A. No.

Q. Even if they were donated, do you think that would be inappropriate?

A. I think that would be inappropriate.

Q. How about donating books on interracial sex—would that be inappropriate if they were donated?

A. No, in my opinion it wouldn't.

Q. Wouldn't be what?

A. Wouldn't be appropriate.

Q. How about donating books advocating homesexuality?

A. No, sir.

Q. How about books advocating free sex— are they appropriate for the public library?

A. If they are paid for by taxpayer's money, in my opinion, no.

Q. Are you familiar with a book *Open Marriage*?

A. No, sir.

Q. Are you familiar with the book *Sex and the Single Girl*?

A. I have heard of it, but I haven't read it.

Q. Are you familiar with a book called *The Joy of Sex*?

A. No, sir.

The questioning proceeds along those lines, establishing that there are certain subjects and words the board member feels are inappropriate for inclusion in the materials held by the library. The questioning then turns to the removal of a specific title from the shelves that seems to have disappeared.

Q. As a matter of fact, the particular book you were looking at didn't get back on the shelf, did it?

A. No, sir.

Q. Why not?

A. I kept it and I loaned it to someone and I have never seen that book since.

Q. Who did you lend it to?

A. I just don't know who I loaned it to. I had it on my desk and several people would come in and see it. Someone said, "May I borrow it?" and it went and I don't know where that book is. In all honesty, I couldn't tell you where that book is today.

Q. I assume you are speaking in all honesty. You are under oath, Mr. Swapp.

A. Yes, sir.

Q. Didn't you destroy that book?

A. No, sir.

Q. You paid for the book, didn't you?

A. Yes, sir.

Q. Why did you pay for it?

A. Because I felt like I should pay for it. I was the last one to have it.

Q. As a matter of fact, you said at that Board meeting in April you apologized to the Board for any anxiety that you might have caused them; is that right? Do you recall apologizing to the Board?

A. I don't recall that, no.

Q. Also the minutes say, "Mr. Swapp stated that he had paid for the book and felt good about what he had done."

A. Yes, sir.

Q. Is that true?

A. Yes.

Q. What did you feel good about?

A. Because I removed that filth from the shelf of the library.

Q. Is it your practice to steal public property?

A. No, sir.

Q. Do you consider it right of any citizen to come into a library and remove books that he doesn't approve of?

A. No, sir.

Q. Do you believe that you occupied a special position that enabled you to do this?

A. I think, as an elected official who has charge of a budget for a library, that I do have some responsibilities in determining the type of material that goes into a library.

Q. Do you believe that you have at the present time the authority to walk into the Davis County Public Library and remove any book you wish?

A. Not particularly.

Q. Particularly or specifically?

A. If I saw a book like that on the shelf I would have it removed again.

Q. Do you think you have the right yourself to go in and remove such a book, yes or no?

A. Yes, I think I do as an elected official.

The examination continues about technicalities, and then turns to the librarian. The board member admits to being disturbed that the librarian's salary is higher than the county commissioner's. The questioner establishes that there are others on the county payroll earning more than the commissioners.

Q. Why doesn't it bother you that the county planner makes more money—but that the librarian does, does bother you?

A. In the first place, his duties are so much greater than the librarian's that there's no comparison.

Q. Does that mean in the amount of time involved in the job?

A. Time, background, schooling.

Q. Do you think... that the county planner has more academic credentials than Miss Layton?

A. Yes, I do.

Q. What does he have?

A. He has a Master's Degree in—I don't know what you call it.

Q. So does Miss Layton have a Master's Degree.

A. That's right.

Q. What else does he have that's superior to Miss Layton?

A. Much more responsibility.

Q. That's a big term, Mr. Swapp. I'm trying to pin it down. What do you mean by that? You mean he spends more money?

A. No. He doesn't spend money.

Q. He doesn't spend much.

A. No.

Q. His budget isn't greater?

A. That's right.

Q. What do you mean by responsibilities?

A. I just mean responsibilities. He's got more technical responsibilities than a librarian will ever have.

Some time later, the moral background of a librarian is explored.

Q. Do you think that the librarian should hold the same moral standards of the majority of people in Davis County?

A. I don't know she needs to hold those kind of standards, but I think she has to exemplify those standards to some degree. I mean, what you do on your own outside of—when you are outside of the public, I think that's your business.

Q. Do you believe the librarian should hold the same religious standards as the majority of the people in Davis County?

A. No, sir.

Q. Would an atheist be a satisfactory librarian in Davis County, in your opinion?

A. No, I don't believe they would.

Q. Why not?

A. Because I don't think they would represent, by ordering their books, the majority of the people of the county. I think they would order books which would be perhaps more to their thinking than they would be to the thinking of the general public.

Q. By the same token, do you believe a Communist would be a satisfactory librarian?

A. No.

Q. By the same token, do you think that a homosexual would be a satisfactory librarian?

A. No.

Q. By the same token, do you believe an Episcopalian could be a satisfactory librarian?

A. Yes.

Q. Why?

A. Because there are mighty fine Episcopalians, I presume. I don't have any qualms about Episcopalians, but I do have qualms about homosexuals.

Q. Or Communists or atheists?

A. Yes.

Q. How about Unitarians?

A. There are some good Unitarians, I'm sure.

Q. Are there any good atheists?

A. I don't know. I don't know any atheists, but if atheists believe what I believe atheists believe, I don't think there's any good ones.

And as the questioning nears its close, the subject of intellectual freedom comes up. In a newspaper article, the board member was quoted as having said, "Anyone fighting for intellectual freedom is a subversive, in my way of thinking." He denies making the statement as quoted, but agrees that "militant fighters for intellectual freedom" are subversive. The questioning continues.

Q. Also in this same article they quote you as saying, "I have known all along who our enemy is. I knew before the election, and it doesn't bother me." Do you remember saying something to that effect?

A. Yes.

Q. What do you mean? Who is your enemy?

A. I'm talking about intellectual freedoms, those who are sponsoring any kind of literature they would like to have in a library that is not conducive to the good of the general public—the good of Americanism—the morale of the community.

Q. You see these as your enemy; is that right?

A. Yes, if they are trying to tear down the morale of the community and the morals of the community, I see them as enemy.

Q. That would include the Friends of the Library and the American Civil Liberties Union?

A. If that's what they stand for, yes.

Q. Do you believe that is what they stand for?

A. I have reason to believe that if they are fighting to keep a book like *Americanna* [sic] on the shelf, yes. I think they stand for those things that are not for the betterment of the community.[5]

That is the reality librarians face. The librarian is adopting the principle that a library should be intellectually free, and is ready to defend that, but those who use or govern libraries are little aware of librarians' credo. Ms. Jeanne Layton found herself resisting censors, and before very long, she was out of a job and involved in a lengthy and costly litigation. Sonja Coleman hauled the Chelsea School Committee into court, which handed down a landmark decision in favor of the First Amendment rights of libraries and librarians. She was restored to her position, but working conditions became unbearable, and she had to leave. She was unable to find another position, but she had the courage to say about her experience, "One thing I hope has become clear is that the First Amendment is *never* abstract. It's *this* book, *this* poem."[6] We don't know Ms. Layton's fate, after twenty years of service, but we do know that taking a stand about the myth of intellectual freedom can leave a librarian without a place to practice. Yet the momentum developed over the past forty years for the librarian professional as a champion of First Amendment rights has created a new mythology, so that it is possible for a person like Sonja Coleman to shrug and ask, "But what else can you do?"

And it is that question that faces the library and information professional today. What is the professional librarian to do when the Tampa City Council votes 5-2 to order the local public library to move six sex-education books from the children's collection to the adult collection and forms a special committee charged with making recommendations "regarding the supervision and control of the library"? A Livermore Valley, California, Unified School

District book-selection committee voted to remove Evan Hunter's *The Chisholms* from the high-school library after a complaint by a parent. The committee was composed of an administrator, a librarian, two teachers and three parents. Said one of the committee members, "I'm not willing to use *The Chisholms* to fight a First Amendment case." (Ms. Coleman, it wasn't *this* book.) A clerk in the San Jose, California, system has asked the city council to remove the head librarian, Homer Fletcher, because he denied the clerk the right to decide which books should circulate and to whom they should circulate. A new classification for books was created by the Alpha Park, Illinois, public library: "certain popular non-fiction treatments of sexual topics," to be housed in an inaccessible section of the library. The action came as a "good compromise" suggestion from the head librarian. (But what else can you do, Ms. Layton?) The Concerned Educators Against Forced Unionism succeeded in getting the Mississippi Textbook Commission to drop thirty-two textbooks from its approved list because they presented unions as a part of American life. Jim Davis, asssistant superintendent of Bellevue, Nebraska, schools, had two pages of an advanced biology text used in the high schools glued together and another page blacked out. A Pennsylvania school district banned *The Adventures of Huckleberry Finn* from its reading lists. In Adair, Oklahoma, students not wishing to participate in Bible lessons must stand in the hall until they are over.

In Albany, Oregon, the public library board voted unanimously to keep *Changing Bodies, Changing Lives*, commenting that the library must serve all of the community. In Abingdon, Virginia, the Washington County Library Board voted to forget about library complaints and voted to remove from library shelves any book ruled pornographic by a court of competent jurisdiction; the board also reaffirmed its faith in librarian Kathy Russell in her battle against those who attempted to remove titles from the library. In Fresno, California, the school board denied a parents-group request to ban a textbook because it did not teach "absolutes." In Onida, South Dakota, the school board refused to remove *Lord of the Flies* from the curriculum and the library. In Waukesha, Wisconsin, the librarian, Dorothy Naughton, was successful in forcing the police to go to the courts to gain access to the name of the person who checked out some library materials in the possession of the police.[7]

That, too, is the reality. There are losses, and there are gains. The myth of intellectual freedom may at times seem to be no more than that. Yet it is obvious that more and more library and information professionals are accepting the principle of intellectual freedom as part of their credo of service. And in so doing, they are finding that, although their position on the totem pole of authority may be low in the eyes of *The New York Times*, they can be proud of the fact that they have at last begun to assume a position on that pole. Through a constant effort, we have managed, with growing sophistication, to articulate and advocate our goals and priorities before those mechanisms in our society designed to resolve conflict. The effectiveness in local, state and federal government agencies of library advocacy is not always great, but we are there—and we plan to stay there. Our appearance in the courts as professionals was nonexistent twenty years ago, but through the legal arm of the ALA, The Freedom to Read Foundation, the concerns of library professionals are being articulated well enough to cause an author (Sidney Sheldon) to contribute $25,000 to support them. The increasing visibility of librarians in conflicts about such issues as censorship, copyright, freedom of information and fees for access has won increasing attention from the nation's press. This is evidence that librarians are exercising what Professor Edward H. Cole calls "The Criteria of Competence," which assume that, in making decisions, some may be more competent than others to pass judgment on particular matters. Cole says that in certain areas affecting library and information services, what professionals have to contribute to the decision-making process should be made to count. And he points out that, in view of such a responsibility, the library and information "profession expertise should not be a cause for political neutrality, it should be a cause for assertion and advocacy. If professionals do not assert their collective and divergent judgments, who will fill the vacuum?"[8]

The need for greater involvement in the political process by professionals is evident. The need for articulated and well-documented priorities in all phases of user service has never been greater, as inflation devours from beneath and ideologues strike from every direction. The myth of intellectual freedom is growing. Our concern with the book on the shelf, the film unspooling in the viewing room, the recording in the bin, is basic, and has been the foundation for our mythology. But there is more. Andrew E. Wessel, engineer and research systems analyst, says it better than we could:

> The computer, automated libraries, and data banks with whatever information may be contained therein raise some rather novel problems. If not otherwise published, what public right can be asserted with regard to information stored in computers? And of more relevance to our inquiry, what public right can be claimed pertaining to information abstracted, culled, edited, combined, and otherwise processed and transformed into computer files, even should the source be published materials? To focus our attention on automated libraries alone, where information in the public domain can be made available to the public, is as much an error as to be solely concerned with the "privacy issue." The importance and power of computers lie not merely in increased capabilities to handle vast amounts of information. Of more concern is the potential computers offer to process and transform such information more in accordance with our various needs. Automated libraries will not, in themselves, offer sufficient countervailing capabilities to the public when confronted by the computerized information retrieval systems of government, particularly the executive arms, industry, and other major societal institutions. It is precisely these existent and near future capabilities to process, manipulate, combine and arrange information offered by computerized information retrieval systems, to make information far more useful by its transformation into forms and arrangements that better match needs, to which questions of public access must be addressed. And to the extent that ownership of such systems implies the control of access to these capabilities, then it is the ownership of information retrieval systems that is of far more concern than the ownership of information per se. Suppose information was as freely available as sunlight. Asserting a public right to sunlight would have little bearing on the question of the distribution of the benefits of solar energy harvested by those who own or control the harvesting machines.[9]

NOTES

1. *The New York Times*, July 20, 1973, p. 30.
2. *ALA Handbook of Organization 1981/1982 and Membership Directory* (Chicago, ALA, 1981), p. 197.
3. Ibid.
4. ALA *Bulletin* (February 1939): 128–130.

5. Herbert I. London and Albert L. Weeks, *Myths That Rule America* (Washington, D.C.: University Press of America, 1981), p. xiv.
6. Extracted from an unedited transcript of a deposition by Morris F. Swapp, January 2, 1980, Salt Lake City, Utah.
7. Nat Hentoff, "What Happened After the Famous Victory in Chelsea?" *Village Voice,* November 20, 1978, p. 41.
8. The examples cited in the preceding paragraphs were taken from the *Newsletter on Intellectual Freedom* (January 1982).
9. Edward M. Cole, "Political Effectiveness: New Dimensions of Professionalism," *Tennessee Librarian* (Spring 1976): 65.
10. Andrew Wessel, *The Social Use of Information, Ownership and Access* (New York: John Wiley & Sons, 1976), p. 63.

Selected Bibliography

NOTE: *There are many other authors and subjects we could have listed here, but we wanted to present a reading list that could provide the reader with a solid overview without having to undertake major research. In addition we should point out that the aware professional should look under "Intellectual Freedom" in the* ALA Yearbook, *a serial published by the American Library Association. The professional should subscribe to the* Newsletter on Intellectual Freedom, *published by the Office for Intellectual Freedom of the American Library Association. And if you wish to introduce the subject to a high-school or adult group, we recommend that you show the filmstrip "Censorship in Schools and Libraries," produced by* The New York Times *in 1978 (79 frames in color, 35mm, 12-minute cassette and discussion manual).*

Adler, Mortimer J. *The Idea of Freedom.* New York: Doubleday, 1958.

    A scholarly study of the concept of freedom drawing on the contributions of thinkers in the development of the philosophies of Western civilization. Through comparative study, differing and similar approaches are classified and analyzed.

Allport, Gordon W. *Becoming; basic considerations for a psychology of personality.* New Haven: Yale University Press, 1955.

    Of particular interest for those seeking to understand the need of the individual in relation to feelings of freedom of the will and social pressure for conformity.

American Civil Liberties Union. *Academic Freedom and Civil Liberties of Students in Colleges and Universities.* 3rd ed. New York: American Civil Liberties Union, 1976.

204 FREEDOM OF ACCESS TO LIBRARY MATERIALS

This 56-page summation of issues and answers is part of a series of issue-oriented materials generated by this agency for which we should all be grateful.

American Library Association. *Intellectual Freedom Manual.* Chicago: American Library Association, 1974.

Currently out of print, and the materials are dated. However, until a new edition appears, this one will serve, for its historical background material is useful. The new edition will contain revised policies that have been undergoing extensive rewriting during the past five years.

Anastaplo, George. *The Constitutionalist: Notes on the First Amendment.* Dallas: Southern Methodist University Press, 1971.

This is a well-researched and -documented argument for the careful preservation of the fragile protections offered under this part of the Bill of Rights. It is heavy going at times but ultimately rewarding.

Anderson, A. J. *Problems in Intellectual Freedom and Censorship.* New York: Bowker, 1974.

Intended as a case-study cum problem-solving text, this a fine substitute for the real thing. It is particularly recommended for relaxing reading and musing. Presentation of one of the cases at a gathering will not only break the ice, but may even cause a barn-burning.

Archer, Jules. *Who's Running Your Life? A Look at Young People's Rights.* New York: Harcourt Brace Jovanovich, 1979.

Intended for the young adult, this easy-to-read, liberal interpretation should be read by all librarians in order to get a feeling for how it feels to be a confused teen.

Association of Research Libraries. Systems and Procedures Exchange Center. *External User Services.* Washington, D.C.: Systems and Procedures Exchange Center, 1981.

This appeared too late for us to use, but it is an essential

Selected Bibliography 205

document for those seeking to discover access problems facing the academic library.

Bartlett, Jonathan E. *The First Amendment in a Free Society.* New York: Wilson, 1979.

For those too intimidated to tackle Anastaplo, this is a more readable interpretation and includes some case examples of interest. Current trends are discussed.

Berninghausen, David K. *Flight From Reason: Essays on Intellectual Freedom in the Academy, the Press, and the Library.* Chicago: American Library Association, 1975.

Purist in attitude and soundly based in the most liberal interpretations of the "neutrality" of intellectual freedom, these essays represent a fair proportion of the thinking of many librarians. It is therefore essential to read them.

Bonk, Walter J. and Rose Mary Magrill. *Building Library Collections.* 5th ed. Metuchen, N.J.: Scarecrow Press, 1979.

A standard work in the field, being continued with a shift toward the emerging collection-development concept of selection and access.

Bosmajian, Haig, comp. *Censorship, Libraries, and the Law.* New York: Neal-Schuman, 1982.

Transcripts of court cases pertaining to library censorship cases.

Boyer, Calvin J. and Nancy Eaton, eds. *Book Selection Policies in American Libraries; an Anthology of Policies from College, Public and School Libraries.* Austin: Armadillo Press, 1971.

Although somewhat dated, this work is a good starting place for the onerous and difficult task facing some librarians who suddenly find that they must create a selection policy. The formats and some of the language are not as dated as some of the methods of handling controversial subjects.

Broderick, Dorothy M. *Library Work With Children.* New York: Wilson, 1977.

A collection of readings including some of the wisdom of the author. We find this renowned spokesperson for children's services always interesting, albeit controversial.

Broadus, Robert N. *Selecting Materials for Libraries.* 2nd ed. New York: Wilson, 1981.

Designed as a text for the beginner, this work has been refined into a statement on the entire process. It will serve as a refresher for the practitioner and is an excellent resource when one is trying to articulate the difference between selection and censorship. Comparable but complementary to Bonk and Magrill.

Busha, Charles H. *An Intellectual Freedom Primer.* Littleton, Colo.: Libraries Unlimited, 1977.

This is a collection of interesting essays on aspects of freedom of expression too seldom discussed by librarians. Data systems, visual arts, erotica, performing arts, cinema and, most needed of all, research into censorship. A good book to dip into from time to time.

Busha, Charles H. *Freedom v. Suppression and Censorship; With a Study of the Attitudes of Midwestern Public Librarians and a Bibliography of Censorship.* Littleton, Colo.: Libraries Unlimited, 1972.

As one can tell from the title, this is a companion study to Fiske (q.v.). It is reassuring to find that you are not alone in your feelings about censorship by librarians, and this book can serve to assist in developing your own personal study of the subject.

Cox, C. Benjamin. *The Censorship Game and How to Play It.* Arlington: National Council for the Social Studies, 1977.

A pamphlet that presents a different approach to the problems of not only confronting, but anticipating, the censor. While somewhat precious at times, it does provide a fresh insight into prevention as well as a "cure."

Emerson, Thomas I. *The System of Freedom of Expression.* New York: Vintage Books, 1970.

——. *Toward a General Theory of the First Amendment.* New York: Random House, 1963.

These two books, particularly in their opening sections, give clear, succinct accounts of our rights and why they are important to us. There are also summaries of pertinent cases. Very highly recommended.

Fiske, Marjorie. *Book Selection and Censorship; a Study of School and Public Libraries in California.* Berkeley: University of California Press, 1959.

A classic study that set off fireworks among librarians and opened the doors to more serious study and involvement by the American Library Association. The fact that Busha's later study (see citation above) supports her findings makes a sad comment on the growth of professionalism among librarians. But it is the reason that all professional librarians should be familiar with the findings of these landmark works.

Haight, Anne Lyon. *Banned Books. 387 B.C. to 1978.* Updated and enlarged by C. B. Grannis. 4th ed. New York: Bowker, 1978.

A classic that appears on many library shelves as a handy reference and source book for high-school and college debaters. Yet very few librarians know its contents. What an exhibit this list would make in a library, spread out over a range of shelves, accompanied by the American Society of Journalists and Authors' snappy red button, which states: "I Read Banned Books."

Hentoff, Nat. *The First Freedom: The Tumultuous History of Free Speech in America.* New York: Delacorte, 1980.

This author's prose is readable and his indignation great. Recommended to arouse your ire and to send as a gift to your wavering peers.

Jenkinson, Edward B. *Censors in the Classroom: the Mind Benders.* Carbondale, Ill.: Southern Illinois University Press, 1979.

The author is a respected researcher and has published rather extensively on this subject. A fine introduction for school librarians and teachers.

Lipset, Seymour Martin and Earl Raab. *The Politics of Unreason: Right-wing Extremism in America, 1790-1977.* 2nd ed. Chicago: University of Chicago Press, 1978.

A textbook, and a credo that has become widely accepted by political scientists. It is important for librarians, who can provide themselves with a basis for interpreting current trends and movements.

Moon, Eric, ed. *Book Selection and Censorship in the Sixties.* New York: Bowker, 1969.

While this is dated, this collection of essays still contains much valuable material about attitude, philosophy and compassion. All one could wish for is an edition from the more interesting 1970s.

Moore, Everett T. *Issues of Freedom in American Libraries.* Chicago: American Library Association, 1964.

This selection of little essays represents the "razor's edge" of library writing about intellectual freedom during the 1950s, when the issue was not only unpopular, but discussing it was thought to be a bit impolite. The stateliness of the prose helped to get the message through to some who were put off by other approaches.

Oboler, Eli M. *Fear of the Word: Censorship and Sex.* Metuchen, N.J.: Scarecrow Press, 1974.

Philosophical and historical musings about the prudish and repressive attitude toward sex by the library world's "Sage of Pocatello." A major voice in library intellectual-freedom matters and long a gadfly to any who ran up against his personal morality; the tone here is liberal, with more conservative overtones of the nineteenth-century philosophers.

Pope, Michael. *Sex and the Undecided Librarian: A Study of Librarians'*

Opinions on Sexually Oriented Literature. Metuchen, N.J.: Scarecrow Press, 1974.

Not as well written or surveyed as the Fiske and Busha studies but the results are much the same. One of the differences here is that the claims of librarians who call themselves "academic," and often state that they have *no* intellectual-freedom problems, are shown to be false.

Rice, Donald L., ed. *The Agitator: A Collection of Diverse Opinions From America's Not-So-Popular Press.* Chicago: American Library Association, 1972.

If you can find this publication in a library, we'll be surprised. Culled from the extremist press, both right and left, these illustrations and articles will shock even today. Getting this kind of information to the American reading public was not popular with collection developers. Many liberals folded their flags and went fishing when this was on sale.

Sutherland, Z. *Children's Access to Services and Materials in School and Public Libraries.* Proceedings of the 41st Conference of the Graduate Library School, May 16–17, 1980. *Library Quarterly,* January 1981.

As is usually the case with this publication, the quality is high, and sometimes dry—but important!

Varlejs, Jana. *Young Adult Literature in the Seventies: A Selection of Readings.* Metuchen, N.J.: Scarecrow Press, 1978.

A collection of reprints of journal articles that contains four very good essays and a bibliography on controversial literature.

Woodworth, Mary. *Intellectual Freedom, the Young Adult, and Schools: A Wisconsin Study.* Madison: Communications Programs, University of Wisconsin-Extension, 1976.

Born right on the threshold of the resurgence in censorship in schools, this study could have been a crystal ball in its day. Now it is a solid model for similar studies in other states.

Appendix

BOOK SELECTION INQUIRY

Author _____ Publisher _____
Title _____ Copyright Date _____
Reader's Name _____
Address _____
Represents ____ Self ____ Organization
   If complainant represents organization:
   Name of Organization _____
   Address of Organization _____
   Name of Officer or Person in Charge _____
1. How did you learn of this book? _____
2. What are your objections to this book? _____
   _____
3. What harm do you feel might be the result of reading this book? ____
   _____
4. Did you read the entire book? ____ Yes ____ No If not, what parts did you read? _____
5. Is there anything worthwhile in the book? _____
6. Have you read any professional reviews of the book?
   ____ Yes ____ No If so, please list names of critics and sources of reviews.
      1. _____
      2. _____
      3. _____
7. What do you believe are the main ideas of this book? _____
   _____
8. What do you think was the author's purpose in writing this book? ____
   _____
9. In view of the author's purpose, would you say he has succeeded or failed? _____

10. What book with a similar purpose would you suggest in place of this book?
    Author: _____
    Title: _____
                         Signature of Reader _____
Additional comments _____

Source: Enoch Pratt Free Library (Baltimore, Maryland).

BOOK SELECTION INQUIRY
(For Book Not in Library)

Author _____ Publisher _____
Title _____ Copyright Date _____
Reader's Name _____
Address _____
Represents ____ Self ____ Organization
   If complainant represents organization:
   Name of Organization _____
   Address of Organization _____
   Name of Officer or Person in Charge _____
1. How did you learn of this book? _____
2. Have you read the book? ____ Yes ____ No
3. Have you read any professional reviews of the book?
   ____ Yes ____ No If so, please list names of critics and sources of reviews.
   1. _____
   2. _____
   3. _____
4. What do you think are the main ideas of this book? _____
   _____
5. What do you think was the author's purpose in writing this book? ____
   _____
6. In view of the author's purpose, would you say he succeeded or failed? ____
   _____
7. Why do you think it is important for the Library to have this book? ____
   _____

Appendix 211

8. What book with a similar purpose would you suggest in place of this book?
   Author: _____
   Title: _____
                     Signature of Reader _____
   Additional comments _____

Source: Enoch Pratt Free Library (Baltimore, Maryland).

REQUEST FOR REVIEW OF MATERIAL

Title _____
Author _____ Publisher _____
Type of Material _____
  1. Have you examined the whole material? _____
  2. What did you find objectionable? (Be specific, including page number)
     _____
  3. What harm do you feel will result from its use? _____
     _____
  4. Did you find anything valuable in this material? _____
     What? _____
  5. What do you think is the main idea or the author's purpose in writing this material? _____
     _____
  6. Do you know of any material that would better suit the purpose? ____
     _____
  7. Would this material be better suited for a different age level? ____
  8. What action do you feel should be taken on this material? _____
     _____
  9. Will you be willing to discuss this material with the review committee? _____
Your name _____ Phone _____
Address _____
Do you represent an organization? ____ -Name of Organization _____
Date _____ Signature _____

Source: Unknown

CITIZEN'S REQUEST FOR RECONSIDERATION OF A BOOK

Author _____ Hardcover _____ Paperback _____
Title _____
Publisher (if known) _____
Request initiated by _____
Telephone _____ Address _____
City _____ Zone _____
Complainant represents ____ himself
                           ____ (name of organization) _____
                           ____ (identify other group) _____

1. To what in the book do you object? (Please be specific; cite pages)_____
   _____
2. What do you feel might be the result of reading this book?_____
   _____
3. For what age group would you recommend this book?_____
4. Is there anything good about this book?_____
5. Did you read the entire book? _____ What parts?_____
   _____
6. Are you aware of the judgment of this book by literary critics?_____
7. What do you believe is the theme of this book?_____
8. What would you like your school to do about this book?
   ____ do not assign it to my child
   ____ withdraw it from all students as well as from my child
   ____ send it back to the English department office for reevaluation
9. In its place, what book of equal literary quality would you recommend that could convey as valuable a picture and perspective of our civilization?_____
   _____

                 Signature of Complainant _____

Source: The National Council of Teachers of English. *The Students' Right to Read.* (Champaign, Illinois: The Council, 1962), p. 17. Reprinted by permission.

PATRON COMMENT ON LIBRARY MATERIALS

Title _____
Author _____ Publisher/Producer _____

Form of the material (e.g., 8mm film, pamphlet, hardcover book, 35mm slide, phonograph record, etc.) _____

Please state your comment, suggestion or criticism of the material as specifically as possible _____

Did you read, see, listen or otherwise use the material in its entirety? _____ If not, then which parts? _____

Are you aware of the judgment of this material by qualified critics? _____ If yes, please identify source _____

Additional comments _____

Date _____ Signature _____
Address _____ Telephone _____

The Library appreciates your interest. Your comments will be forwarded to the Selection Committee of Librarians having responsibility for this form of material.

Source: Vigo County (Indiana) Public Library. Reprinted by permission.

CITIZEN'S REQUEST FORM FOR RE-EVALUATION OF LEARNING RESOURCE CENTER MATERIALS

Initiated by _____
Telephone _____ Address _____
REPRESENTING Self _____ Organization or Group (name) _____
School _____
MATERIAL QUESTIONED:
Book: Author _____ Title _____
_____ Copyright Date _____
A-V MATERIAL: Kind of Media (film, filmstrip, record, etc.) _____
Title _____
OTHER MATERIAL: Identify _____
Please respond to the following questions. If sufficient space is not provided, please use additional sheet of paper.
 1. Have you seen or read this material in its entirety? _____
 2. To what do you object? (Please cite specific passages, pages, etc.) _____

3. What do you believe is the main idea of this material?_____

4. What do you feel might result from use of this material?_____

5. What reviews of this material have you read?_____

6. For what age group might this be suitable?_____

7. What action do you recommend that the school take on this material?_

8. In its place, what material do you recommend that would provide adequate information on the subject?_____

Date _____ Signature _____

Source: Anchorage (Alaska) Borough School District, Joe D. Montgomery, Superintendent. Reprinted by permission.

Index

by Marilyn Delson

Abortion Eve, 81
About Sex (Texture Films), 38, 82
Access restriction, 166
  book mutilation, 74
  closed shelf, 72-3
  fees, 77
  labeling, 75, 117-8 (films), 164
Across 110th Street, 147, 153
Addict in the Streets, 147
Adler, Mortimer, 2-4, 14
Adventures of Huckleberry Finn, The, 88, 101, 199
Affluent Society, The, 81
After the First (film), 82
Age of Keynes, 81
All The King's Men, 82
American Civil Liberties Union (ACLU), 144, 159
American Heritage Dictionary of the English Language, 79-80
American Libraries, 36
American Library Association (ALA), 59
  American Association of School Librarians, 147
  "Best Books for Young Adults," 94
  circulation record inspection and, 64
  Code of Ethics, 184-6
  Freedom to Read Foundation, 144, 179, 200
  Library Bill of Rights, 12-13, 16, 92-3, 120-1, 147, 163, 173, 186-9
  material selection guidelines, 154
  Newsletter on Intellectual Freedom, 129
  special interest groups and, 103
  Staff Committee on Mediation, Arbitration, and Inquiry, 181
  during World War I, 16
American Nazi Party, 11
Anarchist Cookbook, The, 45, 46
Art of Loving, The, 49
Asheim, Lester, 75, 76, 167
Asimov, Isaac, 37
Astrology, 82-3
Auden, W. H., 38

Baldwin, James, 84
Banned Books, 78
Bernier, Charles, 113
Bettelheim, Bruno, 21n, 46
Bible, 44-5, 59
Birds, The (film), 81
Birth of a Nation (film), 82
Bishop, Claire, 95
Black Boy, 82
Booklist, 148
Born Innocent (TV movie), 40, 45-6
Bradley, Julia Turnquist, 32
Brain, James Lewton, 78-9n, 80
Broderick, Dorothy, 50n, 130-1, 137
Butler, Cynthia, 90

Cable television, 5
Caldwell, Erskine, 41

Index

Car and Driver, 37
Carson, Rachel, 10
Catcher in the Rye, 80, 82, 117
Catch-22, 117
Censorship, 8, 9, 58
   case studies, 146-65, 176-82, 189-99
   education and, 32
   federal government and, 63-6
   of films, 38, 63, 81, 82
   group tactics, 66-71
   laws and, 14
   librarians and, 71-7
   of library exhibits, 83-4
   power of language and, 79-80
   pressure groups and, 59-62
   of recordings, 83
   in school libraries, 36-7, 52, 54-5
   side effects of, 78
Central Intelligence Agency (CIA), 65-6
CIA and the Cult of Intelligence, The, 66
Changing Bodies, Changing Lives, 199
Chelton, Mary K., 89, 99
Children
   access controversy and, 36, 49-55
   school libraries and, 31-2
   sex education and, 42-3
   stereotyping and, 91-4, 97
Children's Literature: An Issues Approach, 93
Chin, Frank, 95n
Chisholms, The, 199
Christie, Agatha, 97
Cline, Victor, 161
Clockwork Orange, A, 28, 147, 153
Cole, Edward H., 200
Comix, 147, 153
Commissioner of Education, U. S., 161
Commission on Obscenity and Pornography, U. S., 40, 161
   cause and effect studies, 41n, 46
   imaginary stimuli, 43n, 114-15

Complaints
   complaint form, 136-9
   effects of, 140-5
   group action and the media, 135-6
   handling of, 126-32
      guidelines, 133-5
   referral of, 125
   review committees, 139-40
Connecticut Law Review, 32
Constitution, U. S., 12
   1st Amendment, 5, 33, 45-6, 159, 198
   14th Amendment, 32
Cook, Fred J., 95
Council on Interracial Books for Children, 93
Covert Action Information Bulletin, 28
Cox, Richard, 42n
Creationism, 82
Cruising (film), 96
Customs Service, U. S., 64-5

Daddy Was a Numbers Runner, 37, 95
Daisy Summerfield's Style, 82
Darrow, Jr., Whitney, 97
Das Kapital, 72
Davidson, Dee Ann, 42n
Death of a Legend (National Film Board of Canada), 38
Death of a Princess (film), 96
Death of a Salesman, 81
Decent Interval, 66
Declaration of Independence, 21
Dictionary of American Slang, 79
Dinky Hocker Shoots Smack, 81
Discarding materials, 101-2
Dorris, Michael, 90-1n
Douglas, William O., 22n, 24, 45n, 46
Down These Mean Streets, 80
Dragonwings, 93
Drums Along the Mohawk, 79
Dunbar, Lawrence Paul, 102

Education libraries, 18-9, 30
  school boards, 32-3, 63
  school libraries, 31
Eliot, T. S., 98, 101
Emerson, Thomas I., 3-4n, 21n, 24n
Esalen Institute, 54
Espionage Act of 1918, 65

Fadiman, Clifton, 42-3
Fantasia (film), 39
Fantastic Voyage, 37
Farson, Richard, 54
Fire Next Time, The, 84
First Blast of the Trumpet Against the Monstrous Regiment of Women, The, 99
Fiske, Marjorie, 166n
Five Chinese Brothers, The, 88, 95, 97, 100
Fixer, The, 88
Florida Action Committee for Education, 62
Flowers for Algernon, 80
Foolish Fig Leaves, 161
Ford, Henry, 141
Forsman, John, 178-9n
For Whom the Bell Tolls, 81
Freedom, 14-5, 20-1, 71
  acquired, 3n
  circumstantial, 2n, 4-5
  natural, 3n, 4
  reason and, 6, 9, 11, 13
  tolerance and, 10-1
Fromm, Erich, 49

Galbraith, John Kenneth, 81
Gay: What You Should Know About Homosexuality, 98-9
Gerhardt, Lillian, 94
Gilbert, W. S., 29, 30
Girls and Sex, 80
Glamour, 37
Go Ask Alice, 147, 153
Godfather, The, 96 (film), 117 (film), 147, 153

God's Little Acre, 41
Goethe, Johann Wolfgang von, 3, 58, 78
Goffstein, M. B., 82
Gordon, Theodore, 25
Gore, Daniel, 178n
Grapes of Wrath, The, 80, 81, 117
Green, Bette, 95
Griffiths, D. W., 82
Guy, Rosa, 94

Haight, Anne L., 78
Harlequin Romances, 97
Harris, Richard, 4
Harrisburg Seven, 182
Hayakawa, S. I., 79, 80
Hemingway, Ernest, 81
Hentoff, Nat, 176-7
Heritage Foundation, 150, 154, 159
Hesse, Hermann, 161
Hitchcock, Alfred, 81
Hitler, Adolf, 99
Hoffman, Abbie, 78
Holmes, Oliver Wendell, 10, 53
Holocaust, 41, 46-7
Honored Society, The, 95
Hoover, J. Edgar, 39-40
Howard, Edward N., 136-7
How To Avoid Social Diseases: A Practical Handbook, 80
How To Say No to a Rapist and Survive, 82
Human and Anti-Human Values in Children's Books, 93
Hunt, Morton, 98
Hunter, Evan, 199

Ideas in Conflict, 25
I'm Glad I'm a Boy, I'm Glad I'm a Girl, 97
Individualism, 7-11, 13-4
In Dubious Battle, 81
International Jew, The, 141
In the Night Kitchen, 74
Introducing Shirley Braverman, 93

Index 219

Invisible Man, The, 38

Jackson, Shirley, 38, 81
Jaws, 72
Jesus Christ Superstar (recording), 83
John Birch Society, 85, 115, 131
Justice Department, U. S., 64

Kanawha County (West Virginia), 68
Kaufmann, Walter, 3*n*, 7*n*
Keats, Ezra Jack, 94
Kesey, Ken, 98
Keyes, Daniel, 80
Knox, John, 99
Kohler, Mary, 55
Kuh, Richard, 161
Ku Klux Klan, 62, 83, 120-1

Labeling. *See* Access restriction.
LaFarge, Oliver, 80
Language of Change, 112
Laughing Boy, 80, 88
Lekachman, Robert, 81
Lewis, Norman, 95
Librarians, personality and, 166-7
Libraries. *See also* Education libraries; Prison libraries; Private libraries; Public libraries.
  as forum for ideas, 13-4
  funding sources, 18
  neutrality and, 16
  youth services and, 16
Library Bill of Rights (1939), 12-3, 16, 92-3, 120-1, 147, 163, 173, 186-9. *See also* American Library Association.
Library of Congress, 30, 181
Life, 37, 40, 80
Little Black Sambo, 88, 97, 100
Little Women, 38
Locke, John, 6*n*, 7, 11
Lofting, Hugh, 101
Loophole, 147, 153

Lorang, Mary Corde, 115
Lord of the Flies, 199
Los Angeles Public Library, 81
Lottery, The, 38 (film), 81 (film), 116

Maas, Peter, 95
Madison, James, 22*n*
Mafia and Politics, The, 95
Malle, Louis, 96
Mandingo, 40
Marchetti, Victor, 66
Marcuse, Herbert, 8*n*, 10
Martin, Allie Beth, 179*n*
Marx, Karl, 72
Material selection, 23-4
  balanced collection, 85
  censorship and, 71, 75
  legal books, 26
  policy development, 167-76
  pornography, 26-8
  school books, 30-3
  science books, 25
  small press materials, 29-30
  violence in books, 28, 46
Mead, Margaret, 100*n*, 103-4*n*
Media, 5, 7, 53, 110
  bias against nonprint materials, 107, 109, 116-18
  computers, 112
  halftone invented, 108
  programming problems, 119-22
  user impact, 112-16
  video equipment, 106, 111
Mein Kampf, 99
Mencken, H. L., 51*n*
Merchant of Venice, The, 88, 101
Merritt, LeRoy C., 167, 168*n*, 180
Merriwether, Louise, 37
Meyers, Duane H., 181
Michael Hendee, 90-1
Mill, John Stuart, 7, 11, 21-2*n*
Miller, Arthur, 81
Milwaukee Public Library, 64
Missouri Citizens for Life, 62
Mitchell, Don, 147

Molz, R. Kathleen, 123n, 144
Monaco, James, 108-9n
Montagu, Ashley, 92n, 99n
Montesquieu, Baron de, 11n
Moore, Everett T., 188
Murder of Roger Ackroyd, The, 97

Nader, Ralph, 10
National Commission on Resources for Youth, 55
National Council of Teachers of English, 59
National Lampoon, 61
National Library Association, 154
New Left, 13
New Right, 13
Newspapers, 5
Newsweek, 37
New York Public Library, The, 96
New York Times, The, 28, 46, 184n, 200
Nicholas, Leslie, 80
North Carolina Libraries, 177-8n

Of Mice and Men, 80, 117
One Flew Over The Cuckoo's Nest, 98
O'Neil, Robert, 22, 23n
Optimism, historical, 11, 13
Our Bodies, Ourselves, 55, 89

Palisades Free Library (New York), 24
Pantaleone, Michael, 95
Parents of New York United (PONY-U), 62
Pessimism, historical, 13-4
Peyton Place, 39
Phantom India (film), 96
Playboy, 30
Pomeroy, Wardell, 80
Popular Photography, 37
Pornography, 26-8
Postal Service, U. S., 65
Potter, Beatrix, 94
Prison libraries, 30-1, 65

Private libraries, 18
Progressive, 63
Psycho (film), 81
Public libraries, 18, 30
    demand vs. elitism, 19-20
    freedom of expression and, 22
    material selection, 23-34
Puzo, Mario, 96, 117

Regional Center for Educational Training (New Hampshire), 90
Retrato De Teresa (Portrait of Teresa, film), 64-5
Richard Scarry's Best Word Book Ever, 97
Rights of minors, 53-4
Riverside (California), 67, 68
Roberts, Don, 74, 107
Roosevelt, Eleanor, 3
Roots (TV program), 40
Ruby, 94
Rudman, Masha Kabakow, 93-4
Run, Shelly, Run, 37

Sade, Marquis de, 27
Samuels, Gertrude, 37
Say Goodbye (film), 82
Scarry, Richard, 97
School Library Journal, 91, 94, 148
"School, Parents, and Textbooks," 161
Secret Rulers, The, 95
Sendak, Maurice, 74
Sexuality, 59, 65, 80
Shapiro, Lillian, 94
Sheldon, Sidney, 200
Siddhartha, 161
Simpson, Elaine, 51, 52n
Skokie (Illinois), 11
Slade, Mark, 112-13n
Small press materials, 29-30
Smith, Lillian, 146
Snepp, Frank, 66
Snowy Day, The, 94

Solzhenitsyn, Aleksandr, 3
Sorrentino, Joseph, 47
Soul On Ice, 147, 153
State Library of Idaho, 65
Steal This Book, 78
Steinbeck, John, 80, 81
Stereotypes, Distortions and Omissions in U. S. History Textbooks, 93
Story of Doctor Doolittle, The, 88, 101-2
Story of Epaminondas and His Auntie, The, 102
Strange Fruit, 146
Streetcar Named Desire, A, 88
Summer of My German Soldier, The, 95, 130
Supreme Court, U. S., 10, 32
   Brown vs. Louisiana, 122
   Warren "Court," 187
Suspicion (film), 81
Sylvester and the Magic Pebble, 74
System of Freedom of Expression, The, 21

Tale of Peter Rabbit, 94
Tales of Witches, Ghosts and Goblins Told by Vincent Price (recording), 83
Tarkington, Booth, 102
Tate, Binnie, 103n
Teacher's Sex Class, 27
Ten Commandments, The (film), 40
Thirty-Nine Steps, The (film), 81
Thomas, Piri, 80
Thumb Tripping, 147
Time, 37, 80
Titicut Follies (film), 63
Tocqueville, Alexis de, 11, 12n

Today's Isms, 81
To Have and To Have Not, 81
To Kill a Mockingbird, 117
Top Of The News, 91, 137
Treasury Department, U. S., 64
Tricontinental Film Center, 64

Underground Dictionary, The, 43-4, 140-41
University of Chicago, 187

Valachi Papers, The, 88, 95
Village Voice, 176
Violence, 46-8

Walker, Gerald, 96
Warren, Earl, 187
Warren, Robert Penn, 82
Washington County Public Library (Virginia), 176
Wells, H. G., 38
Wessel, Andrew E., 201n
Where Do We Draw the Line?, 161
White, Howard, D., 167n
Wiese, Kurt, 95
Winston-Salem Public Library (North Carolina), 120-21
Wizard of Oz, 39
Wolitzer, Hilma, 93
Wright, Richard, 82

Yep, Laurence, 93
Yerkey, A. Neil, 113
Young adults
   access controversy and, 36-7, 49-55
   school libraries and, 33
   stereotyping and, 94-5